ANCIENT SLAVERY
AND MODERN IDEOLOGY

ANCIENT SLAVERY AND MODERN IDEOLOGY

By

M. I. FINLEY

*Master of Darwin College
and Professor Emeritus of Ancient History
in the University of Cambridge*

1980
CHATTO & WINDUS
LONDON

Published by
Chatto & Windus Ltd
40 William IV Street
London WC2N 4DF

*British Library Cataloguing
in Publication Data*

Finley, *Sir* Moses I
    Ancient slavery and modern ideology
      1. Slavery in Greece – Historiography
      2. Slavery in Rome – Historiography
    I. Title
    301.44′93′0938   HT863

    ISBN 0-7011-2510-1

© M. I. Finley 1980
Set, printed and bound in Great Britain by
Fakenham Press Limited, Fakenham, Norfolk

To
Jean-Pierre Vernant
and
Pierre Vidal-Naquet

CONTENTS

Preface 9

I. Ancient Slavery and Modern Ideology 11

II. The Emergence of a Slave Society 67

III. Slavery and Humanity 93

IV. The Decline of Ancient Slavery 123

Notes 150

Bibliography 185

Index 195

PREFACE

Although slaves have been exploited in most societies as far back as any records exist, there have been only five genuine slave societies, two of them in antiquity: classical Greece and classical Italy. This book is about those two societies, examined not in isolation but, in so far as that is meaningful, in comparison with the other three (all in the New World). I consider how the ancient slave societies came into being and how they were transformed in the long process that brought about medieval feudalism; how slavery functioned within the ancient economy and in ancient political systems, and how it was judged socially and morally; what modern historians have made of ancient slavery, and why. These topics are interwoven throughout: the book is not arranged along conventional chronological lines but pursues four major themes one at a time. In other words, although the inquiry is both historical and historiographical, these chapters do not constitute a history of ancient slavery.

Over the past twenty-five years, the study of slavery in the United States, the Caribbean and Brazil has reached an intensity without precedent. The debate has often been bitter, and it has become a public debate, not merely an academic one. It is clear why that should be so: modern slavery was black slavery, and therefore cannot be discussed seriously without impinging on present-day social and racial tensions. Obviously, ancient Greek and Roman slavery has no such immediate significance. Nevertheless, other contemporary ideological considerations are active in that seemingly remote field of historical study – active in the sense that they underlie, and even direct, what often appears to be a purely 'factual', 'objective' presentation. For that reason, the disagreements in this field are also profound, the controversies conducted polemically. I believe that a full, open account of how modern interest in ancient slavery

9

has manifested itself is a necessary prerequisite to the substantive analysis of the institution itself, and I have therefore begun with that theme. It then recurs in the subsequent chapters, primarily as a foil for my own views on the particular subject under examination.

The core of the book consists of four lectures that I had the honour to give at the Collège de France in November and December 1978. The invitation gave me the welcome opportunity to discourse on a subject on which I have been reflecting for a long time. My interest in ancient slavery began in the early 1930s, when I was a graduate student at Columbia University under W. L. Westermann, and I have been writing and lecturing directly on the subject for the past twenty years. I have accumulated many debts during those years, but here I shall restrict myself to thanking John Dunn, Peter Garnsey, Keith Hopkins, Orlando Patterson, Elisabeth Sifton and C. R. Whittaker, who kindly read the whole work in draft; Yvon Garlan, Elio LoCascio, Dieter Metzler, Pierre Vidal-Naquet and my wife, who either read individual chapters or offered help in other ways. I am also most grateful to Douglas Matthews for preparing the index.

Darwin College, Cambridge   M.I.F.
October 1979

Chapter 1

ANCIENT SLAVERY
AND MODERN IDEOLOGY

The volume and the polemical ferocity of work on the history of slavery are striking features of contemporary historiography. That is easily understandable for American slavery: it was black slavery, and even a 'purely historical' study of an institution now dead for more than a century cannot escape being caught up in the urgency of contemporary black-white tensions. One commentator has recently remarked rather bitingly that because of the 'coercion of the times', every 'new interpretation of slavery has professed to be more antiracist than the one it replaces'.[1] Similar concerns are evident in the study of slavery in the Caribbean or Brazil and of the impact of the slave trade on Africa. But they obviously cannot explain why ancient slavery is being subjected to a similarly massive and not much less heated inquiry. No one today need feel ashamed of his Greek or Roman slave ancestors, nor are there any current social or political ills that can be blamed on ancient slavery, no matter how distantly.

Some other explanations must be sought, and I shall argue that they are deeply rooted in major ideological conflicts. For the analysis a crude and partly artificial distinction can be drawn between a moral or spiritual view and a sociological view of the historical process. Such a distinction cannot be neatly maintained, of course, either by the historian or by the activist: in the debate over the abolition of the modern slave trade, 'it is no more unusual to find humanitarians using economic arguments than to find their opponents using humanitarian ones'.[2] Nevertheless, my distinction is serviceable for my purposes, as the different stresses in the following superficially similar quotations illustrate (both of them easily paralleled in other writers).

The first is from Arnold Heeren, the extremely influential Göttingen philosopher and historian, writing at the very beginning of the nineteenth century: '. . . everything that moderns have said about and against slavery may also be applied to the Greeks. . . . But one should not try to deny the truth that, without the instrument of slavery, the culture of the ruling class in Greece could in no way have become what it did. If the fruits which the latter bore have a value for the whole of civilized mankind, *then it may at least be allowed to express doubt whether it was bought at too high a price in the introduction of slavery'* (my italics).[3]

The contrasting quotation is from Engels' *Anti-Dühring*: 'It was slavery that first made possible the division of labour between agriculture and industry on a considerable scale. . . . Without slavery, no Greek state, no Greek art and science; without slavery, no Roman empire. Without Hellenism and the Roman empire as the base, also no modern Europe. . . . It costs little to inveigh against slavery and the like in general terms, and to pour high moral wrath on such infamies. . . . But that tells us not one word as to how those institutions arose, why they existed, and what role they have played in history.'[4]

The moral-spiritual approach has dominated the discussion of ancient slavery since the early nineteenth century and almost monopolized academic study (apart from 'neutral' antiquarianism), so much so that it is now the common view that modern interest in ancient slavery 'awakened out of the idea of freedom in the eighteenth century with the beginning of modern social constructive criticism',[5] and that the climax of that initial impulse came in 1847 with the appearance of Henri Wallon's *Histoire de l'esclavage dans l'antiquité*. When Wallon published his three volumes, he introduced them with a 164-page chapter on 'Slavery in the Colonies'. The reason was explicitly given in the short preface: 'Slavery among the ancients! It may seem strange that one should seek so far away, when slavery still exists among us. In taking this path, I do not at all divert minds from the colonial question; on the contrary, I wish to bring them back to it and concentrate them on a solution.'

The solution could not have been simpler: abolition of an institution that was un-Christian to its very roots, one that corrupted slaves and masters alike and therefore the whole of society. In 1847 abolitionism was a live issue in Europe. By 1879, however, when Wallon published a second edition, slavery had been banned in virtually all the New World colonies, abolitionism had become an issue of the past, a dead issue. Nevertheless, Wallon, now permanent secretary of the Académie des Inscriptions et Belles Lettres, dean of the Faculté des Lettres in Paris, and 'Father of the Constitution', chose to reprint his out-of-date chapter on the colonies, because, as he wrote in a new preface, 'it may give an idea of the colonial regime and of the state of opinion among us at the precise moment when the debate was resolved, much sooner than one might have believed' – 'thanks to God', he piously added.

Wallon's *Histoire* remains unrivalled in its scale and its deployment of the literary and juristic sources, of the patristic literature, and (far more than is usually allowed) of inscriptional evidence. Yet today it normally receives mere lip service, with a pejorative remark or two about what Westermann has called 'the abolitionist prejudices of the time'. Its 'influence', he continues, 'in establishing the modern religious-moralistic assessment of the ancient institution has probably been the most harmful and the least challenged.'[6] Joseph Vogt avoids Westermann's denunciatory tone, but the two-page account that he calls paying 'special attention to this outstanding work' is restricted almost entirely to the value judgments (which 'needed revision') about the negative influence of slavery on society and the healing role of Christianity in bringing the institution to an end.[7] I need not go on calling the roll: from such comments and 'summaries' no one could imagine the contents of Wallon's three volumes or the magnitude of his scholarly contribution. He himself was not wrong when he wrote, in closing the long introductory chapter on the modern situation: 'Besides, this book is not a pleading but a history. Without banishing the modern question from my mind, I have remained face to face with the ancient fact' – tens of thousands of facts, I should add, about the size of the slave population, the sources of slavery, the price and employment of slaves, helots, manumission and so on.

Several things need to be said about this mixture of denunciation and neglect of Wallon. The first is that it is a twentieth-century phenomenon.[8] The second is that, much as one may legitimately criticize, or disagree with, Wallon's interpretations of the data, the case is weak for a charge of deliberate distortion or omission of the evidence in consequence of his Christian piety or his abolitionist fervour. And the third is that anti-Wallonism does not reflect a shift away from the moral-spiritual approach to history, as may appear on the surface, but results from a shift, and also a clash, in the moral values of historians. Crudely stated, the conflict is between Heeren's view that slavery, though an evil, was not too great a price to pay for the supreme cultural achievement (and legacy) of the Greeks, and Wallon's insistence that there can be no defence for an evil which so grossly violates the essence of Christianity. Rarely have the issues been posed quite so bluntly, but it is not difficult to disentangle them from the complex interplay of value-systems. Wallon has suffered posthumously because, good Christian though he commendably was, he allowed no mitigating nuances on behalf of classical traditions and classical values. So have some other twentieth-century historians who, from different premises, attributed the 'decline of antiquity' to the single factor of slavery.

Although I hold that the stress on moral values has led to a distortion of both the study of ancient slavery and the current accounts of the historiography of the subject, I want to pursue the matter of the relationship between Christianity and ancient slavery a bit further, because it has been a central theme in the ideological debates about ancient slavery; indeed, a prime example of what happens when the past is summoned as witness in moral or theological disputation. Westermann, for example, a religious agnostic, or at least not a believer, made his attack on Wallon in a polemical chapter in which he had no difficulty in demolishing the view that Christianity was responsible, even if only by delayed action, for the disappearance of ancient slavery. In a world without ideology that polemic would not have been necessary: it had been done nearly a century before at much greater length and with deeper insight, by that radical theologian, friend of Nietzsche and precursor of Karl Barth, Franz Overbeck.[9] Indeed, it had been done sufficiently in three or four pages in 1771 by John Millar.[10] The position was summed up by Ernst Troeltsch half a century ago: Inwardly 'the nature of the slave relationship was neutralized by the claims of the ideal. Outwardly, however, slavery was merely part of the general law of property and of the order of the State, which Christianity accepted and did not try to alter; indeed, by its moral guarantees it really strengthened it.'[11]

The heat of Overbeck's arguments and the intemperance of his language may be attributed to the fact that he was making a powerful theological argument about the nature of Christianity, not merely correcting a historical fallacy – and perhaps to the magnitude of the Augean stables he wished to clean. By 1875, when he was writing, it had become dogma that the early church was opposed to slavery: it would require many pages merely to list the books and essays in which this doctrine appeared, not all of them contemptible and some of them of considerable scholarly quality. Wallon was not the creator of the dogma or even its most popular spokesman: the latter was probably Paul Allard, whose *Les esclaves chrétiens* went through five editions in French alone after it first appeared in 1876 and was 'crowned' by the Academy.

The difficulty with the dogma is the apparent incompatibility with the actual record. That had become a serious worry by the early nineteenth century, and there was an outburst of studies of the church and ancient slavery. Wallon, it is worth recalling, won a competition sponsored by the Académie des Sciences Morales et Politiques in 1837 on the theme, the replacement of slavery by serfdom, and his was one of three works ultimately published as a consequence.[12] In 1845, before Wallon's three volumes had appeared, the Trustees of the Hulsean Prize in the University of Cambridge set as the subject of their competition in that year 'The Influence of Christianity in Promoting the Abolition of Slavery in Europe'; the winning dissertation, by Churchill Babington, published the following year, ran to 181 learned pages. In 1862, under the direct stimulus of the American Civil War, the Society for the Defence of the Christian Religion in The Hague invited a more differentiated approach by the two-part formulation of its theme: 1) a 'scientific explanation' of the Biblical passages pertaining to slavery, and 2) an inquiry into how slavery should be considered 'according to the spirit and principles of Christianity'. They were rewarded with at least one lengthy, worthwhile response, the prize-winning essay by a German schoolmaster, Heinrich Wiskemann, published in Leiden in 1866 under the title, *Die Sclaverei*. Wiskemann, a classical scholar, theologian and historian, with a long list of serious publications, undermined the view that the New Testament offers any comfort for abolitionists, and then argued that slavery is nevertheless 'an evil that can be accepted by religion and by reason only under circumstances (*unter Umständen*)'.

In sum, men of firm belief were compelled to find some sort of explanation of the long survival of slavery after the triumph of Christianity. Wallon's third volume opens by acknowledging the problem and returns to it time and again. His way out of the dilemma – slavery was an evil practice inconsistent with moral requirements – is not a very satisfying one. Neither is Wiskemann's: Christ and the apostles either maintained silence about slavery or they endorsed it for sound tactical reasons (that is what he meant by 'accepted under circumstances'). However, a lame answer is better than the line adopted by Joseph Vogt: he holds to the dogma of a fundamental opposition by Christianity from the outset, without ever attempting to reply to the arguments and the evidence that have been marshalled against it, not even to those of Westermann, for whom he has expressed much, though not altogether uncritical, admiration. Although 'it is true', he is content to write, that Christianity accepted 'slavery as an institution', what matters is that 'the contrast between slave and master within the new Christian community could only be a relative one. . . . A new kind of evaluation of property and power had appeared.'[13] That is close to Wallon, though with a slightly less activist overtone. Vogt's quarrel with Wallon is therefore not over Christianity but over the latter's denial of the spiritual excellence of the pagan Greeks and Romans.

That Vogt is wrong in believing, against Troeltsch, that 'a new kind of evaluation of property and power had appeared', seems to me certain. It seems equally undeniable that it is an evasion of the central dilemma to rest on the casually dismissive clause, 'although it is true that Christianity accepted slavery as an institution'. But I do not discuss those aspects; my immediate concern is with the methodological fallacy that pervades Vogt's account, a common one in the history of ideas, which we may call the 'teleological fallacy'. It consists in assuming the existence from the beginning of time, so to speak, of the writer's values – in this instance, the moral rejection of slavery as an evil – and in then examining all earlier thought and practice as if they were, or ought to have been, on the road to this realization; as if men in other periods were asking the same questions and facing the same problems as those of the historian and *his* world.[14] The false proposition that modern interest and research into ancient slavery had its roots in the Enlightenment and abolitionism is another example. 'Interest' and 'study' are assumed to be constants, and are assessed and judged according to the nineteenth- and twentieth-century practice of academic scholarship and the academic monograph. It should not have to be said that there are, and always have been, levels of interest, or that the research monograph is not the only measure of interest.

Throughout antiquity itself the interest in slavery as such was a contemporary, not a historical, one. The few apparent exceptions are only apparent – the various wrong-headed explanations of the origin of Spartan helots; the assertion by the fourth-century B.C. historian Theopompus (quoted in Athenaeus 4.265B-C), that the Chiots were the first to have *bought* slaves from the barbarians, made in the context of

17

Spartan decline and of the Graeco-Macedonian invasion of
'barbarian' Persia;[15] Dionysius of Halicarnassus (*Roman Antiquities* 4.24) on the good old days as a blatant contrast to the
degeneration which provoked the Augustan enactments of his
own day curbing manumissions. Such references to the past,
historical or mythical, made in order to explain or justify or
illuminate a current situation, belief or action, were common –
one need only think of Pindar's odes – but they did not constitute an interest in the past as such, or in history, let alone in a
history of, or an historical inquiry into, a particular institution.
To hold otherwise is a modern illusion, generated by the
creation of a discipline called 'history' and its introduction into
school and university curricula.

The illusion is heightened, when we come to more recent
centuries, by the unique status and authority of classical culture
in western civilization. The citation of Greek and Roman
authors was a familiar technique in numerous contexts, but
neither Aquinas's reliance on Aristotle nor Dante's choice of
Virgil as his guide nor the classical quotations of the American
Founding Fathers had anything to do with a desire to study and
understand Graeco-Roman society or its history. For certain
purposes, individual Greek and Roman writers and thinkers
were selected as models of excellence, in style or education or
morals or logic, to be deployed in suitable contemporaneous
ways. For many purposes they were not serviceable, and then
other authorities replaced them, for example, in the seventeenth-
century debate about English law, for which the historical (and
more often the pseudo-historical) paradigms were English, not
Greek or Roman.[16] And so with the defenders of slavery:
Aristotle offered no more than learned embroidery to the main
argument, which rested on Scripture.[17] To justify the enslavement of some of God's creatures, the support of God was
needed, not of history or of pagan philosophy, which knew
neither sin nor baptism.

The one sphere in which the ancients could, and did, provide
major assistance was the practical one of the law. Roman law
offered unbroken continuity, first through the Germanic codes,

then through the revival of Roman law in the later Middle Ages. The basic texts survived in more than sufficient quantity and there were learned commentaries.[18] Hence the Europeans who peopled the New World with imported African slaves had a ready-made legal system at their disposal, which they adopted almost *in toto*, modifying it slowly to meet certain new conditions, for example, in the eventual restriction of manumission to a minimum. Not surprisingly, no serious study of ancient slavery was stimulated by this juristic activity. Not even Jacques Cujas, greatest of the early modern commentators on the *Corpus Iuris*, contributed anything fresh or penetrating, nor did the occasional dissertation *de iure servorum*.

Neither did the great men of the Enlightenment, despite the current easy assumption to the contrary. Although historical information was for them an essential weapon in their emancipation from the 'domination of metaphysical and theological thinking',[19] their concern with history was purely as a source of paradigms, not as a discipline.[20] The culmination came with Montesquieu, the first thinker, in Cassirer's words, 'to grasp and to express clearly the concept of "ideal types" in history. *The Spirit of the Laws* is a political and sociological doctrine of types', in which the facts are sought 'not for their own sake but for the sake of the laws which they illustrate and express'.[21] In lesser exponents of the new spirit, especially in the political arena, 'facts' were invented as much as sought; history became neither paradigmatic nor sociological but counterfeit. The French Revolution, Marx noted in the opening of *The Eighteenth Brumaire*, 'draped itself alternatively as the Roman Republic and the Roman Empire'. Sparta was preferred over Athens, then to be replaced in the post-revolutionary era by the legend of 'bourgeois Athens'.[22]

When men of the Enlightenment wrote about ancient slavery, as they did often, though briefly, the paradigmatic approach was obvious and universal. The eighteenth century in France (and in England) was deeply concerned with both slavery in the New World and serfdom in the Old, which were treated as essentially identical (for example, by John Millar and Adam

Smith) or were distinguished in purely formal Roman-law terms, as personal and real slavery (in the *Encylopédie*, for example). The dominant trend was opposed to slavery, though Voltaire and Montesquieu were rather ambiguous in contrast to the unqualified hostility of Diderot or Holbach.[23] Not even the latter, it is worth saying, condemned slavery more bitterly, or with greater knowledge of the Greek and Roman sources, than Jean Bodin in the sixteenth century (*République*, Bk. I, ch. 5).

The key eighteenth-century figure was Montesquieu. There are several well known enigmas about his relatively brief discussion of slavery in Book XV (we should say 'chapter') of the *Esprit des lois*: this is the second of four books within the larger context of climate; it is entitled 'In what Manner the Laws of Civil Slavery Relate to the Nature of the Climate'; and it offers a curious justification of slavery in tropical zones. Nevertheless, these few pages constituted the most influential intellectual attack on slavery written in the eighteenth century. Thus, the chevalier de Jaucourt began his article on 'esclavage' in the fifth volume of the *Encyclopédie* (1755) with an acknowledgement of his reliance on Montesquieu, proceeded to label slavery as a nearly universal institution 'to the shame of mankind', and made no concession at any point in his abolitionism. Behind Montesquieu's analysis there lay wide reading in classical authors, of course, but also in the Roman and Germanic law codes and in the great 'voyages' describing the customs and manners of the New World, the Middle and Far East, more or less in equal measure.[24] Nothing could better illustrate Cassirer's conclusion that the facts were sought 'not for their own sake but for the sake of the laws which they illustrate and express'. No historical *inquiry*, no *historia* in the original Greek sense, was stimulated, let alone a study of ancient slavery.

Exceptions can of course be cited. In one direction, there is the failure of the Abbé Barthélemy, a celebrated *érudit* influenced by Montesquieu, Voltaire and especially Rousseau, to take account of slavery in all the seven volumes of his *Voyage du jeune Anacharsis en Grèce*, published in 1789, reprinted at least five times in French and translated into several languages by the end of the century, though his few references are thoroughly hostile.[25] In another direction, there is the stimulus which the Enlightenment gave to historical study in Germany. Between 1800 and 1805 there appeared in Leipzig a massive multi-volume history of Sparta by J. C. F. Manso, a Breslau educator, poet and historian, and an important, controversial Enlightenment figure in his day (though I believe hardly known outside Germany). This remarkable narrative, which carried the story down to the Roman incorporation of Greece into its empire, concentrated on political and military history, but it also devoted dozens of appendices to a wide range of other topics, such as the costs of the Peloponnesian War, and it is punctuated by lengthy reflective digressions in which the man of the Enlightenment reveals himself. The most notable, in our present context, is Manso's assessment of the 'constitution of Lycurgus' (I 178–92), a severe critique of Sparta, primarily because of its base in the exploitation of helots and its concentration on military virtues. Manso's *Sparta* was soon undeservably obliterated by the appearance in 1824 of that perniciously influential 1000-page fantasia, Karl Otfried Müller's *Die Dorier*, in which the helots and the dependent labour in other so-called Dorian states were together squeezed into twenty pages of blatant apologetics. Müller was neither 'enlightened' nor liberal;[26] if he nevertheless called the chattel slaves of such 'commercial states' as Athens a permanent danger to 'morality and order' (I 39), that was not because he was an abolitionist but because this incidental remark served to sharpen the glorification of Sparta and the denigration of Athens.

As a historian, Manso clung to the subject-matter that had been traditional ever since the Greeks: helots appeared in the narrative when necessary and were otherwise dealt with in a single appendix. So too with the greatest 'exception' of them all, Edward Gibbon. Although he 'was entirely at home in the new Paris of the encyclopedists and he shared many of their convictions' as well as adopting his 'leading political, moral and religious ideas' from them,[27] he wrote *The Decline and Fall of the Roman Empire*, the first modern history of any period of antiquity (and arguably the first modern history *tout court*). Roman history had been a recognized university subject for the previous hundred and fifty years, but the practice everywhere, in England and on the continent, often imposed by statute or charter, was essentially no more than a reading, with commentary, of one or more Latin historians. Gibbon took a revolutionary step by writing his own history, not (or not so much) by transforming the proper subject-matter of history. Slavery was relegated to a few decorous paragraphs in the second chapter, which betrayed the influence of Montesquieu but without the latter's subtle analysis or moral fervour (or even Manso's), and it was then ignored, except fleetingly when it was directly involved in a particular event and therefore was required in the narrative.[28]

The distinction is further exemplified in the first history of Greece, by the Scottish classicist and royal historiographer, John Gillies, a substantial two-volume work published in 1786, ten years after Gibbon's first volume. The helots received adequate attention in the narrative of the Messenian wars and of the fifth-century revolt, but only a single sentence in twenty-two pages on the Lycurgan reorganization of the Spartan government and social system. Slaves elsewhere in Greece were virtually ignored, though one isolated sentence is so astonishing that I cannot refrain from quoting it: the system introduced by Solon, Gillies explained, 'would be attended with the inconvenience of withdrawing the citizens too much from their private affairs' were it not for the fact that slaves outnumbered the free by four to one (p. 457). Gillies was no Enlightenment figure, as is evident, for instance, from the violence of his diatribes against the Sophists, yet he could refer to slavery with as much moral outrage as any abolitionist of the day.

To pursue the trail through Mitford, Niebuhr, Thirlwall and the other major historians of Greece and Rome in the ensuing decades would be a profitless exercise. It is enough to look briefly at George Grote, a philosophical radical far along the political spectrum in his distance from John Gillies. Early in his *History*, in the context of the social structure of Thessaly, Grote wrote: 'As a general rule, indeed, the cultivation of the soil by slaves or dependents, for the benefit of proprietors in the cities, prevailed throughout most parts of Greece.'[29] Yet in a work many times longer than Gillies', slavery occupied no more space, and that in the same context – Sparta and bits of narrative. That he was more penetrating in his observations and far more 'modern' in his source criticism goes without saying – but is irrelevant to my theme.

The inescapable conclusion is that those who assert that the modern interest in ancient slavery began with the Enlightenment and abolitionism have been looking for the wrong things in the wrong places. They have forgotten that, in Momigliano's terse formulation, in the seventeenth and eighteenth centuries 'modern people wrote "antiquitates", not Roman (or Greek) histories'.[30] And among the antiquarians the study of ancient slavery (more precisely, Roman slavery) attained monographic scale at an early date. I restrict myself to a few out of a considerable number, in particular those which were widely used and cited to the end of the nineteenth century and sometimes in the twentieth, among them two of the earliest.[31] In 1608 the Frisian Titus Popma published in Leiden his *De operis servis liber*, consisting essentially of a series of 'definitions' of terms, such as *vicarius* or *dispensator*, followed by a relevant quotation or two from ancient authors. Five years later the Paduan cleric and antiquarian Lorenzo Pignoria produced a tome of more than 200 pages, *De servis, et eorum apud veteres ministeriis commentarius*, erudite and systematic with a very modern-looking index of sources that included not only literary and juristic texts but also inscriptions and figured monuments. The bulk of the book consists of a detailed account of the urban occupations of Roman slaves, not to be surpassed until the late nineteenth century.[32] Both books went through at least three printings in the course of a century, and that is measure enough of the interest in ancient slavery in the pre-Enlightenment era. So is Joachim Potgiesser's account of Germanic slaves and freedmen from the time of Caesar to the end of the Middle Ages, originally published in 1703, reissued in 1736 in a volume of 985 pages.

These early antiquarian works were well known to, and often found in the private libraries of, the French *érudits*, a few of whom continued research into ancient slavery, even during and after the Revolution. The *Mémoires* of the Académie des Inscriptions et Belles Lettres were the main outlet. I do not propose to provide a catalogue: it is enough to mention the long and hostile account of the revolt of Spartacus published in volume 37 (1774), by Charles de Brosses, one of the leading magistrates and parliamentarians of his era; and the two studies by the polymath Jean Levesque de Burigny (author, among other works, of biographies of Erasmus and Grotius) on Roman slaves and freedmen (in volumes 35 and 37).

Some of this basic bibliography, beginning with Popma and Pignoria, opened the appropriate chapter in Friedrich Creuzer's *Abriss der römischen Antiquitäten*, published in 1824, in order, he himself explained, to meet the need for a collection of sources and references to accompany university lectures. Creuzer — friend of Schlegel and other dominating figures of German Romanticism, author of two seminal works, one on Greek historiography,[33] the other on symbolism in ancient religion and mythology, who knew his Grotius, Montesquieu and Hegel as well as the most esoteric Byzantine scholia — made no apology for writing an antiquarian work of such austerity that it avoided continuous prose in favour of mere headings and phrases followed by massive citation and quotation of sources and commentaries. He considered slavery important enough to assign it the third chapter, immediately following the origins and the topography of Rome. His nineteenth-century successors, such as Marquardt in the *Privataltertümer*, shared that assessment, and they had the advantage over Creuzer of possessing a model antiquarian monograph published in 1833, *An Inquiry into the State of Slavery amongst the Romans*, by William Blair, neither an academic nor a classical scholar but a Scottish lawyer.

It is noteworthy that all this antiquarian research into ancient slavery was almost exclusively devoted to the Romans. With the important exception of the demographers and of the philologist and jurist J. F. Reitemeier, to whom I shall return, Greek slaves attracted no inquiry on their own. They made their appearance in such monographs as Everhard Feith's book on Homeric antiquities (Leiden 1677) or Samuel Petit's *Leges atticae* (Paris 1635), but not independently. Obviously Greek sources had nothing to offer comparable to the revolts of the second and first centuries B.C. or the Roman agrarian writings or the enormous bulk of the *Corpus Iuris*. Yet I am neither persuaded that this is a sufficient explanation of the difference nor able to offer a better one. Even August Böckh produced only a few pages in his *Staatshaushaltung der Athener* (1817), and they were narrow in scope (restricted to numbers and prices), less complete and less sophisticated than earlier English and French treatments of the same figures, and showed a surprising incomprehension of the arguments of David Hume, for example.[34] Two years earlier, in a monograph on the Attic silver mines, Böckh opened the half-dozen pages on slavery with a sharp attack on the institution and then proceeded to a series of fantastic miscalculations and misjudgments of the numbers of slaves employed in the mines and of the profits derived by their owners.[35] Even feebler were the few pages, a generation later, in K. F. Hermann's *Lehrbuch der griechischen Antiquitäten* (1852), though he had Wallon available to him. It was not, so far as I know, until Büchsenschütz brought out his *Besitz und Erwerb im griechischen Alterthume* in 1869 that Greek slavery received a full antiquarian account, 104 pages in a work of 624 pages covering the period from Homer to Alexander (and excluding the western Greeks).

Büchsenschütz closed with the brief statement (pp. 207–8) that slavery was not only bad economically, though the ancients could not have judged that, but also bad morally and demographically. This may serve to remind us of the fact, often forgotten, that the antiquarians of the past were far from bloodless. Generally they saw ancient slavery as an evil, though they differed in the tone of their condemnation. One must then ask what has led Vogt to single out William Blair's book for special praise: 'how objective this kind of antiquarian research was. . . .

25

His analysis . . . avoided value-judgments in its reconstruction of ancient institutions'.[36] I should not myself select avoidance of value judgments as the best way to characterize an author who referred to 'the odious traffic in human beings' (p. 24); who introduced a seven-page section on punishment and torture (supported by more than five pages of end-notes) with the words, 'The industry of slaves was excited, and their obedience enforced, by severe discipline', and noted that 'punishments were not thought too revolting spectacles to be exhibited before visitors' (p. 112); and who ended his book with a summary of the evil effects of the institution on Rome, 'one of the main causes of the decay of her empire'.

However, one may, if one has the right predilection, find 'objectivity' here in another sense. Blair and the other nineteenth-century antiquarians held fast to that tradition of the genre which had already evoked the hostility of the eighteenth-century 'philosophical historians'. They 'aimed at factual truth, not at interpretation of causes or examination of consequences' or at 'a reinterpretation of the past which leads to conclusions about the present'.[37] An enthusiastic anonymous review of Blair closed with these words of praise: 'He has no splendid theory to illustrate; no object but that of diffusing the valuable knowledge which his industry has enabled him to collect'.[38] The sweeping final generalizations of Blair and Büchsenschütz were mere assertions, neither properly developed at the end nor integrated into the account in the body of the work. There was also a silence about contemporary slavery too pervasive to have been accidental. Blair, indeed, declared in his introduction: 'I do not attempt to institute any comparison between modern colonial, and ancient slavery.' He gave two reasons: first, 'the two systems differ so widely, that they could serve but little to illustrate each other'; second, he himself is 'not sufficiently informed' on the modern side.

Creuzer provides even more decisive evidence. In 1827, three years after the publication of his *Abriss*, he was invited to give a lecture in Paris under the auspices of the Académie des Inscriptions et Belles Lettres, of which he was a member, and he chose as his topic 'Glimpses of Slavery in Ancient Rome'. In the version published nine years later (in German),[39] he gave three reasons for his choice: the current French and English interest in abolitionism, the recent discovery of such important texts as Cicero's *De republica* and the *Institutes* of Gaius, and the opportunity to inform a French audience about German ideas and research. These considerations apart, he continued, *the subject in itself* (*der Gegenstand an sich*: his italics) must occupy the antiquarian, the historian, the philosopher, and every thinking man. He proceeded to a bitter attack on ancient society and morality: 'among the Greeks and Romans slavery is the chief limitation on the so renowned, so exaggeratedly praised nobility (*Herrlichkeit*) of ancient life. . . . Slavery is the great world-historical dividing-line that forever separated paganism and Christianity'.[40] Every branch of public or private life, he concluded, was linked directly or indirectly to the existence of slavery. And then, in the lecture proper, in the annotation which was as long as the text itself, and in addenda (written in 1835) as long as the text and notes together, he devoted his vast erudition solely to the most dogged antiquarianism, on the etymology of the words *servus* and *Sklave*, on slave garments, and the like.[41] The conclusion seems to me inescapable that the contemporary discussions of slavery had little interest for Creuzer despite his strong moral stance, and that they were certainly not the stimulus to his own study of ancient slavery, that he made a bow to them in his Paris lecture only in order to please his hosts. If that is right, it would help explain why in the citations of his wide reading there is no reference to Hume or the early 'economists', to whom I now turn.[42] They were the fountainheads of the second of the two approaches, the sociological one, I singled out at the beginning.

I employ the label 'economists' loosely for the writers who, chiefly from the middle of the eighteenth century, examined wealth, labour, production, trade, in what we should now call 'economic' terms, and often with a historical dimension or perspective.[43] They did not abandon moral categories: virtually every man I shall discuss in this section condemned slavery wholeheartedly, though few were in any sense abolitionists and not all can legitimately be identified with the Enlightenment. But they moved the discussion of slavery – my main concern – into a radically new institutional nexus.

The first, and prime, point that emerges from an examination of this literature is the unanimity with which it was agreed that slave labour was less efficient, because more expensive, than free labour. So obvious did this seem both to Benjamin Franklin, living in the midst of the slaveowners of the New World, and to John Millar or Adam Smith in faraway Scotland, that they found detailed argument unnecessary. A few general considerations sufficed.[44] Their explanations of the persistence of slavery in the face of its relative costliness were equally brief and simple: cheap land for Franklin, habit and lack of economic insight for Millar, man's 'love to domineer' for Smith. The latter two are not very 'economic', admittedly, but they at least lack the apologetic quality of the traditional explanations, which were designed to save the morality of slavery, such as original sin or the preservation of captive barbarians from death.

None of this required, or stimulated, any serious historical inquiry. However, slavery became entangled in the increasingly sophisticated demographic debates of the eighteenth century, with a perhaps unexpected but certainly decisive consequence. I oversimplify, but, with that caveat, it is fair to say that it was generally agreed, first (in David Hume's words), that 'there is in all men, both male and female, a desire and power of generation', so that, in the absence of restraints of one sort or another, 'the human species . . . would more than double every generation';[45] second, that a growing population contributed to the prosperity and well-being of a nation. A considerable body of pamphleteering arose on different aspects of these propositions that can be traced back to the sixteenth century, some of first-rate quality and significance, laying the foundation for modern demography, much, on the other hand, that can safely be labelled fantastic or ridiculous. Two of the debated questions concern us and they will have to be examined jointly: 1) was the world more heavily populated in ancient times than now? 2) what effects, if any, does large-scale employment of slaves have on population growth?

The affirmative answer to the first question had much support, thanks in particular to the early books of the Old Testament and the generations of Methuselah. Explanation was then required not only for the supposedly sharp drop in population at some point in the past, but also for the failure of contemporary society to achieve a return to the lost numbers. Much of the explanation was heavily moralistic, as well as intellectually weak, but the quality changed once the problem was taken over by those I have been calling 'economists'. And they, predictably, brought slavery into account. The first two for us to consider were Benjamin Franklin, writing in a purely contemporary context of trade and protectionism, and David Hume, who set out openly to disprove the alleged demographic superiority of the ancients.

In 1751 Franklin wrote a short pamphlet, 'Observations concerning the Increase of Mankind', only eight pages in the standard modern collection of his papers, which circulated by hand until it was published in Boston in 1755 and immediately reprinted several times in London. Section 13 listed six things which 'must diminish a nation', among them 'the introduction of slaves'. His explanation deserves to be quoted in full: 'The Negroes brought into the English Sugar Islands have greatly diminish'd the Whites there; the Poor are by this means depriv'd of Employment, while a few Families acquire vast Estates; which they spend on Foreign Luxuries, and educating their Children in the Habit of those Luxuries; the same Income is needed for the Support of one that might have maintain'd 100. The Whites who have Slaves, not labouring, are enfeebled, and therefore not so generally prolific; the Slaves being work'd too hard, and ill fed, their Constitutions are broken, and the Deaths among them are more than the Births; so that a continual Supply is needed from Africa. The Northern Colonies having few Slaves increase in Whites. Slaves also pejorate the Families that use them; the white Children become proud,

29

disgusted with Labour, and being educated in Idleness, are rendered unfit to get a Living by Industry.'

Simultaneously, and presumably without knowledge of Franklin's seminal pamphlet, Hume was writing his 'Of the Populousness of Ancient Nations', a lengthy essay (published in 1752), which, despite its title, ranged so widely as to earn McCulloch's accolade a century later, 'the most perfect specimen ever published of an inquiry into any matter connected with the public economy of the ancients'.[46] Hume had been stimulated, as I have already noted, by the argument over the relative populousness of the ancients and the moderns, and the starting-point of his own analysis was the following: The 'chief difference between the *domestic* economy of the ancients and that of the moderns consists in the practice of slavery' (pp. 385-6). Not only is slavery 'more cruel and oppressive than any civil subjection whatsoever', he concluded, but it is also 'in general disadvantageous both to the happiness and the populousness of mankind' (p. 396). The bulk of the essay was occupied with a systematic, critical examination of the population figures in Greek and Roman literary sources, which are 'often ridiculous' (p. 419), including the numbers of slaves. On any account, this study must rank as one of the first original *historical* inquiries into ancient social and economic history. Beloch praised it as 'the basis for every inquiry into the population statistics of antiquity',[47] but that is too narrow a view of its range and quality.

Now a third name has to be introduced, that of the Scottish divine Robert Wallace, who had read a paper on the same subject to the Edinburgh Philosophical Society 'several years earlier', and who was now provoked to publish his effort with an appendix, a reply to Hume twice as long as the latter's essay.[48] Wallace was learned enough to catch Hume out in some factual errors, but his method with the evidence, set out in minute detail from Homer's Catalogue of Ships to the fantastic slave numbers quoted by Athenaeus, was one of uncritical acceptance: the larger the figure in any ancient text, the better for his argument. McCulloch's verdict was that he had 'wholly failed to shake its [Hume's] foundations', but by no means everyone agreed, then or now.[49]

The Hume-Wallace controversy stirred up extensive interest and discussion both in Britain and on the continent,[50] which continued to the mid-nineteenth century, as McCulloch reveals. Among the most active discussants were the *philosophes* and the demographers, but their interest, which was never directed to either the Graeco-Roman data or the special problem of the slave population, soon evaporated: thus Malthus, though acknowledging the contribution to demographic theory of Hume and Wallace (and Adam Smith) in his opening, totally ignored these sections of their work. The *érudits*, in contrast, seized on precisely what Malthus passed over, and they produced a series of learned studies of ancient population in general and of slave numbers in particular: Guilhem de Sainte Croix and Letronne on Athens, then Dureau de la Malle on the Romans and particularly on Italy under the Republic.[51] These studies were among the essential building-blocks underpinning the nineteenth-century antiquarian works on ancient slavery.[52]

However, just as Malthus and his successors abandoned one side of the Hume-Wallace debate, the interest in the size of ancient slave populations, the latter-day antiquarians abandoned the other, more important side, that which led McCulloch to praise Hume's essay as an inquiry into the *public economy* of the ancients. I have already mentioned August Böckh's failure to comprehend what Hume was getting at, and I could repeat that dismissive judgment about virtually every antiquarian and historian who went over the slave-population ground thereafter.[53] I shall restrict myself to Wallon. Two of his longest chapters are on slave numbers, revealing his customary knowledge of the ancient evidence and the modern discussions, but total indifference to the fundamental demographic issues, and in essence these chapters are pointless. Nor is there a serious consideration of labour efficiency anywhere in the three volumes. There are only the conventional, meaningless generalities about growing trade and industry. Slavery is intrinsically wrong on ethical grounds, and its destructive effect on the free people is also a moral one: by its example and by its unfair competitive position, slavery destroys the work ethic, driving the free, and especially the free poor, into sloth and vice.

In other words, Wallon's work on ancient slavery was the climax of antiquarianism in this field. His moral fervour also helped divert the subject from the already available, though still embryonic, institutional approach. That is hardly surprising. It seems regularly to be overlooked that the book was written for a prize competition set by the Académie des Sciences *Morales* et Politiques, whose themes for their competitions were regularly moral and philosophical. On this occasion they had selected the following: '1. Through what causes was ancient slavery abolished? 2. In which epoch was there only serfdom (*servitude de la glèbe*) in western Europe, ancient slavery having come to an end?' I have been unable to discover who or what was behind that choice of topic, but it is not to be seriously doubted that they expected moral disquisitions within an historical frame. One unsuccessful entrant had had the presumption, in Michelet's words, to attribute the abolition to a single cause, interest: 'The masters found it to their advantage to free the slaves in return for rents, in other words, to become rentiers instead of masters; it was a question of industry, not a moral question.' This competitor never even asked himself whether Christianity or 'barbarian customs' or the feudal system had any influence. So, though he submitted 'a clever, brilliant, paradoxical work, full of talent and of rash views', it did not receive even honourable mention.[54]

The successful competitors did not make that mistake. All three, Wallon, Biot and Yanoski, produced the same answer to the question set: Christianity was the key. All three were also honest and intelligent enough to perceive, and to try to cope with, the obvious difficulty, the delay of many centuries before Christianity took effect. All three also found substantially the same way out, in Biot's formulation: 'Christianity does what it should; it accepts the political disposition of society as a given condition to which it must submit; it accepts temporal slavery as a fact. It directs its efforts only to the morality of men . . .

legislation favourable to the social position of the slave was indeed rare, and one should not be too surprised by that . . . it is evident that laws too favourable to the slaves would have strongly tended to upset the whole social edifice, already crumbling under the repeated blows of foreign invasions. It was preferable, in order to maintain public tranquility, that improvement in the lot of the slave be brought about progressively through improvements of the master'.[55]

What other answers to the Academy's demand for causes were in fact available? One possibility, under the influence of the new German historical school of law, was to look to the Germanic invaders of the Roman empire, and two competitors took that line, one a German who specifically dismissed Christianity as impotent in the matter. He shared honourable mention (presumably for his excellent analysis of documents of the tenth and eleventh centuries) with a long contribution of extreme piety which concluded that the abolition of slavery was brought about not by 'the influence of Christianity in general but by the Catholic and pontifical influence in particular'.[56] Biot and Yanoski, in contrast, went to some lengths to deny any Germanic contribution.

Another possibility was to build on the foundations laid by the earlier 'economists', but in 1837 men who had that kind of interest had none in the question posed by the Académie (or they were discouraged from competing by knowledge of the interests and bias of the Académie). No fourth possibility comes to mind, and so the moral answer had the field virtually to itself.

In sum, far from marking the beginning of modern research into ancient slavery, Wallon's *Histoire* was a dead end. I am not referring to the contingent fact that he, like the other prize-winners, young products of the Grandes Ecoles, was not a classical historian. Biot was a Sinologist who had already written a memoir on slavery in Chinese history. Yanoski was a protégé of Michelet's and for a period his assistant: he and Wallon went on to further historical study and publication, but always in fields far removed from either antiquity or slavery.

The essential point is that, along Wallon's lines, subsequent consideration of ancient slavery was restricted to still more antiquarian examination or, on the moral side, to either propagation of the faith – it is enough to cite the article on slavery by J. Dutilleul in the *Dictionnaire de Théologie catholique* (1924) – or to theological debate, as with Overbeck. No basis was laid for continuing *historical* inquiry. There could be no better demonstration than his own words in the concluding section of his work: 'But the reintroduction of slavery in modern times was an act of violence against the spirit of the Gospels, . . . an abruptly retrogade step. If it pleased some greedy merchants, some inhuman politicians, to return to slavery, it is not for Christianity to retreat with them.'

The strength of Wallon's abolitionist feelings is beyond question, but so is the fact that it had little connection, if any, with either the Enlightenment or the rise of 'modern social constructive criticism'. A puzzle remains. Why did Wallon devote a decade of hard, sustained labour on a 1500-page *introduction* to the 'abolition' of ancient slavery, leaving the account of the abolition itself to others; 1500 pages, furthermore, that were largely irrelevant to his central concern? What difference did it make, for example, morally or otherwise, whether classical Athens had 100,000, 200,000 or 400,000 slaves? Perhaps there is an answer to that question, but none is to be found in Wallon's many pages on those particular figures. I have no explanation and I suggest that it is lost in irrecoverable individual psychology.

At the same time another work appeared, beginning in 1854, which, on the subject of ancient slavery, was equally exceptional and equally a dead end – Mommsen's multi-volume *Roman History*. Slavery is treated from the outset in an unprecedented way, as fundamental to Roman society and history. There is no need in the present context to examine Mommsen's views concretely, beyond registering this central location of slavery (he uses such terms as *Sklavenhaltersystem* and *Sklavenwirtschaft*) and the bitterness of his moral condemnation.[57] Why Mommsen broke from the tradition of historical writing about antiquity in this as in other respects – in so far as he had a model, it was Macaulay – is another enigma I am unable to resolve. Neither his liberalism nor his early experience in political journalism offers a sufficient explanation, and his biographers appear to be oblivious to this interesting aspect of his work. Whereas the *Roman History*, enormously popular with the reading public, has always had an ambivalent reception among professional historians of antiquity, his stress on slavery has met with no response at all: subsequent general histories of Rome (as of Greece) have simply abandoned it.[58]

This is not to deny that, after Wallon and Mommsen, articles and monographs on ancient slavery proliferated, as part of the increasing flow of academic publication. Informative as some of them are, they are of no interest collectively: they are merely a nineteenth- (and often twentieth-) century manifestation of the older 'works of curious erudition', though they are now called 'scholarship' rather than 'antiquarianism'.[59] Were they the sum total of research into the subject, the sharp, important, and often (as today) heated debates about the place of slavery in Greek and Roman history would never have come into being. The stimulus was provided elsewhere, by men who were not by vocation students of classical antiquity and who transformed the eighteenth-century doctrine of stages in social evolution based on modes of subsistence into a new model (or, rather, into several competing models).

The first work on the new lines, published in 1789, was in fact without influence, but it deserves to be rescued from oblivion. Johann Friedrich Reitemeier has been described in the *Allgemeine Deutsche Biographie* as 'a man of great gifts and the best education, whose widely ranging activity and originality of mind proved virtually fruitless because of the flaws in his character and way of life'. A devoted pupil of Heyne's in Göttingen, he edited the text of the early Byzantine historian Zosimus and wrote monographs on mining in antiquity, on luxury in Athens, and on torture in Greek and Roman law-courts, before turning to legal history, the field in which he could fairly claim to have been the founder of the German historical school, the forerunner of Hugo and Savigny. In 1783, during his first phase, he won the prize in a competition of the Gesellschaft der Alterthümer in Cassel (in which the entrants were free to choose their subject), and six years later he published his essay in Berlin under the title, *Geschichte und Zustand der Sklaverey und Leibeigenschaft in Griechenland*, which won enthusiastic approval from his teacher Heyne. It appears to have had little circulation and it rapidly became a scarce item: Blair wrote in 1833 that he had never succeeded in seeing a copy and the *Allgemeine Deutsche Biographie* does not even mention it. Today it is virtually unobtainable.[60]

Wallon knew it and dismissed it as a 'work of slight dimensions and medium accuracy' (I 62), citing it only twice, both times for generally accepted points of fact. But it is also an original and sophisticated historical-sociological essay, with a sustained argument that is maintained through its 175 pages, towards which Wallon was characteristically insensitive and indifferent.[61] Reitemeier's long opening sentence would have been enough to put Wallon off: 'Universal human equality, to which everyone without exception may lay claim according to the first principles of natural law, appears to be incompatible with civil society (*bürgerliche Gesellschaft*); for everywhere among the peoples of both ancient and modern times we find inequality, the consequence of subordination, without which there can be no civil society.' What has changed in the course of history is not the fact of dominance and submission (*Herrschaft und Dienstbarkeit*) but the dimension (*Mass*) of the ties between the two. The interest in ancient slavery lies there, in its historical place as the oldest expression in a civil society of the dominance-submission relationship. How did it come into being? What were the advantages and disadvantages 'for the mass of the population and their situation'? For the working population itself?

Reitemeier's springboard in answering the first question was Millar's *Origin of Ranks* (which he knew as he knew Hume and Wallace). Women and children were the first 'to serve men in the production of the means of sustenance and shelter' (p. 11), but with the rise of pastoralism (he writes 'nomadism'), a greater labour supply was required. Under prevailing conditions, workers were obtainable only through compulsion, by rapine, war and purchase. The victims became 'personal' slaves, members of the master's household, and to that extent had a secure existence, more so than casual hired workers but less so than the later 'public (öffentliche) slaves', notably the Spartan helots, who were in effect serfs and were most like the bound peasants of today, especially in 'old Germany'. The first signs of transition from the 'nomadic' type of slavery appear in the Homeric poems (to which Reitemeier devotes an unusually long section, pp. 18–34), but the 'great revolution' came about in the fifth century B.C. Although Athens is the one city in which that can be fully seen in the available evidence, the implication is safe that a similar change occurred wherever the arts and trade flourished (p. 35). The sharp rise in demand for urban labour, driven by a great increase in the standard of living, in the new hunger for luxuries of every kind, prostitutes, fine public and private buildings, fine jewelry and metalwork, and so on, led to the emergence of the classical form of slavery, distinct from the 'personal' slavery found in pastoral and agrarian households.

The dynamic role of luxuries was already a familiar notion: Reitemeier had no doubt read the two relevant essays of David Hume's, 'Of Commerce' and 'Of Refinement in the Arts'. What was brilliantly original with him was the close link with the transformation of Greek slavery.[62] The landowning aristocrats, he argues (pp. 55–58), seized upon this new and growing demand to move into urban investments, without surrendering their base in the land or their hostility to the arts and crafts: they established workshops, trading organizations and brothels which were slave-managed and slave-worked. They thereby blocked the healthy development of an urban middle class of traders and craftsmen, and they thus set the future course of the Greek city-state, economically, politically and ideologically.

The monograph closes with a lengthy balance-sheet. Classical slavery offered two advantages: it was a cheaper form of labour and it solved the problem of labour shortage. But the disadvantages tipped the balance: flight and revolts created an atmosphere of insecurity; the class structure was lopsided; 'enlightenment and the spread of knowledge' (*Aufklärung und die Verbreitung der Kenntnisse*) were much impaired (p. 146); social mobility was too restricted; the state (*Staatsherrschaft*) remained weak as against 'stern household rule' (*strenge Hausherrschaft*). Therefore, the freedom of the 'serving sector' (*dienende Antheil*) of the population, as it exists among 'the present German and other European countries', is much better for the state and for the subordinate classes as well.

The magnitude of Reitemeier's leap from both antiquarianism and the narrowly moral view of ancient slavery can scarcely be exaggerated. How right or wrong he may have been in either his generalizations or his details is beside the point. What matters is, first, that he anticipated by half a century the Rodbertus-Bücher concept of the 'household-economy' of classical antiquity, and that he anticipated Marx and Weber in assigning a central role to slavery in shaping the *evolution* of ancient society;[63] second, that he seems to have had no influence whatever on subsequent inquiries into the subject. Nothing like this monograph had appeared before; nothing like it was to appear again until the end of the nineteenth century.

Whatever Reitemeier's personal failings, they cannot explain the total neglect of his monograph on Greek slavery. The key lay elsewhere, in a profound cleavage that set in at precisely the turn of the century with the rise of the modern university and its departmentalization, notably and most completely in Germany. What may be called professional interest in the world of classical antiquity became virtually a monopoly of that sector of the university population that named its discipline variously as philology, classical philology, or *Altertumswissenschaft*. There were bitter rivalries and conflicts among them, but they shared the fundamental conviction that their goal, their duty, was to apprehend the mind, the high culture, the *Geist*, the essence, of those incomparable models of spiritual achievement, the Greeks and the Romans, or perhaps the Greeks alone.[64]

The exceptions were the continuators of the antiquarian tradition and the new-style historians of Greece and Rome, neither of whom, we have seen, significantly furthered the study of ancient slavery, much as a few of them may have added to the stock of information on the subject.

I shall have more to say about the new classical philology and the 'philological method', but first we must turn to another intellectual stream, the nineteenth-century successors of the eighteenth-century economists. It was they (more precisely, some among them) who, in a specific and limited way, introduced a new dimension into the consideration of ancient slavery.[65] Three preliminary points about them are important: first, their concern was a contemporary one; second, they were historically minded, not merely in the old sense of paradigmatic history, but in an evolutionary sense, which meant that they conceived contemporary society to be a stage in human history, and were to a greater or lesser extent interested to establish the sequence of stages and to explain the rise and fall of each; third, they were all educated on the classics, knew the sources and read them in the original. There was no communication between them and the philologists. The latter's ties outside their own discipline were with the idealist philosophers and the theorists, chiefly romantic, of the arts and of letters. Seekers after the *Geist* of the Greeks understood barbarism, renaissance, enlightenment; their conceptual world excluded production, capital, labour or rent. August Böckh, a towering figure in the projection of the new classical philology, was no exception: his *Public Economy of Athens* was an uncharacteristic, purely antiquarian work without significant progeny.

By a 'new dimension' I do not mean systematic inquiry or research: not one of the nineteenth-century 'economists' wrote anything about ancient slavery even approaching in scale Reitemeier's essay or the hundred-odd pages of Büchsenschütz's *Besitz und Erwerb* (let alone Wallon's *Histoire*). What was new was the concept of stages (or periods) in the history of society defined, or determined, by the way the economy – property, production, distribution – was organized. Such a concept of history inevitably places greater stress on, and assigns a more complex role to, slavery within the context of ancient society than hitherto. One need only examine the way in which Wilhelm Roscher, in an essay first published in 1849, built an historical model on David Hume's generalization that 'the chief difference between the *domestic* economy of the ancients and that of the moderns consists in the practice of slavery',[66] a model much beyond anything Hume himself conceived.

However, it is not Roscher whom one thinks of first but Karl Marx. Today it requires a considerable effort to remember that the total of Marx's scattered comments on ancient slavery amounts to no more than a few pages, and that most of those are contained in seven notebooks, now generally known as the *Grundrisse*, written in the winter of 1857-8, first published in Moscow in 1939 but hardly noticed before the appearance of the Berlin edition in 1953.[67] Nearly a full century of study and writing based on Marx, specifically about his conception of the evolution of society through stages defined by the nature of the property regime in the land and by the mode of production,[68] proves to have rested on an incomplete and substantially over-simplified pattern. In the *Grundrisse* Marx suggests 'Asiatic', 'Germanic', 'ancient' systems as well as the familiar 'slave', 'feudal' and 'capitalist'. Notebooks are notebooks, not analyses in their final shape, ready for public communication, but a thinking aloud, extraordinarily subtle, complex, dense, bu also often opaque, elliptical and unfinished. Any attempt to convert those pages into a complete, watertight system requires Procrustean treatment of the evidence; for example, by those who wish to distinguish between an ancient mode of production (classical Greece) and a slave mode (Italy from the second century B.C.).[69]

In the subsequent published writings of Marx and Engels the historical scheme became simplified and took on what was soon understood as a unilinear look, particularly in Engels' *Anti-Dühring* and *Origin of the Family*. Why that occurred is not my concern, nor is the contentious question of the extent to which Engels, especially in the two works just mentioned, accurately reflected the views of Marx. What is essential for this discussion is to appreciate the nature and limits of their interest in the Graeco-Roman world. *Das Kapital* was the crown of Marx's career, and that fact must be accepted in its full literal implication. Pre-capitalist (or non-capitalist) forms of property and production were of the greatest significance, not in themselves but as the basic structures in the unfolding of human history. Profound as Marx's interest was in the historical process, at no time in his life did he (or Engels) attempt a study of ancient society or the ancient economy. As Eric Hobsbawm has pointed out, Marx never discussed 'the internal dynamics of pre-capitalist systems except in so far as they explain the preconditions of capitalism', or 'the actual economic contradictions of a slave economy', or 'why in antiquity it was slavery rather than serfdom which developed', or why the ancient mode was replaced by feudalism.[70]

It may even be said, without being paradoxical, that Marx paid little attention to slavery as such. In antiquity it was one of the modes of production which he subjected to brief, abstract analysis. In the modern world it was first one of the means of 'primitive accumulation', in the colonies, then a peculiar anomaly (in the American South) within a capitalist framework. 'The fact', he wrote in the *Grundrisse* (p. 513) 'that we now not only call the plantation owners in America capitalists, but that they *are* capitalists, is based on their existence as anomalies within a world market based on free labour.'[71] In contrast, 'all philologists who speak of *capital* in antiquity, of Roman, Greek capitalists', commit a gross error. Therefore it is also a major error to draw on Marx's various acerbic remarks about *American* slavery in order to fill out his views on *ancient* slavery. Of course there were similarities, common elements – if there were not, there would be no justification for the single label 'slavery' – but there was an unbridgeable divide at the base, the system of production, and that was the determining factor in the analysis.[72]

In the following generation, the followers of Marx (as well as the socialists who disagreed and disputed with him on various points) understandably did not expand his restricted interest in slavery in general, and in ancient slavery in particular. The world of philology or *Altertumswissenschaft* revealed no signs of awareness of his existence, any more than they paid attention to earlier or contemporary economists and economic historians. Only at the turn of the century did a break come, in Italy explicitly with Ettore Ciccotti and Giuseppe Salvioli, in Germany implicitly with Karl Bücher and Max Weber.

Ciccotti's *Il tramonto della schiavitù nel mondo antico* ('The Decline of Slavery in the Ancient World'), published in 1899, was the first full-scale account – it is essential to stress 'full-scale' – of ancient slavery, since Reitemeier's a century earlier, to examine the institution as part of a complex and continuing historical process.[73] The sympathetic though critical reviewer in the *Wochenschrift für klassische Philologie* described it as not only a history of Graeco-Roman slavery but 'along the way virtually a complete economic history'.[74] He was not wrong and there is no cause for surprise: the first Marxist to attempt such an inquiry had no choice in the matter. Even the title Ciccotti adopted, which seems to have attracted insufficient attention, was designed to point to the underlying theory of history. It was also, of course, the theme set early in the century by the Académie des Sciences Morales et Politiques, in the competition that stimulated three books, all of which had come to the same conclusion. And so Ciccotti's introduction began with a detailed critique of the view that Christianity (or Stoicism or any other ethical system) was responsible for the decline of ancient slavery. The alternative approach, he concluded (pp. 73–77), was provided by Marx and Engels; that was to examine ancient slavery (unlike modern) as 'a general and indispensable instrument of production' (p. 57) and to follow its changing role as the ancient economy was transformed under the Romans in a way that not only reduced the need for slaves but also exposed their inherent character as an economic handicap. In other words, in order to explain the decline of ancient slavery it was essential to examine its entire history, and that Ciccotti proceeded to do.[75]

He did not do it very well, not even in his own terms. He was obsessed with both the moral flaw of slavery and the inadequacy of slave labour as an instrument of production; he drew grossly exaggerated picture of a numerous free proletariat in fourth-century B.C. Greece and again in the Roman Empire, openly competing with the slaves; he repeatedly based broad conclusions on data that did not warrant them; his understanding of Marx's theory of modes of production was vague in the extreme. On this last, essential objection, one need only compare two contemporaries who were not Marxists but were very knowledgeable about, and much influenced by, Marx, namely, Karl Bücher in *Die Entstehung der Volkswirtschaft*, published in 1893 (and known to Ciccotti when he wrote *Il tramonto*), and Max Weber in *Die Agrarverhältnisse des Altertums*, published in 1909;[76] and a third, who was a Marxist and a better one than Ciccotti, Giuseppe Salvioli, in a work originally published in French (1906) under the title *Le capitalisme dans le monde antique*, with the subtitle *Etudes sur l'histoire de l'économie romaine*.[77] None of these three wrote about ancient slavery as such, but their incorporation of slavery into their analyses is what matters, and the way that was achieved.

I cannot undertake to expose the full richness of their views, but must content myself with a few quick pointers. For Bücher, it was slavery which permitted 'the most fully developed form' of household-economy to emerge in Graeco-Roman antiquity.[78] Salvioli agreed without accepting Bücher's general historical scheme, but went on, under Marx's influence, to look at Roman slaves as perhaps the first commodity to be bought and sold 'with profit as the aim'. Unlike Ciccotti, he concluded that there was no meaningful competition between free and slave labour in antiquity because no genuine proletariat came into being (and no capitalism).[79] Max Weber, finally, who had studied the work of Ciccotti and Bücher (though apparently not Salvioli) and referred to them favourably if critically, cannot be dealt with adequately in brief compass, both because of the density of his thought and because he continued to re-think and re-consider his views to the end of his life. However, a single longer quotation from a popular lecture on 'The Social Bases of the Decline of Ancient Civilization', delivered and published in 1896, will suffice for my purposes: 'Ancient civilization was a *slave civiliza-tion (Sklavenkultur)*. . . . As in the Middle Ages, the antagonism between both forms of cooperative human labour also existed in antiquity. Progress depends on *progressive* division of labour. With free labour that is more or less identical with progressive *expansion of the market*. . . . With unfree labour that is achieved by progressive *amassing of men*; the more slaves or *coloni*, the greater the specialization of unfree occupations that is possible. But whereas in the Middle Ages *free* labour and the *exchange* of goods were increasingly victorious, the development in antiquity was the *reverse*' (his italics).[80]

None of this made any lasting impact (indeed, hardly any at all) on ancient historians. In the case of Ciccotti that is a puzzle. Unlike Bücher, Salvioli and Weber, he was an ancient historian by profession, holder of the chair at Milan until his dismissal in 1898 because of his political (socialist) activity. *Il tramonto* came at the end of nearly two decades of great productivity, as he published scholarly books and articles on a wide range of major topics. *Il tramonto* was favourably reviewed not only by R. Lange in the *Wochenschrift* but also by Pöhlmann, who called it an important advance, and later by Henri Francotte.[81] And, for all its weaknesses, it is a book filled with insights, the first (and the last) modern work to examine the history of ancient slavery within the framework of the ancient economy and ancient society. Yet it was an almost total failure. It went through two editions in Italian and was translated into French, Spanish and German, but, it appears, for readers who were not academics, or at least not classicists and ancient historians.[82] Only in Italy did he remain an intellectual figure of major consequence;[83] elsewhere he disappeared from sight. The seemingly obvious explanation, his Marxism, does not seem to me to be sufficient. I believe we must also look in another direction.

That means first and foremost Eduard Meyer, the most prestigious ancient historian in the Germanic university world in the generation after Mommsen. Those were the years in which Meyer was writing the third, fourth and fifth volumes of his *Geschichte des Altertums*, published in 1901 and 1902. They dealt with the classical period of Greek history, the fifth and fourth centuries B.C., and, following the orthodox tradition, slavery is allowed no more than one three-page section and two or three additional references. However, the three volumes were preceded by a stream of special studies, including a brief excursus on the size of the slave population in fifth-century Athens, published in the second volume of his *Forschungen zur alten Geschichte* (1899); and by two quickly published lectures, *Die wirtschaftliche Entwicklung des Altertums* (1895) and *Die Sklaverei im Altertum* (1898), subsequently reprinted in the first volume of his *Kleine Schriften* (1910 and again 1924). The *auctoritas* of these two lectures can hardly be exaggerated: a recent account of Eduard Meyer says that 'they quickly acquired the rank of a binding synthesis';[84] for Vogt he 'pointed the way in two excellent sketches of economic history' in which 'proper credit is awarded to the unique character of each age and each civilization';[85] Westermann opened his encylopaedia article with the sentence, 'The basis of our contemporary understanding of slavery in Greek and Roman history was laid by Eduard Meyer.'[86]

The two lectures, which must be taken as an integrally linked pair, are the expressions of a complex ideology, and a no less complex personality. One strand is the doctrine, widely and firmly held by German historians and political theorists, that the state is the decisive organism in history, that modern attempts to shift the focus to cultural and economic history must fail in face of the 'facts'.[87] A second is the wish to rescue the study of antiquity from both the aesthetic/moral idealization of the early nineteenth century and the antiquarianism of the second half of the century by a reconstruction of the 'real picture', which, it turned out, was increasingly 'a mirror-image of the modern world'.[88] A third, which ties the first two together, is total rejection of all conceptions of historical stages defined by economic structures. Marx is of course included, but I have found no evidence that Meyer was particularly concerned with Marx (or had any serious knowledge of his work); he normally spoke contemptuously of 'die Nationalökonomen' (the political economists) as a group, reserving his obsessive fury (that is the right phrase) for Karl Bücher, nor Karl Marx.

Ancient slavery presented an obvious difficulty for a man who wrote, with an evident measure of inconsistency, that the economic conditions pre-supposed by the Twelve Tables 'already carry, in fact, a relatively modern character'; that the seventh and sixth centuries B.C. in Greece correspond to the fourteenth and fifteenth centuries 'in the development of the modern world'; that 'in all respects' the Hellenistic world 'cannot be conceived in too modern a way', though in comparison with the seventeenth and eighteenth centuries rather than the nineteenth; that Athens of the fifth and fourth centuries B.C. 'stands under the banner of capitalism' just as much as England since the eighteenth century, Germany since the nineteenth.[89] What about slavery, then? Meyer's answer was to dismiss it as an historical irrelevance, a by-product of the peculiar political development of the city-state.

He achieved his objective in the lecture on slavery by a series of steps. (1) War was 'the natural relationship' between ethnic groups (*Stämme*). (2) Within the group, slavery was not permissible, whereas serfdom (*Hörigkeit*) was not only allowed but became the common practice, in Israel and throughout the ancient Near East as in archaic Greece and Rome. (3) Therefore the archaic period was a medieval one in the literal sense, and that demolishes any notion of a succession from antiquity to the Middle Ages to the modern world in a series of stages. (4) In the age of tyrants in Greece and in the fifth and fourth centuries B.C. in Rome, urbanism and the great increase in wealth and the standard of living brought capitalism into being, with a corresponding development of trade and industry. (5) However, because of the political transformation and the extension of full rights to the lower classes, free hired labour could not meet the tremendous needs of the capitalists, partly because the free poor were unable and unwilling to take the jobs, partly because they were too expensive when they were willing. (6) Therefore the capitalists, taking advantage of the natural state of war with the outsider, turned to large-scale slave labour. Had slaves not happened to be available, the capitalists 'would have found another way to create the required labour force for themselves'.

(7) The consequence was endless conflict between the slaves and the ruined proletarian masses, who demanded that the state support them, putting the state in an increasingly impossible position, from which the Greeks were saved by Philip and Alexander, the Romans by the *pax Augusta* and the consequent drying up of sources of slave supply. (8) An exact parallel to this development occurred in early modern times, with the minor difference that the second time round serfdom was replaced by free, not slave, labour, because 'the Christian-Germanic development' made the latter impossible (and in the New World, mysteriously, because 'the possibility was lacking of any industrial development'). 'Nowhere,' Meyer writes, 'does the modern character of ancient slavery reveal itself more clearly than in the fact that, under favourable conditions, the slave, like the modern industrial worker, had the possibility of achieving prosperity and wealth.' Besides, slavery was like modern migratory labour in bringing about race mixture. (9) That slavery had nothing to do with the decline of the ancient world is demonstrated by the absence of slave revolts in the Roman Empire. (10) Slaves no longer being available in sufficient numbers, free labour continuing to be too expensive, and tenancy having become unprofitable, the capitalists returned to serfdom. 'And so the circle was closed. The development returned to the point from which it began: the medieval order became dominant for the second time.'

My summary is not in the least a caricature. I called it a 'series of steps' rather than an argument because there is no argument: there is only a succession of *ex cathedra* assertions, in highly rhetorical dress, without either evidence or a discussion of the views under attack. In forty pages there are exactly eleven references to, or quotations without citation from, Greek and Roman sources, and on at least two of those, one of them being Aristotle, the presentation is grossly distorted, and on a third he indulges in tendentious textual criticism. The argument from silence is deployed in opposite directions when it suits him: on the one hand, Bücher is 'crushed' in *Wirtschaftliche Entwicklung* with the (false) statement that his *oikos* (household) does not appear in the sources, but, on the other hand, Meyer himself is permitted, in *Sklaverei*, to sketch a development that was 'generally unknown to contemporaries'.[90] As for modern writers, Meyer's way was always imperious: he could be savage, as with Rodbertus and Bücher, but usually he either ignored others or made prejudicially selective reference to them. Thus, he cited Ciccotti's 'very noteworthy' preliminary study of the numbers of slaves in Athens and ignored everything else Ciccotti had to say; when he quoted a sentence from Weber's *Agrargeschichte* criticizing Rodbertus, he omitted the comment that Rodbertus' work was 'an otherwise very intelligent exposition', and he paid not the slightest attention to the remainder of Weber's analysis.[91]

In sum, Meyer's lecture on ancient slavery is not only as close to nonsense as anything I can remember written by a historian of such eminence, but violates the basic canons of historical scholarship in general and of German historical scholarship in particular. The question then arises, How did it achieve the standing it so rapidly acquired? There were objectors, not only disreputable ones like Bücher and other *National-ökonomen* but also as eminent a historian as Mommsen's pupil, Ludo Hartmann.[92] Hardly anyone listened, and I cannot believe that the spell Eduard Meyer had woven by then, not to be underestimated, is a sufficient explanation. What Meyer provided, I suggest, was authoritative support and comfort, in a general way rather than in its chain of specific propositions, for already generally accepted views, or at least predispositions, for the ideology of professional ancient historians. And it was so welcome that they closed their eyes to the technical weaknesses.

Paradoxically, the lessons drawn were not always compatible with Meyer's own deeply felt views. He was a political being to an unusual degree of intensity and with increasingly deep pessimism, notably revealed in his long review in the *Deutsche Literaturzeitung* for 1924 of Spengler's *Decline of the West* or in the introduction to the second edition of his *Kleine Schriften*, published in the same year.[93] Socialism was the worst symptom of everything that was going wrong with his world, not only socialist politics but any kind of socialist thinking. In that respect his views were generally shared in the conservative German academic world. But he was also, in his lights, a methodologist and philosopher of history.[94] That concern kindled the fury against Bücher and the *Nationalökonomen*: their kind of historical periodization was a threat to Meyer's social and political beliefs, to his world and his world-view, not just to his conception of the ancient world. And here he parted company with most of his admirers, who both fled from philosophy of history or theory and clung to their dogged positivism, their scholarship for its own sake, and also largely isolated themselves from their colleagues in economics, social science, economic history and even modern history.

My concern, however, is not with the 'modernism' of Meyer and his followers and all its implications, but with ancient slavery. Admittedly it would be erroneous to consider the 'modernists' as if they spoke with one voice: Pöhlmann, for example, who in the closing years of the nineteenth century wrote the classic polemic against socialism in the name of ancient history,[95] approached slavery with different nuances, which his final editor, Friedrich Oertel, then tried to reconcile with Meyer's account.[96] But they both remained firmly opposed in principle to all stage theories and therefore felt free to proceed in the language, and with the concepts, of their own world. Pöhlmann wrote, in a section entitled 'Capital and Labour', that the frequent accumulation of slaves in different enterprises by a single entrepreneur was 'often deplored by anti-capitalist social critics' (citing Plato, *Laws* 12.846E, and Diodorus 1.74), and that the free workers 'knew perfectly well' that the competition of slaves was responsible for mass impoverishment; Oertel insisted that slavery made a qualitative difference, that it alone provided 'different bases and a different coloration' to mass impoverishment because otherwise there was no significant difference, given the presence in antiquity of both the capitalist spirit and technical talent (*Veranlagung*).[97]

49

These are brave generalizations, quoted that way in isolation, but unfortunately they led to no analysis of the economics or economic implications of slavery. In 1907 a pupil of Pöhlmann's, Kurt Riezler, published a 100-page essay dedicated to his teacher, quite important in some respects, in which he argued that the political and social constraints inherent in the *polis* blocked economic growth, without once mentioning slavery.[98] In 1930 Oertel himself wrote an article on the inheritance of Demosthenes, under the resounding title 'On the Question of Large-scale Industry in Attica', which was unavoidably all about slaves, given the nature of the inheritance, but which never got round to the qualitative difference that he had himself stressed in his Pöhlmann edition.[99]

And these were among the few men who showed a concern for theoretical considerations. The others had no problems. If they had an interest in social, economic or legal history, slavery continued to be one of a series of institutions and practices available for scholarly research into the 'facts'. The uncomfortable implications raised by Marx and the other political economists could be put aside, though there were still controversial questions, seemingly moral (to which I shall have to return once again later on). And those with primarily political and cultural interests could happily ignore the institution altogether.

Thus far I have been speaking solely about German scholars, simply because the debate was largely monopolized by, and restricted to, the German-speaking world. Elsewhere there was almost total indifference, except of course among economists, economic historians and sociologists. Even in Italy, as early as 1908, Calderini could produce a useful monograph on manumission and freedmen in Greece[100] – still the only one we have – which was quintessentially antiquarian, seemingly unaware of, and certainly unconcerned with, the efforts Ciccotti, Salvioli, Barbagallo, Ferrero and Pareto were then making to transform the study of ancient history.

French indifference, which has been noted elsewhere,[101] is puzzling because French intellectuals generally, including academicians, were open to the socialist and revolutionary tradition, unlike the Germans. Yet wherever one turns on our subject one finds no trace of the ferment we have been considering. Paul Guiraud wrote a 650-page book on Greek landed property in which slavery receives two pages, helots fourteen, and 'socialist theory and practice' forty, with a conclusion that warns against drawing universal laws: 'If Greece perished because of agrarian socialism, it does not follow that we are condemned to suffer a similar fate.'[102] Paul Louis, in the Roman volume of the *Histoire universelle de travail*, tells us explicitly that there are no 'mysteries', that everything developed with 'manifest and irrefutable' logic; that, for example, Roman institutions 'permitted this proletariat to live in idleness'; that there was certainly capitalism – 'it mattered little whether labour were servile or free'; that the colonate (the tied peasantry of late antiquity) 'established itself in the place of the servile system by a transition which was almost unnoticeable'.[103] Paul Louis happened not to be an ancient historian but a specialist in the history of French socialism and syndicalism and as much a modernist as Eduard Meyer, though with a lurch to the left (as the Italians say). Gustave Glotz, on the other hand, author of the Greek volume in the same series, was the outstanding Greek historian of his generation in France; yet all he could offer was a chapter on slavery in no way an advance over Büchsenschütz's *Besitz und Erwerb*, except for the astounding generalization, 'the absence of machinery is at once the cause and, to a certain extent, the effect of industrial slavery' (repeated throughout the book more times than I can count); and a final two-page peroration on the reasons why it is impossible to agree with either Bücher or Meyer, whose notions receive no consideration anywhere in the book.[104] And finally there was Jules Toutain, who proclaimed in the introduction to *L'économie antique* (1927) a rejection of all theories and hypotheses in favour of an 'objective' account of the documents alone – a method applauded by Henri Berr who commissioned the volume for his series, *L'Evolution de l'Humanité* – and who managed to find in the documents no more about slavery than would occupy some three continuous pages of text if they were not scattered through the book. 'Slaves, employed in work on the land, were very numerous in all the Greek city-states' (p. 52) is a typical, complete quotation.

There is no point in continuing this catalogue, among the French as elsewhere, in examining Tenney Frank's *Economic History of Rome* (1919, 1927), for example, or the multi-volume *Economic Survey of Ancient Rome* which he edited. Nothing is changed, nothing has advanced. There were rare exceptions, and two should be noticed. In 1900–1 Henri Francotte published his two-volume *L'Industrie dans la Grèce ancienne* which was, and still is, without parallel or peer. Francotte could assemble and cite the documentation with the best of the antiquarians, but he also never lost sight of his stated intention, 'to link my subject to the whole (*ensemble*) of the history of Greece, to bind the destinies of industry to those of society itself'. Quietly but persistently, he proceeded to examine the Bücher-Meyer debate; to strike a balance on the side of Bücher on the particular issue of industry, while rejecting Bücher's *Hauswirtschaft* (household economy) as a sufficient account of the Greek economy; to evaluate and locate industry within the larger framework; and to offer the best assessment we have of the complex interplay between slave and free labour in manufacture – all done so quietly that this excellent book has been largely forgotten.[105] One man who did not overlook Francotte was W. E. Heitland, and his *Agricola* (1921) has many of the same virtues, though it is less sophisticated in its economic analysis and tends to amalgamate economic and moral considerations. It also suffers from a major vice, organization of the material according to ancient authors, and that, evidently, is why Heitland is still regularly consulted while Francotte is not: there is no more convenient place to look up what Demosthenes has to tell us about agriculture, or the Roman jurists or Symmachus.

Not many years later Westermann was invited by Wilhelm Kroll, on the recommendation of Rostovtzeff, to write a 'synthesis of the history of Greco-Roman enslavement'[106] for the multi-volume classical encyclopaedia commonly referred to as

'Pauly-Wissowa'. The first volume of the encyclopaedia had appeared in 1894 and publication had been progressing steadily for a generation before anyone thought it necessary to include a substantial article on slavery. I do not know whether the initiative came from Kroll, then the editor, or from Rostovtzeff. The latter's involvement with the subject was of long standing: the Russian historians under whom he had trained had a social (and sociological) interest that was untypical among European scholars at the time. As early as 1910 Rostovtzeff had published a major, wide-ranging book on the colonate, whereas Westermann had nothing in print to explain his Pauly-Wissowa assignment, though he had written a few articles on one or another economic topic. He set to work in the most diligent tradition of German scholarship, absorbed while he was a pupil of Eduard Meyer's, of whom he was in awe. Like Meyer, he had little use for, and little understanding of, the *Nationalökonomen*, and a predisposition to play slavery down whenever a reasonable opportunity seemed to present itself.[107]

But Westermann was equally in awe of Rostovtzeff (to whose memory the book on slavery that followed the Pauly-Wissowa article was dedicated); 'It is difficult', he once wrote when he presumed to disagree, 'to differ with the great authority of the late Professor Rostovtzeff upon social and economic problems of the Hellenistic and Roman periods of antiquity'.[108] And that created a dilemma. Rostovtzeff could be as 'modernist' as anyone, and as contemptuous of economic theory, in particular of Marxism, which was his generic term for a whole range of theoretical position.[109] However, his background – he was almost fifty when he left Russia during the Revolution – and his liberal *Weltanschauung* were utterly unlike Meyer's, for whose judgments on most economic matters he showed little sympathy. 'Modern scholars', he wrote in an important summary statement, 'recoiling from the grossly exaggerated and untenable Marxian doctrine regarding the role of slavery in ancient times, are inclined to minimize the numbers of slaves and the part played by them in pre-Hellenistic Greek economy'.[110]

Underpinning this generalization was a serious effort to

grapple with the apparent 'crisis' that beset the classical *polis* in the fourth century B.C., and in particular with the mutual impact of slave and free labour on each other.[111] There followed equally serious, and carefully nuanced, accounts of Hellenistic slavery, region by region. My own disagreement with Rostovtzeff's conception of the ancient economy needs no reassertion at present. I am here concerned with the way slavery is examined dynamically within an historical account, not with the rightness or wrongness of that account. Nor am I concerned with the inconsistencies: he could assert, on the one hand, that by the Hellenistic period the economy 'differed from the modern economy only quantitatively, not qualitatively';[112] on the other hand, that 'if we consider the extent of the services that the citizens were expected to render to the State . . . , we shall not be surprised that the economy of [Hellenistic] Rhodes was based . . . on . . . foreigners and slaves.'[113]

One can dispute Rostovtzeff's analysis of the fourth-century *polis*, whereas Westermann's chapter, entitled 'From the Persian Wars to Alexander. The Social Setting of *Polis* Slavery', reveals total indifference to, if not unawareness of, the central issues. Or, to take another example, his brief criticism (p. 37) of Rostovtzeff's assessment of the role of slavery in Hellenistic Rhodes employs an invalid statistical argument as a supposedly sufficient answer to a serious structural view. Paradoxically, the influence of Meyer's essential doctrine is also absent, apart from the persistently 'negative' tone. It is in fact impossible to discover why Westermann says at the outset that Meyer laid the basis for the modern study of ancient slavery. He makes about a dozen references to Meyer's *Sklaverei*, most of them unnecessary, while he implicitly rejects Meyer's absurd cyclical conception, and overtly repudiates the latter's interpretation of the actions of the tyrant of Corinth, Periander.[114] Meyer's crusading against the *Nationalökonomen* makes no noticeable appearance. Only the ghost of Meyer is omnipresent.

Westermann's mistakes have been repeatedly exposed, in reviews of the book and in subsequent publications on ancient slavery.[115] Although the scholarly achievement was nonetheless considerable, it is necessary to ask what went wrong, badly wrong. A brief review of the Pauly-Wissowa article, concluded as follows: 'The organization and essentially antiquarian character of this encyclopedia prohibit a real theoretical discussion and synthesis of many fundamental questions. . . . For such a discussion we must await W.'s forthcoming volume.'[116] I wrote that myself in 1936, a young student obviously treading on eggshells – hence the disingenuous shifting of responsibility to the encyclopedia – and desperately trying to flash signals. In vain. Westermann worked on, systematically and almost obsessively, for nearly twenty more years, and when the volume at last appeared in 1955, nothing had changed beyond the insertion of still more documents and several marginal topics; nothing, that is, except the new final chapters, which contained the one sustained argument in the whole work, directed against the view that Stoicism and Christianity contributed in any substantial way to the decline of ancient slavery. Those final chapters bring the question into sharp focus whether it was (or is) possible to write a better 'synthesis of the history of Greco-Roman enslavement'.

I shall return to that question in the end. Meanwhile we have reached the middle of the present century in this survey without having found many traces of the heated debates I promised at the beginning. Apart from the single question of Christianity and slavery, the heat was generated by the larger question of the nature of the ancient economy, and the still larger one of stages in historical development, in which slavery was only a factor. The heat over slavery did not erupt until the 1950s, and then with little advance warning.

The first sign, easily missed as such, was the announcement in 1951 that the Mainz Academy was about to embark on a great research programme into ancient slavery, under the direction of Joseph Vogt, who had studiously ignored the subject until then but has orchestrated the Mainz programme ever since (though his own publications in the field are only articles, not books). Within the decade Vogt had published essays on 'Slavery and Humanity' and 'The Structure of Ancient Slave

Wars' and his Tübingen rectoral address on 'Human Relationships in Ancient Slavery'; and three monographs in the Mainz
series had appeared, Micknat's short one on Homeric slavery,
Lauffer's two volumes on slavery in the Laureion mines, and
the first of Bömer's four volumes on slaves in religion. The signs
of the coming ideological controversy were now plainly to be
seen, but hardly any one appears to have taken notice, until the
International Historical Congress at Stockholm in 1960, where
sharp conflict broke into the open.

Again the epicentre of the storm was in Germany, but this
time it was concentrated on slavery as it had not been before.
To trace the source, it is necessary to turn back briefly to two
developments during the preceding half-century. The first is the
revival of the 'classical humanism' of the early nineteenth
century, with its glorification of the eternal, universal validity
of Hellenism and its identification of the Hellenic and German
'spirits'.[117] That 'faith' (*Glaube*) had largely given way among
German classicists in the late nineteenth century to 'pure'
scholarship. That is to say, they did not abandon a reverence of
Greek virtues or the conviction of close affinity with it, but the
earlier evangelism was stifled by increasing quantities of
specialized (antiquarian) publications. The sense of purpose
was thus lost. One reaction came from Eduard Meyer, another
from what is sometimes known as the 'third humanism', led
first by Wilamowitz and then by Werner Jaeger. Like that of
Humboldt and his disciples, whose spiritual ancestry they
warmly acknowledged, the third humanism amounted, in
Momigliano's words, to a 'religion of classicism', an 'intuitive'
(or 'demonic') 'classicistic mysticism'.[118] Like the humanism of
Humboldt, too, it was a *German* mysticism. For Eduard
Schwartz, 'the aim of the *Gymnasium* can be only to educate
Germans through antiquity'; for Stier, *Deutschtum* and *Griechentum* are bound together; for Jaeger, classical humanism was the
work of 'the German-Protestant *Geist*'.[119]

Among the chief spokesmen, clearly, there were some of the
greatest philological scholars of their epoch and that strengthened their impact. In their return to Humboldt, however, they

adopted a different stance with respect to slavery, following Eduard Meyer's lead but generally going further. Whereas the Humboldt school openly accepted slavery as a necessary condition of 'that liberal spirit which has not reappeared to a similar extent among any other people, that is to say the spiritual role of noble and great attitudes truly worthy of a free man',[120] the third humanism simply turned its head. Saluting Wilamowitz on his eightieth birthday, Eduard Schwartz said: you brought us back to 'the knowledge of *Hellenentum* as an historical phenomenon, in all its manifestations from the beginning to the end, in its gods, heroes and men, in all its constructions, in the forms of its poetry and its speech, in everything that it did and suffered, that it created and that it willed'.[121] That long catalogue of the components of *Hellenentum* patently did not include slavery. In Wilamowitz's book on 'Greek State and Society', they are entitled to a single paragraph, the core of which is the amelioration brought about by 'religion and custom', and to another dozen miscellaneous phrases or sentences, two of which consists of no more than 'putting slavery aside'.[122] Jaeger was more thorough: the word 'slave' does not appear in the detailed indices of his three-volume *Paideia*.

The other development occurred outside Germany. The Russian Revolution stimulated an unprecedented volume of Marxist historical writing; on ancient history that remained largely, though not wholly, within the confines of the Soviet Union, and I shall limit my brief consideration to the Russian writers.[123] In the first decade or two following the Revolution, the older generation of historians, many of whom remained in the country, were largely involved in orienting themselves to Marxism. That concern stirred a renewed interest in the Bücher-Meyer controversy, at a time when it had sunk into silence elsewhere: Bücher's *Entstehung der Volkswirtschaft* was translated into Russian in 1923, the Greek section of his *Beiträge* in 1924. But ancient slavery as such did not become a subject of major research, still less so as the mid-1930s approached and the Engelsian periodization became official dogma: all ancient society, including the ancient Near East, was neatly pigeonholed into a 'slaveowning society' and the 'slave mode of production'. Formulas replaced inquiry, except in minor byways of the subject. When, therefore, the great debate began in 1951, there was no Marxist work on slavery (in or out of the Soviet Union) of any genuine significance later than Ciccotti and Salvioli. In effect that was acknowledged by Soviet ancient historians by the early 1960s. At the beginning of 1963, for example, G. G. Diligenskii, hard-line editor of *Vestnik Drevnei Istorii (Journal of Ancient History)*, regretted that 'the cult of personality had exercised a determining negative influence on research work in the field of history and, in particular, ancient history'. Such problems as the diverse forms of slave relations, he continued, 'were sometimes resolved with the aid of schematic formulas applied without the requisite concrete analysis of all the phenomena of a multifarious historical reality'.[124]

Here, as in many more important affairs, the second World War was a watershed. Again I single out two elements, both of which had an impact in many countries but most powerfully in Germany. The first was the growing pressure to reexamine higher education, in particular the place of classical education, based in Germany on the traditional *humanistische Gymnasium*. In Germany, in fact, reconstruction would be a more precise word than reexamination, among other reasons because of the hasty retreat from the central determining concepts of race and *Führertum*.[125] The second was the creation of the eastern bloc of countries, in the whole of which Marxism was the official philosophy of historical study, and again Germany was in a special position, in consequence of the division into West and East Germany, West and East Berlin.

These elements are already visible in the early publications on slavery of Vogt himself and of the Mainz project. The abruptness of their emergence is perhaps surprising: the second edition of Vogt's history of the Roman Republic, published in 1951, reveals even more than normal disinterest in slavery, hardly finding space in which to mention the great slave revolts of the second and first centuries B.C. Perhaps I should therefore say explicitly that in what follows I have no private information and I attribute nothing to cold deliberation, to a conscious decision to adopt a certain line. All my inferences and interpretations arise solely from the published work behind which there lies of course, the *paideia*, the *Bildung*, of Vogt and his co-authors. I should also say, as I have already said in an earlier and different context, that the Mainz project, taken altogether, includes works that vary in quality and approach. There are among them good and inferior books and articles, as in most projects, and there are a number which are 'old-fashioned' in their more or less neutral positivism. I shall be frankly selective, as my concern is with ideology, and for the moment I shall concentrate on Vogt's own articles, especially the earliest, which, I propose to show, already contain the main ideological elements that have since dominated the debate; and which, it is important to note, he was willing to reprint, essentially unchanged, in an English translation as late as 1974.

In 1961 Vogt addressed the Deutscher Altphilologenverband on 'Research on Ancient Slavery from Humboldt to the Present Day', and the lecture was then published in the journal *Gymnasium*, which likes to think of itself as spokesman for the *humanistische Gymnasia*. Why Humboldt, who did no research whatever into ancient slavery and scarcely mentioned it in all his voluminous writing? The answer is that Vogt identifies himself with the German tradition of 'humanism' fathered by Humboldt.[126] His earliest essay, 'Slavery and Humanity', closes with these words: 'Slavery was essential to the existence both of this [Greek] basic will to live and of the devotion to spiritual considerations. . . . Those forces fundamental to Hellenism succeeded in wrestling the miraculous creation of the polis and its civilization from the poverty of the land, the inclemency of the climate and the opposition of a hostile world. Slavery and its attendant loss of humanity were part of the sacrifice which had to be paid for this achievement.'[127]

But that is not the whole story. 'Perhaps', he writes in a later essay, 'it has been left to the Classics to uphold the existence of intellectual standards in all areas of knowledge and skill, under conditions of general equality and universal freedom.' If 'the Humanism of classical studies is to survive in our world', we must abandon the old humanist 'tolerance of the inhumanity that enabled the Greeks and Romans to secure their development as human beings'; we 'must portray human society as it really was without concealing or extenuating its negative aspects'.[128] There, I believe, is one key to the whole exercise, a kind of 'saving the phenomena', rescuing 'classical humanism' by certain concessions. I would add that 'human society as it really was' turns out to be not all that bad, as Vogt seeks and finds the 'humanity' that was constantly cropping up in the practice of slavery itself. It can hardly be irrelevant that in the 'from Humboldt' survey only one major figure comes through unscathed and that is Eduard Meyer.

In the crude dichotomy I suggested at the outset, Vogt's interest in ancient slavery is entirely a moralistic, or perhaps 'spiritual', one, not a sociological one. Hence his obsession with Marxism treads a restricted path. The 'salient feature' of Eduard Meyer's article on slavery, he writes, is 'that it destroys the notion of the supposedly regular development from Primitive communism . . . to the proletariat of modern capitalism. Political factors and various other forces are placed alongside economic ones. . . .' Marxism, on the contrary, 'can only approach the subject in terms of material production and the creation of a class structure'. Therefore, in his repeated expressions of disagreement, Vogt can never go beyond generalized objections to Marxism as such, as he understands it. His concerns are spiritual, theirs material. Anyway, 'the purpose and the basic premises of Marxist historical scholarship in countries under Communist rule have been fixed in advance for all time', making 'understanding' with them 'very difficult'.[129]

Vogt has throughout retained his characteristically cool tone, but the temperature shot up at the International Historical Congress in Stockholm in 1960 (a year before the construction of the Berlin Wall, it is not irrelevant to point out). The full bitterness, above all between East and West Germans, is blunted in the printed reports: one needed to sit through the meetings to catch it. And the session on ancient slavery, included in the programme at the suggestion of the German Historical Association, was one of the main combat-zones. 'The result of the confrontation was catastrophic', Van Effenterre later reported.[130] That the confrontation was not 'spontaneous' is demonstrable. The German periodical *Saeculum* devoted all the issues of 1960 to a critique of Marxism, and what that meant is revealed by the titles of the twelve articles: three refer to Marx or historical materialism, one to Czech history, the remaining eight to Soviet historiography. The volume was described by the distinguished French historian Robert Mandrou as an 'indictment', filled with 'excommunications and anathemas', for a trial in which the accused was to be denied the right of counsel.[131] The first fascicule was prepared beforehand and distributed at the congress. It included a lengthy piece by Vittinghoff entitled 'The Theory of Historical Materialism about the Ancient "Slaveowners' State"' and subtitled 'Problems of Ancient History in the "Classics" of Marxism and in modern Soviet Research'. This essay fits Mandrou's description exactly: Vittinghoff ignored publications that did not support his case and restricted himself to generalities and programmatic statements.[132] That was too easy: even some Soviet historians were beginning to say the same in essence, if not in language. Not once did Vittinghoff discuss a question of substance with regard to ancient slavery, contenting himself in a footnote (in the wrong context) with the inevitable, 'Everything essential was already said by Eduard Meyer in his fundamental lecture of 1898'.[133]

In the Congress programme Vittinghoff had only a brief 'communication', on the significance of slavery in the transition from antiquity to the Middle Ages in the west.[134] Despite the broad title, his exclusive concern was again with absurdities to be found in Soviet writing on the subject between 1933 and 1953. In closing, he conceded that the approach which he had no trouble in dismissing was no longer acceptable to Soviet historians. Why bother, then? I believe I had myself given the answer two years beforehand: 'in the guise of a discussion of ancient slavery, there has been a desultory discussion of Marxist theory, none of it, on either side, particularly illuminating about either Marxism or slavery.'[135] In the context of the Stockholm Congress in 1960, the hammering, the wholly negative presentation, and the insistence on restricting Marxism to Soviet writers, seem, taken together, to constitute an intentional political act.

I have deliberately selected an extreme manifestation within a cultural-political situation that was in reality multifarious, and I ask forebearance while I continue a little longer. In 1963 Vogt commissioned a monograph on slavery and technology in the Roman Empire. When the book, by Franz Kiechle, appeared in the Mainz series in 1969, its by no means obvious opening sentence was, 'Consideration of the methods of production had basic importance in the Marxist conception of history from the outset.'[136] The penultimate sentence, 176 pages later, rejected a statement by Edward Thompson (identified as 'the English historian influenced by the Marxist view of history') on the ground that 'the social structures of the fourth century A.D. and of the period at the turn from the Middle Ages to the modern era were not at all radically different'. The volume itself contains much factual information about technology in the Roman Empire. My present concern, however, is solely with the way it was conceived and written, as an unrelenting attack on Marxism. Kiechle begins with the prejudicially incorrect assertion that 'The view that the use of slave labour was an impediment to technical progress was originated by Karl Marx.'[137] He then follows throughout his book with the equally incorrect implication that only Marxists have held such a view, an implication he can project only by unrelenting selectivity in his citation of modern authorities.[138]

In the meantime, Kiechle had suggested to a pupil, Wilhelm Backhaus, that he write his dissertation on Marx, Engels and slavery. It was duly submitted in 1971 and published as a book in 1974 (not in the Mainz series). Again the reader is surprised: the first quotation on the first page of the text proper is from

Stalin, not from Marx or Engels, and throughout, later 'Marxism' competes for attention with Marx and Engels, 'Marxism' being equated with writers from eastern Europe. In the preface he lays down the most remarkable methodological principle I have ever encountered in the history of ideas. 'In what follows the author identifies as "Marxist" all authors who claim this predicate for themselves. To differentiate terminologically in this respect is not within his competence, and it is not his task.'[139] The abdication of intellectual responsibility does not end there. By the time Backhaus had completed his work, Marxist writing about antiquity was appearing in the West at an accelerating pace, and anyone familiar with it will know how much of it is frankly groping, tentative and mutually polemical. Today the quantity of this writing is almost beyond the capacity of any single historian. Backhaus resolves the difficulty by ignoring all of it: there is not a single Marxist work on ancient slavery in his bibliography that was written in English, French or Italian (other than by Marx, Engels or Ciccotti). The monolithic picture he then succeeds in drawing, apart from other flaws, is a caricature of the current situation in Marxist thinking, one to which Mandrou's assessment of Vittinghoff's 1960 article applies with equal force, and one that is equally a political act.[140]

The habit of using the ancient world as a springboard for a larger political polemic is of course not a monopoly of any one camp or school. However, I shall not pursue the examination of current trends any further. My aim has not been to provide a complete bibliographical survey. Omissions, which have been considerable for the period since the first World War, carry no implication about the importance or unimportance of any historian or any particular publication. I have, after all, said nothing so far about my own research in the field and little about my assessment of ancient slavery. I have rather sought to demonstrate the extent and depth of ideological significance inherent in the modern study of ancient slavery, by concentrating on major examples of scholarly work of stature in which, on my view, the ideological impulses are strongest, though rarely acknowledged as such in academic circles (in contrast to Marxist writing, which is automatically criticized for its 'bias'). Backhaus closed his book on Marx and slavery with these words: we must regret that 'virtually the only historians who make an effort to achieve an integrated approach to slavery are those who tread the path marked out by Marx and Engels'. The implication, curious coming from him, is that anti-Marxism is not of itself an integrated approach. I agree, and I have tried to show how powerful an ideology it has nevertheless been. But my aim is not a plea for the end of theoretical concerns. In historical study that can lead only to a heaping up of discrete data, of raw material for the historian, not to history itself. The difficult discrimination that has to be made is between appropriate social theory and political ideology in the narrow sense.

Nor does my critique of the moralistic approach imply an end to moral judgments. I return to the rhetorical question I posed earlier, about Wallon: What difference did it make to him whether Athens had 100,000, 200,000 or 400,000 slaves? Was the evil less if there were only 100,000? I see no validity in an ethical system that holds such a question to be meaningful, any more than in Vogt's belief that detailed research will one day produce a moral calculus with which to determine whether slavery 'was a beneficial growth or a malignant cancer on the ancient body-politic'.[141] Slavery is a great evil: there is no reason why a historian should not say that, but to say only that, no matter with how much factual backing, is a cheap way to score a point on a dead society to the advantage of our own: 'retrospective indignation is also a way to justify the present'.[142] The present-day moralistic approach has taken a different turn. It starts from the high evaluation of ancient culture and then tries to come to terms with its most troublesome feature, slavery. Anyone who clings to the cause of neo-classicism or classical humanism has little room for manoeuvre, except in the way he prefers to abate the nuisance of ancient slavery, or, as with Vogt, in the way he tries to 'rescue' the record of Christianity.

The rest of us must tread another path, and it is to us that I address the question once again, in a variant form, Why should we struggle to establish the number of slaves in classical Athens? To reply, in the language of Wilamowitz and Eduard Schwartz, that we want to know everything about the classical world, is insufficient. First, their answer presupposes the neo-classical valuation; secondly, 'knowing everything' easily degenerates into collecting all known butterflies (or postage stamps or matchboxes). To locate slavery within ancient society, in order to understand that society, is a much more difficult and more rewarding enterprise. But it requires asking the right questions, and the historian must ask them himself. The ancient sources do not do that often enough, and, when they do, they often fail to ask the right questions. They are asking their questions, not ours. There lies the incurable flaw in the famed 'philological method': it forgets the elementary methodological truth stated in the following way by Charles Darwin in 1861: 'About thirty years ago there was much talk that geologists ought only to observe and not theorize; and I well remember someone saying that at this rate a man might as well go into a gravel-pit and count the pebbles and describe the colours. How odd it is that anyone should not see that all observation must be for or against some view if it is to be of any service!'[143] In more formal language, all statements of fact 'presuppose concepts whose meaning is at least partly given by the context of theory'.[144] Neither the philologist nor the historian has any claim to exemption.

Buckland noted that 'there is scarcely a problem' in Roman law 'the solution of which may not be affected by the fact that one of the parties to the transaction is a slave'.[145] That is too narrow. I should say that there was no action or belief or institution in Graeco-Roman antiquity that was not one way or other affected by the possibility that someone involved *might be* a slave. It follows that slavery cannot be abstracted from its context. It follows, too, that my answer to the question I posed and left earlier, whether we may look forward to a qualitatively better 'synthesis' than Westermann's of 'the history of Graeco-Roman enslavement', is a mixed one. Beyond doubt there can be one which is more accurate, more complete in its knowledge and control of the ancient evidence, more tightly and coherently organized. However, the more profound difficulty is not with Westermann's details but with his view of ancient society in particular and of the social process in general. Every such book, like any historical work on warfare, religion or the economy, ancient or modern, eastern or western, implies, and can make explicit in only a limited way, these basic views. It is noteworthy how much of the current debate about American slavery moves beyond disagreement about the immediate data and their interpretation to 'other' matters, to Catholicism and Protestantism, to racism, absentee landholding, the world cotton market, the limitations inherent in a federal state structure, ad infinitum. Serious debate about ancient slavery is no different qualitatively, though the 'other' matters are not identical and the available data are despairingly slight in quantity. In the end, therefore, a genuine 'synthesis' of the history of ancient slavery can only be a history of Graeco-Roman society.

Chapter 2

THE EMERGENCE OF A
SLAVE SOCIETY

Fustel de Coulanges began his remarkable study of the Roman colonate in this way: 'The colonate is one of the most obscure institutions of the Roman Empire. . . . Slavery is more easily explained.' He was wrong about the latter. No doubt, as he continued, slavery 'was a primordial fact, contemporary with the origin of society; it had its roots in an age of the human species when all inequalities had their *raison d'être*.'[1] But the Greeks and Romans, independently so far as we can see, transformed this 'primordial fact' into something new and wholly original in world history (and something rare throughout history), namely, an institutionalized system of large-scale employment of slave labour in both the countryside and the cities; in Marxist language, 'the slave mode of production was the decisive invention of the Graeco-Roman world'.[2] That invention is not 'easily explained'.

We must begin with a crude, but fundamental and indeed commonplace, distinction between labour for oneself and labour for others. 'Oneself' is to be understood not in a narrow individualistic sense but as embracing the family, nuclear or extended as the case may be in any particular society. That is to say, the work of the women and children within the family, no matter how authoritarian and patriarchal its structure, is not subsumed under this category of labour for others (though I am aware that I face objections from several directions when I say that). Nor is interfamily cooperative activity, as during harvest periods. 'Labour for others' implies not only that 'others' take some of the fruits but also that they customarily control, in direct ways, the work that is done and the manner of its doing, whether in person or through agents and managers. Neither the independent peasant nor the tenant-farmer normally satisfies the

67

second of those conditions, though he pays taxes or rents or both, and may be restricted in various ways by public law. That is again a commonplace, but I must insist on it at the outset because failure to draw so elementary a distinction has plagued much of the debate about ancient slavery in the past century.

The need to mobilize labour-power for tasks that are beyond the capacity of the individual or the family reaches back into prehistory. Such a need was present whenever a society attained a stage of sufficient accumulation of resources and power in some hands (whether king, temple, ruling tribe or aristocracy). And the requisite labour force was obtained by compulsion – by force of arms or by force of law and custom, usually by both together – for all purposes (or interests) not amenable to straightforward cooperation: in agriculture or mining or public works or arms manufacture. Compulsory labour takes a considerable variety of forms, today as in the past[3] – debt bondage, clientship, peonage, helotage, serfdom, chattel slavery, and so on. But whatever the form, the compulsion is fundamentally different from that lying behind hired labour, which implies the conceptual abstraction of a man's labour power from the man himself. The wage-labourer also surrenders some of his independence when he accepts employment, but such loss cannot be classed with that suffered by slaves or serfs.

In early societies, free hired labour (though widely documented) was spasmodic, casual, marginal. Significantly, in neither Greek nor Latin was there a word with which to express the general notion of 'labour' or the concept of labour 'as a general social function'.[4] Only with the development of capitalism did wage labour emerge as the characteristic form of labour for others. *Labour power* then became one of the main commodities in the market-place. With slavery, in contrast, the *labourer himself* is the commodity. The slave is in that respect unique among types of labour despite overlapping with, for example, the most oppressive kinds of serfdom or with convict labour.[5] The slave and the free wage-labourer thus stand at the extreme poles of labour for others, but historically the important contrast is rather between slaves and other types of compulsory labour. As institutionalized systems of organizing labour, other kinds of involuntary labour preceded chattel slavery, and both preceded (and then coexisted with) free hired labour. In order to understand ancient slavery, therefore, some preliminary consideration is required of the labour systems within which it arose and which it largely displaced in key areas of the classical world, though by no means in all.

It must be acknowledged at the outset that in current historical and sociological writing the classification of types of labour is in a bad state. Behind faulty classification there is of course faulty theory, or at least inadequate conceptualization. Only a few years ago Meillassoux complained, 'In the present state of research, there is in fact no general theory which permits us to identify slavery or the objective bases of its coming into existence (*existence eventuelle*). . . . No formal criterion has been brought to light that permits a categorical distinction between slaves and all other components.'[6] At one extreme, marginal distinctions are insisted on so fiercely that all institutions are reduced to an infinity of discrete instances, stultifying any possibility of analysis or understanding. Thus Lauffer assured us at the Stockholm Historical Congress that we must not translate the Greek *doulos* or the Latin *servus* as 'slave' because that word is too reminiscent of modern Negro slavery, whereas 'the ancient "slave" is a wholly different social type' (though he never told us why).[7] At the other extreme there is the tendency to create a 'supra-historical mélange' that 'defies all scientific principles'.[8] One variant, common among Anglo-American anthropologists, goes like this (and it is by no means restricted to slavery). First, a host of, let us say, African statuses and status-terms are translated as 'slaves'; second, it is observed that at essential points these so-called slaves are extremely unlike the slaves of classical antiquity or of the Americas; third, instead of reconsidering their appellation 'slaves' to their own subjects, these anthropologists angrily protest the 'ethnocentrism' of 'western' historians and sociologists and demand that the latter redefine and reclassify slaves in order to provide a place for their own pseudo-slaves.[9]

An even worse situation prevails with regard to the other forms of compulsory labour that have appeared throughout history. It is a sign of our grave difficulty in comprehension that we are unable even to translate the labels into modern western languages: 'helot' is not a translation but an adoption; 'debt-bondsman' is an artificial coinage; *pelatai, laoi, clientes, coloni* have not even been adopted but merely transliterated.

When I say that we cannot translate these terms I do not imply that historians do not translate them all the time, writing about the Graeco-Roman world and even more about the ancient Near East. The magnetism of the traditional tripartite division of labour into slave-serf-free appears to be irresistible. Procedures vary. The most common is to label everyone who is not obviously a slave or a free man a serf – the helots of Sparta, the *penestai* of Thessaly, the *laoi* of Hellenistic and Roman Asia Minor, and the varying dependents who made up the bulk of the population of Mesopotamia. The exotic feudalisms that so irritated Marc Bloch[10] have proliferated considerably since his day, only to reach what has been called 'the impasse of a quasi-universal feudalism'.[11] One current Marxist school has taken another tack. In a recent article with the revealing title, 'Slaves, Helots and Serfs in Early Antiquity', the distinguished Leningrad Assyriologist Diakonoff asserts that 'there is no difference between these two types of workers [slaves and helots/serfs] in regard to the main points, *viz.* both were exploited by extra-economic coercion, and both were entirely devoid of property in the means of production'. Underlying that conclusion, factually incorrect in part, there is a desperate rear-guard action designed to 'save the phenomena' of the Engelsian unilinear scheme. 'All ancient societies', says Diakonoff, 'in Europe as well as on all other continents', belong to 'a typologically identical socio-economic formation', sharing 'a common system of production typical of antiquity'.[12]

Not surprisingly, attempts at classification, good or bad, turn out to depend on underlying theoretical or ideological considerations. Whereas Lauffer defends the humanist valuation of classical society by insisting on the uniqueness of the ancient slave as a social type, Diakonoff and his school defend their version of Marxism by creating an 'easy supra-historical mélange defying all scientific principles of classification'. In effect the latter fall back on a tautology: the slave is an instrument in the slave mode of production. However, to quote Meillassoux once more, 'It is really not obvious that slavery is only a relationship of production.'[13] Whether it is or not is a matter for demonstration, not an axiomatic premise. One fact is at least indisputable, that chattel slavery existed as a major institution in such different social formations as the Roman Empire and nineteenth-century America.

That all forms of involuntary labour can formally be classed in a single category is self-evident. But is that a useful classification? Do extra-economic compulsion and lack of ownership of the means of production exhaust the 'main points', as Diakonoff asserts? Are the self-evident differences among the various kinds of compulsory labour unimportant? A few examples will, in my view, suggest the inadequacy of Diakonoff's simple scheme as a tool of historical analysis.[14]

It can scarcely be disputed, first, that helots were 'collective bondsmen', that is to say, they were a whole population (or populations) subjected to bondage, whereas debt-bondsmen and slaves fell into bondage individually, one by one. That distinction holds even for the hundreds of thousands of captives sold off by Julius Caesar or for the shiploads of African captives transported to the Americas: their fate was an individual one, not a collective one. It is equally certain, secondly, that all categories of compulsory labour other than chattel slaves possessed, in different degrees, restricted rights of property and usually much wider rights in the sphere of marriage and family law. These rights were *de iure* in at least some societies, well documented in the 'law code' of Gortyn in Crete, perhaps only *de facto* in other communities, though that suggestion may be grounded on nothing more than the paucity of evidence. Either way there were significant consequences: helots and *clientes* and the rest were self-reproducing, unlike the chattel slave populations, requiring no reinforcement from outside in order to maintain the requisite numbers; and they were looked upon and feared by their masters, with good reason, as potentially rebellious as a group, I might almost say as a subject community.[15] The debt-bondsmen of archaic Athens and Rome offer the extreme example (and there may have been similar dependent classes in other early communities about which we are uninformed). They succeeded in freeing themselves *en bloc* and thereby automatically reestablishing themselves as full members of their respective communities. That was civil strife, a conflict within the community, not a slave revolt: the aims of the latter were to emancipate themselves as individuals, not to incorporate themselves into the masters' community or to transform the social structure. In this context, it is also noteworthy that when the Messenian helots were freed (again *en bloc*) by the Thebans after they had defeated Sparta at Leuctra in 371 B.C., the Messenians were at once accepted by the Greeks generally as a proper Greek community.

Objection has been raised in the past to my stress on such distinctions among types of compulsory labour: the whole scheme is only a 'juristic abstraction', or a mere description of institutions 'without inquiring into their function'.[16] True, no classification or taxonomy, no matter how detailed, is a sufficient account of the nature of a given society and its transformations. It can only be deemed to be more or less useful than competing classifications as an analytical tool in a particular inquiry. The question in the present context is whether or not such distinctions, the existence of which cannot be seriously denied, contribute substantially to an understanding of the emergence of a slave society, in other words, to the replacement of other forms of compulsory labour by chattel slavery where that occurred. In Diakonoff's vague terminology, are they or are they not 'main points'? I shall not try to answer on the level of grand theory, in a more or less metaphysical debate about the dynamic or dialectic of history.[17] Instead, I shall proceed immediately to a more detailed examination of the slave and slavery.

As a commodity, the slave is property. At least since Westermarck writing at the beginning of the present century, some sociologists and historians have persistently tried to deny the significance of that simple fact, on the ground that the slave is also a human being or that the owner's rights over a slave are often restricted by the law.[18] All this seems to me to be futile: the fact that a slave is a human being has no relevance to the question whether or not he is also property; it merely reveals that he is a peculiar property, Aristotle's 'property with a soul' (*Politics* 1253b32). Reciprocally, the old Latin word *erus* also implies the peculiarity of a slave-property. Defined in the Oxford Latin Dictionary as 'a man in relation to his servants, master', *erus* was regularly and frequently used by slaves in the comedies of Plautus and even of Terence, in preference to *dominus*. Later poets continued to employ the word as an occasional archaism, but they extended it to mean also the owner of an animal or other property, thus sacrificing the original implication that the slave-master relationship was odd, indeed unique, among property relations.[19]

Legal restrictions on the rights of a slaveowner are also a side-issue: in modern sociological and juridical theories of any school, all property is understood to be a matrix of rights, rarely if ever unlimited. The precise rights that constitute the matrix vary with kinds of property and kinds of society. Property, in other words, is an historical category, and that is one more commonplace that I must regretfully enunciate in order to remove the confusions that still prevail on the subject. When Roman lawyers defined a slave as someone who was in the *dominium* of another, they used the quintessential property-term *dominium*.[20] They were not dissuaded by the slave's human quality (not even when they used the word *homo* to refer to a slave, as they did frequently).[21] Nor were the millions of slaveowners who bought and sold slaves, overworked them, beat and tortured them, and sometimes put them to death, precisely as millions of horse-owners have done throughout history. Other millions did not exercise their rights to the full in this way: that is interesting, even important, but it does not undermine the slave-property link conceptually.

The failure of any individual slaveowner to exercise all his rights over his slave-property was always a unilateral act on his part, never binding, always revocable. That is a critical fact. So is its reverse, the equally unilateral, always revocable grant by a slaveowner of a specific privilege or benevolence. As for promises, one of Plautus' slaves succinctly exposed their standing: no master can be brought to court over a promise to a slave (*Persa* 193–4). Even the act of manumission could be, and frequently was, qualified in a multitude of ways. Failure to appreciate the fundamental significance of this unilaterality – as when Eduard Meyer compared the chances of ancient slaves and modern wage-earners to achieve wealth and social position[22] – destroys the possibility of fixing and comprehending the nature and history of slavery within any given society.

Paradoxically, it was precisely this quality of the slave, as property, that offered the owning class flexibility (to which I shall return shortly) not available with other forms of compulsory labour. That is one reason why I stress what is a juristic category and therefore of itself not a sufficient 'definition' of the slave. How individual owners chose to treat their peculiar property was normally not a matter of mere whim or of differences in personality. Owners frequently offered slaves the incentive of eventual manumission through various arrangements which automatically brought into being a chain of behaviour and expectations that affected the master, too. Although in law and in fact he could always revoke the offer, the material gains to be derived from slavery would have been sharply reduced if such arrangements were not as a rule honoured.

The slaveowner's rights over his slave-property were total in more senses than one. The slave, by being a slave, suffered not only 'total loss of control over his labour'[23] but total loss of control over his person and his personality: the uniqueness of slavery, I repeat, lay in the fact that the labourer himself was a commodity, not merely his labour or labour-power. His loss of control, furthermore, extended to the infinity of time, to his children and his children's children – unless, again, the owner by a unilateral act broke the chain through unconditional manumission. And even then, only children born subsequently were beneficiaries, not those already in existence at the moment of manumission. There is indeed ample evidence that manumission was not rarely withheld until a slave had progeny who could replace him (or her) in servitude, though there is no way of determining how frequent a practice this was, or whether it was largely restricted to certain categories of slaves, such as those in the Roman imperial employ.

This totality of the slaveowner's rights was facilitated by the fact that the slave was always a deracinated outsider – an outsider first in the sense that he originated from outside the society into which he was introduced as a slave, second in the sense that he was denied the most elementary of social bonds, kinship. '*Quem patrem, qui servos est?*' (Plautus, *Captivi* 574). 'What father, when he is a slave?' The contrast with Spartan helots, Thessalian *penestai* or the *clientes* of early Rome provides the clearest delineation, as has already been suggested: never did the master-class need or attempt to replenish the supply of dependent labour of this kind from outside. In stressing the kinlessness of slaves, I am concerned less with the juridical position, primarily the exclusion of slaves from legally recognized marriage (hence the Roman insistence on the word *contubernium*) than with the *de facto* position. There were slave unions and slave families, beyond a doubt, but they counted among the privileges that could be granted unilaterally by a slaveowner, and withdrawn unilaterally. The very possibility could be totally withdrawn by castration. As the poet Statius wrote in praise of Domitian's (ineffectual) prohibition of the practice (*Silvae* 3.4.76–7), 'nor by a harsh law are slave mothers fearful of the burden of sons'.

Complete and brutal withdrawal of the kinship privilege also took the form of dispersing a slave family through sale. In A.D.

75

325 Constantine ordered an official to stop the break-up of slave families on imperial estates in Sardinia which he had transferred to private ownership (*Theodosian Code* 2.25.1), and that was almost certainly the earliest governmental interference with the practice.[24] A little earlier the jurists were ruling that in an intestate succession or in certain other situations in which the contrary intention was not made explicit, slave families should not be broken up.[25] That reflects a humane tendency, no doubt, but the more significant point is the stress on intent: the slave-owner's freedom in this respect was not being challenged as late as the third century.

We shall never know how common the practice was in antiquity to break up slave 'families'. On the one hand, the presence in substantial numbers of slave children may be thought to argue for a relative permanence of slave unions. On the other hand, one body of evidence is highly suggestive in the opposite direction. We now possess sixty-odd original documents (nearly all from Egypt) recording the private sale of slaves, and in not one case is an adult male slave sold together with a wife or children. Furthermore, a study of the twenty-nine papyri that record the sex and age of female slaves sold in Egypt under the Roman Empire shows only two instances of the sale of a mother with child or children.[26] Eleven of the girls in the catalogue were under the age of seventeen, seven under the age of thirteen. One fourteen-year old had already been sold three times previously. Unless one is prepared to believe that all the girls were orphans, all the mature women either unmarried or widowed and childless, even such limited documentation has serious implications. As a pointer, I quote from a recent American study in which it was calculated that even on the low estimate that a mere 1·92 % of the slave population of the southern states was sold in any given year, the statistical consequence was that any given slave had a virtually 50 % 'chance of being sold at least once in the course of a 35-year lifetime' and on average 'would witness 11.4 sales of members of his family of origin and of his own immediate family'. After all allowance is made for personal, regional and temporal variations, the authors rightly conclude that 'the threat of sale was sufficiently large to affect the life of every slave'.[27]

A priori these three components of slavery – the slave's property status, the totality of the power over him, and his kinlessness – provided powerful advantages to the slaveowner as against other forms of involuntary labour: he had greater control and flexibility in the employment of his labour force and far more freedom to dispose of unwanted labour.[28] In consequence, a hierarchy arose within the slave population. One need only think of the following contemporaries: the slaves in the Spanish gold and silver mines or in the chain-gangs on Italian estates, the slaves in the imperial civil service, the slave overseers and stewards on the land, the urban slaves conducting their own commercial and manufacturing establishments in Rome and the other cities of Italy through the device of the *peculium* (to which we shall return). The slaves, in other words, constituted a type within the larger class of involuntary labour, but they were at the same time significantly divisible into sub-types. Stated differently, the slaves were a logical class and a juridical class but not, in any usual sense of that term, a social class.[29]

Yet, for all the advantages (or apparent advantages), slavery was a late and relatively infrequent form of involuntary labour, in world history generally and in ancient history in particular. Advantages and disadvantages are not essences but historical attributes that come and go under changing social and economic conditions. The critical question in the development and decline of ancient slavery can therefore be examined only by an inquiry into the necessary and sufficient conditions. What, in other words, brought about the transformation from the 'primordial fact' of individual slaves to the existence of slave societies, and what subsequently brought about a reversal of that process?

The process was not only complex, but uneven and in a sense incomplete. Free labour was never eliminated, not only incidental hired labour but the central labour of the independent peasants and artisans. The coexistence of free and slave labour, furthermore, was more than a coincidence in time and place; it was often a symbiosis, as in Italian agriculture where an adequate supply of free seasonal labour was a necessary condition for both the proper operation of slave *latifundia* and the economic survival of the free peasantry.[30] That is straightforward enough, unlike the survival of non-slave forms of involuntary labour. The latter opens up the very large question of the unity we implicitly posit when we speak of the Graeco-Roman world, a question I cannot discuss except in the one aspect immediately relevant to the matter of involuntary labour.

So long as the individual communities remained relatively small and self-enclosed, embracing urban centre and rural hinterland within a single structure, the *polis* in Greek, the rule seems to have been that slavery and other forms of compulsory labour did not coexist: in Athens, the rather mysterious groups known as *pelatai* and *hektemoroi* were replaced after Solon's reforms at the beginning of the sixth century B.C. by slaves (or by free peasants); whereas, in contrast, the survival of helots rendered slaves unnecessary for the Spartans. That was the pattern, however, only in the old Greek world – the Greek mainland and the Aegean and Ionian islands. Elsewhere, Greek dispersion from early in the eighth century B.C. into territories occupied by peoples whose social structure was less advanced often brought about a mixed system: in the countryside widespread non-slave involuntary labour was introduced, as on the shores of the Black Sea, in parts of Asia Minor, and even for perhaps two centuries in Syracuse; whereas in the cities proper (Greek innovations in these areas) genuine slavery developed, though I do not believe we can say much more about it than those few, admittedly vague words. The subject is one about which we have hardly any documentation, but, in broad outline, recent study has substantiated the picture I have sketched so briefly.[31]

Later the establishment of territorial states through conquest had similar consequences with respect to exploitation. The Graeco-Macedonian rulers in the eastern lands conquered by Alexander left the rural labour regime basically unchanged, and that means perhaps 80 or even 90% of the total labour force. Why should they have done otherwise? But the ruling class in the newly created Greek *poleis*, in their determined effort to continue their old way of life, expected slave labour and obtained it.[32]

The Romans behaved in the same way as their Hellenistic predecessors. In Sicily, where the Syracusan Kyllyrioi had apparently disappeared by the early fourth century B.C. at the latest, slave labour became the sole form of involuntary labour and remained so after the Roman conquest. The same was largely true in Italy, though I take the view that in the areas of latest conquest on the peninsula debt – bondsmen were a significant element, and that throughout Italy tenants who fell into debt were in effect held on the land by compulsion.[33] Everywhere else, apart perhaps from the northern provinces, the common pattern until the late Empire seems to have been one of urban slavery and rural dependent, rather than slave, labour, though more study is still necessary, for Spain and Gaul in particular.[34] Once more, I had better repeat that free independent peasants and artisans survived all the political changes, in large numbers, and that nothing I have said implies that there were no slaves in the provincial countryside. A pattern does not require unanimity.

In sum, slave societies, as distinct from societies in which there were slaves, were not to be found in all parts of what eventually became the Roman empire. What we accept as a political unit, and in a sense as a cultural unit, was not *ipso facto* an economic or social unity. In Wallerstein's conceptual scheme, it was a 'world-empire', not a 'world-system'; a structure in which different labour-regimes and modes of production co-existed and were tied together politically rather than economically.[35] An account of the development of Graeco-Roman *slavery* must therefore restrict itself, at least initially, to the central areas of Greece, Italy and Sicily, and that is what I shall do.

It is conventional to begin the analysis by what I have repeatedly called the 'numbers game'. I shall not join in, both because it has long been clear that the evidence does not permit genuine quantification and because most of the players start from the false assumption that they must either produce astronomical figures in order to justify the label 'slave society' or, in opposition, that they somehow eliminate a slave society by demolishing the extreme figures. In 1860 the slaves made up 33% of the population in the southern states of the United States, a slightly lower percentage in Cuba and Brazil.[36] On conservative estimates – 60,000 slaves in Athens at the end of the fifth century B.C., 2,000,000 in Italy at the end of the Republic – the comparable percentages are in precisely the same range, about 30 and 35%, respectively. That is more than sufficient, especially since the signs all say that slave-owners in antiquity were found considerably lower in the social and economic scale than in the New World,[37] and since this proportion of slaves was retained in antiquity over a long period of time: the entire history of slavery in the United States lasted no more than the period from Augustus to Septimius Severus.

It is equally impossible to quantify the distribution of slaves among the free men. However, a few indisputable figures will give an idea of the concentration at the upper end. Early in the fourth century B.C., the father of Demosthenes had two groups of slaves, making furniture, swords and cutlery, 52 or 53 in total; in the previous generation, the orator Lysias and his brother jointly inherited about twice that number, engaged in producing shields, the largest single manufacturing establishment on record in the whole of antiquity; the slave work-force in the Athenian silver mines during the classical period often ran into five figures; a prefect of the city of Rome in the reign of Nero, Lucius Pedanius Secundus, had 400 slaves in his town house alone; at about the same time, the administration of the Roman aqueducts maintained a permanent staff of 700 slaves, including the 'architects'.

I have cited these few, admittedly outsize figures as a prelude to the general point that an assessment of the place of slaves in a society is not a matter of their totals, given a reasonably large number, but of their location, in two senses – first, who their owners were; secondly, what role they played, in the economy but not only in the economy. There were no slave employments, apart from mining as a general rule and domestic service, the latter defined as service in households other than those of one's immediate family. Equally there were no free employments, other than law and politics (as distinct from administration) and normally the army (but not the navy, and excluding the servants of individual soldiers). In practice, however moralists such as Aristotle or Cicero may have evaluated the work, all other occupations were shared by slaves and free men, often working side by side on identical tasks. Xenophon's remark that 'those who can do so buy slaves so that they may have fellow workers' (*Memorabilia* 2.3.3) is not mere sententiousness.[39] The ratios between slaves and free men in any occupation varied greatly in time and place: one need only contrast the normally free, respected physicians of Greece and their often unfree, always low-status counterparts in Rome and Italy. Such distinctions are interesting but marginal. The location of slavery cannot be determined by occupational tests.

One fundamental nuance in Xenophon's remark is that the fellow-workers were a slaveowner together with his slave or slaves, not slaves alongside hired free labour. In all Greek or Roman establishments larger than the family unit, whether on the land or in the city, the *permanent* work force was composed of slaves (or of other kinds of involuntary labour where that regime survived). I stress the word 'permanent', for, as I have already indicated, free casual and temporary hired labour was common enough, and indeed indispensable, in agriculture and in such abnormal activities as temple building. Not many generalizations about the ancient world can be substantiated with such certainty, with so few exceptions in the documentation.[40] Farm tenancy, which is often adduced as an alternative to agricultural slavery, was no exception to this rule. Tenants were not employees: they either took on family-size farms which they worked without additional labour or they leased larger holdings and themselves employed slaves. Either way they did not breach the normal structure of labour on the land. Nor was there a slave 'level' of work: in the larger establishments, urban and rural, slaves performed all tasks from the most menial to the professional and managerial.

We may therefore locate slavery neatly and simply. With one exception which I shall clarify in a moment, free men dominated small-scale farming, much of it subsistence farming, as well as petty commodity production and small-scale trading in the cities; slaves dominated, and virtually monopolized, large-scale production in both the countryside and the urban sector. It follows that slaves provided the bulk of the immediate income from property (that is, income from other than political sources, such as the vast sums pocketed by Roman Republican commanders and provincial officials or tax-farmers, and other than the secondary income obtained by the rich from moneylending) of the élites, economic, social and political.[41] The exception I mentioned is primarily a procedural one: the practice, probably much more common in Italy than in Greece, whereby slaves enriched their owners by working as 'independent' craftsmen, shopkeepers and 'businessmen' – through what the Romans called *peculium* – was merely a variant procedure for the benefit of the élite; in one sense it led to considerable slave participation in petty commodity production, with important social consequences, but economically it did not disturb the location of slavery as the basic source of élite income. Manumission, finally, was often but a further extension of the *peculium*-idea.

I have of course been referring only to those 'central' areas in which other forms of involuntary labour were displaced by slavery. They were the slave societies of Graeco-Roman antiquity, and they were that precisely because of the location of slavery within them. And so the time has come to consider how and why that rare phenomenon came into being. The conventional starting-point has almost always been the 'natural' state of war that has supposedly existed in early times and in simple societies among different tribes and peoples. Already in antiquity, and in modern times ever since the international lawyers of the sixteenth and seventeenth centuries, it has been repeated like a litany that slavery was in the first instance a mitigation of barbarian modes of warfare. That was Fustel's 'primordial fact'.

Historians of antiquity have then gone a step further, and insisted on war and conquest as the necessary condition for the creation of a slave society. I must demur at some length. The fallacy arises from a view of Roman history that is so dazzled by the vastness of the conquests and enslavements of the last two centuries before Christ that it is blind to the unmistakable, considerably earlier growth of slavery in Rome.[42] No one will deny the enormous leap that occurred after the second Punic War. A similar leap occurred in the course of American history, for different reasons, but that does not invalidate the view that the southern states were already a slave society in the first half of the eighteenth century. So was Rome not later than the third century B.C. All vigorous new institutions develop and expand, but that process follows their introduction and cannot be confused with the latter.

Admittedly the two centuries before 200 B.C. are a wasteland for the student of Roman social and economic history, but the signs all point in the same direction. A first tax on manumissions is reported to have been levied as early as 357 B.C. (Livy 7.16.7). By the last quarter of that century controversy arose over the votes of freedmen in the Roman assemblies (Livy 9.46.10–14). In 296, during the third Samnite War, freedmen were called up for military service (Livy 10.21.4). In that same war, Livy records the enslavement of nearly 40,000 captives, a figure which may not be accurate but is also not complete.[43] In 262 came the first of a long series of mass enslavements during the Punic wars, 25,000 after the capture of Agrigento.[44] No one will seriously suggest that all these men, women and children were sold off to Carthage or to the Greek east rather than in Italy. Nor can it be maintained that, faced with an unprecedented and 'unexpected' phenomenon of many tens of thousands of slaves, the Romans quickly, whether consciously or unconsciously, slid into the habit of employing slave labour on a considerable scale for the first time.

Another approach is available. The tradition of social conflict in Rome from the foundation of the Republic stresses the persistent efforts to restrict the landholdings of the oligarchy, and

particularly the amount of *ager publicus*, conquered land, occupied by individuals for both farming and grazing. It is enough to
mention the Licinian-Sextian laws of 367 B.C. and the three
occasions in the 290s when men were prosecuted for exceeding
either the maximum holding or the permitted number of grazing animals.[45] No single detail need be correct – the maximum
supposedly fixed by the Licinian-Sextian laws is a highly
improbable duplicate of Tiberius Gracchus' 500 *iugera* in 133
B.C. – but it would require remarkable scepticism to ignore the
tradition totally. No one will deny that there were wealthier
Roman landowners in the fourth and third centuries, and that
they were not working farmers in the style of the legendary
Cincinnatus. Who worked their land? The choice lies between
clients, men bound by *nexum* (abolished, at least formally, by the
lex Poetelia Papiria of 323 B.C.), and hired labour on the one
hand, and slaves on the other. The choice seems to me an easy
one to make. In the sources, Gelzer, noted long ago, 'special
emphasis is laid . . . on the way in which only the wealthy
gained by the system of *occupatio*, because the use of slave labour
gave them the advantage over the free peasant-farmers.'[46]

Were the authors whose work lay behind Livy and other later
writers all creating a fiction? Surely not, at least for the third
century. Much has been made by some historians of the fact that
the word *vilicus* is not in evidence before about 200 B.C. and that
archaeologists have not found what they loosely call villas before
the second century.[47] I am unimpressed by this argument from
silence. During the Hannibalic War, one in every two citizens
of military age was mobilized in the armies and navies, and that
is inexplicable, indeed unthinkable, without the presence in the
labour force of large number of slaves and of a well established
system of slave labour.[48] There were even enough slaves by then
to permit *their* enlistment in substantial numbers.[49]

None of this is to deny the peculiar importance of conquest in
the history of Roman slavery. Its essential role, however, was in
creating the basis for large estates, with all the consequences that
followed for Roman society and therefore for the 'structure' of
Roman slavery. The 'conquest theory' thus helps to explain the

specific character of the Roman slave society, not its emergence.
Comparative evidence reveals that a necessary condition for an
adequate supply of slaves is not conquest but the existence, outside the society under consideration, of a 'reservoir' of potential
slave labour on which the society can draw systematically and,
as it has been neatly phrased, 'on institutionally agreeable
(legal and cultural) terms'.[50] Need I recall that neither the
Americans nor their slave traders from Portugal and later
England made war in Africa (with the possible exception of the
Portuguese in Angola) in order to draw on that reservoir? Nor
did the ancient Greeks systematically make war on their main
sources, the 'barbarians' of the east and northeast. Neither
Chios nor Corinth, two of the city-states singled out by Greek
writers as slave centres, was a conquering or imperial state.
That the 'barbarians' fought each other and sold their own
captives to ancient Greek (and modern Portuguese) slave-
traders is irrelevant. So is the question whether or not the
'barbarians' themselves employed slaves.[51] And so is the fact
that, whenever the captives of wars within the Graeco-Roman
world were sold off, some of them were slaves to begin with,
especially when a city had been captured: such actions merely
redistributed the existing slaves, they did not add to the total
stock.

One illustration is worth pursuing because it has broad
implications. The police force of Athens, from possibly *c.* 477 to
c. 378 B.C., consisted of a corps of state-owned Scythian slaves,
originally numbering three hundred.[52] That is a remarkable
institution. How did the Athenians come to think of it, and how
did they maintain it? Scythians were famous archers and some
had been employed as mercenaries under the Pisistratid tyranny.
But hired mercenaries and slave policemen are qualitatively
very different. One precondition for the introduction of the
latter was the prior existence of an established slave system; the
second was the existence of an organized slave trade. Warfare
and piracy, if frequent enough, might conceivably maintain a
general supply of slaves; they could not possibly have guaran-
teed the necessary supply of such specialists as Scythian archers.

Even war, furthermore, produces captives, not slaves; captives are transformed into slaves by the consumers, who obtain them through the agency of slave traders.[53] In sum, war and conquest were no doubt important contributing factors to the establishment and preservation of a slave society, they were not a necessary condition (at least not in a direct way) and certainly not a sufficient condition.

Stated differently, my argument is that, logically, the demand for slaves precedes the supply. The Romans captured many tens of thousands of men, women and children during the Italian and Punic wars because the demand for slaves already existed, not the other way round. Existence of a sufficient demand requires at least three necessary conditions.[54] The first, in a world which was overwhelmingly agrarian, is private ownership of land, with sufficient concentration in some hands to need extra-familial labour for the permanent work-force. The second is a sufficient development of commodity production and markets (for the present discussion it does not matter whether the market is a distant one, an export-market in the popular sense, or a nearby urban centre). Hypothetically, helots and other forms of dependent labour can be employed in non-commodity-producing societies, but not slaves, who must be imported regularly, in quantity, and therefore paid for. The third is a negative condition, the unavailability of an internal labour supply, compelling the employers of labour to turn to outsiders. All three conditions must exist at the same time, as they did in Athens and other Greek communities in the sixth century B.C. and in Rome by the third century B.C. at the latest.

As documentation, the Roman evidence is unsatisfactory, as I have already indicated, though I myself have no doubt about the chronology and the broad outlines of the development. In contrast, the Athenian evidence, both archaeological and literary, is good enough, and I shall concentrate on Athens.[55] Before 600 B.C., the population of Attica had grown spectacularly from the 'Dark Age' nadir, a ruling class of 'Eupatrid' families held much of the land, there had been a measure of urbanization, and some commodity production had developed

86

in both rural and urban sectors. Several of the necessary conditions for slavery were in existence, therefore, little as we may understand the processes by which they arose. Solon then provided the vital negative condition: however one imagines the status of the pre-Solonic *hektemoroi* and *pelatai* (Aristotle, *Constitution of Athens* 2.2), there can be no denial that after Solon debt-bondage and other non-slave forms of involuntary labour effectively ceased to exist in Attica (though not, it is unfortunately necessary to repeat over and over, in many areas of the Greek world). The Eupatrids and presumably some non-aristocratic wealthy families now required a labour-force to replace those they had lost through the Solonic reforms; they were unable to find it internally and they turned to outsiders, which means to slaves. Why?

That is the critical, and most difficult, question. I do not pretend that I am able to answer it satisfactorily, but we can at least get rid of some persistent, bad arguments. One such argument dismisses the whole problem by stressing the paltry scale of Athenian wealth and landholding as compared with the Roman and Italian (a comparable argument to dismissing Italian slavery before the second century B.C.). No doubt a Pompey or an Ahenobarbus would have laughed at the wealth pretensions of a sixth-century *pentakosiomedimnos*, a member of the highest census-class in the Solonic constitution. But the latter had to produce his 500 *medimnoi* annually to retain his status, and what matters is not how that figure compares with wealth-standards in another society but how it ranks within its own society: two-thirds higher than the qualification for a knight, two and a half times the qualification for military (hoplite) service. What matters even more is that some, at least, of the 500 *medimnoi* were commodities. Even if one believes that the whole of Plutarch's life of Solon is a fiction, including his stress on olive production and export, the fact remains that every scrap of metal employed in Attica for civilian and military purposes had to be imported; that silver was being mined at Laureion in the Bronze Age, and in the archaic period from the ninth century B.C. at the latest;[56] that fine Athenian pottery was being exported from well before Solon's time and achieved virtually monopoly status by the middle of the sixth century; that the urban population, relatively small though it may have been, required pots and pans and work-tools as well as food and drink.[57]

It is no objection that, on present evidence, Athens did not begin to coin money until some decades after Solon: Near Eastern trade had managed for millennia without coins, as had the earlier Greeks, and the Phoenicians and Cathaginians continued to do so long after the Greeks adopted coinage. Without a sufficient cash-income, the Athenian élites could not have acquired the necessities for even their relatively low life-style, for their indispensable weaponry, or for the taxes which paid for public works, public festivals and public cults.[58] None of this requires a revival of the Beloch-Meyer 'modernism'; it requires merely an acceptance of some commodity production, in particular by the élites, and of the notion that members of the élites did not personally perform all the requisite labour, aided solely by members of their individual families.

And so we are back to the critical question. Why was it necessary to seek the labour outside? Slavery as such did not have to be invented – it was a 'primordial fact', as familiar to the Greeks as to anyone else. But slavery as *the* form of labour for others was a radically new idea. I assume that the decision was imposed not by those who needed to employ labour but by those Athenians whom they sought to employ. It is the unavailability of the latter, *en masse* not as miscellaneous individuals, that requires explanation. In the complete absence of documentation, we have no choice but to speculate, and that speculation is not helped by the experience in the New World. The latter was a settlement area, with vast quantities of land becoming available as time went on; without a resident labour force (other than the native Indians who proved insufficient, when not useless); with the possibility, realized at an early date, of a small number of export-crops, cotton, tobacco, sugar, in great demand in a world-market. Nothing could have been more unlike Attica, with little arable land, none of it 'free', and with a sufficient, and often excess, population, in a pre-industrial, pre-capitalist world. In Attica, slavery was never accompanied by the massive growth of concentration in land-holding that occurred in Italy through the dispossession of peasant smallholders (what may be called the peculiar Roman substitute for the land 'freely' available in the New World).[59] Yet even in Attica slavery was an agrarian as well as an urban institution.[60]

There is a way, however, through which land ownership offers an initial approach to our speculation about the origins of the slave society. Fundamental to the *polis*, Greek or Roman, from the time when it emerged in its archaic form out of the pre-*polis* stage, was the deep conviction that membership in the *polis* (which we may call citizenship) was inextricably bound up with possession of the land, the obligation of military service, and religion. I do not know of a single exception to the rule that land ownership was restricted to citizens by law, except for those rare individuals to whom the state granted the right as a personal privilege in reward for public service of one sort or another. The standard 'revolutionary' slogan was 'Cancellation of debts and redistribution of the land', the slogan of a dispos-sessed peasantry: it was raised in Solonic Athens and it was ack-nowledged by Roman senators and emperors alike in their col-onies and their veteran settlements. The psychology was briefly and pathetically summed up by Thucydides (2.16.2) in reporting the reaction of the country people to the Periclean strategy, which required them, a clear majority of the whole citizenry, to withdraw behind the city walls when the Spartans made their first raid, in 431 B.C.: 'They grieved and could hardly bear to leave their homes and ancestral shrines which had always been theirs from the establishment of the ancient constitution.'

Psychology is all that we have to fall back on – the political and social psychology that prevailed in the period when the élite, having lost their older forms of involuntary labour, turned to slave outsiders. The peasantry had won their personal free-dom and their tenure on the land through struggle, in which they also won citizenship, membership in the community, the *polis*. This in itself was something radically new in the world, and it led in turn to the second remarkable innovation, a slave society.

My model, I need hardly add, diverges radically from Eduard Meyer's, despite certain apparent similarities. His revolutionary proletariat – making up at least half the citizen population, engaged in a great three-way class war with agrarian aristocrats and urban capitalists, jealous of the growing body of slaves, lacking skills themselves, unwilling to work for others, and therefore demanding public support – is one gigantic fiction.[61] One need only ask, Which ancient states supported their poor citizens in idleness? Not even Athens, though Athens in the fifth and fourth centuries B.C. went much further than any other state in providing ways of supplementing income; and surely not the Ionian cities or Aegina, Rhodes, Corinth, which Meyer includes in his fictitious account. He surely knew that, but he apparently allowed his strong political convictions to confuse the picture by linking ancient slavery to democracy, a patently false link.

Nothing I have said implies deliberative action, a consideration of choices followed by a decision to select one of them, namely, slavery. Everyone knew the impossibility of compelling the peasant- or artisan-citizens to become a hired labour force, the citizens who were themselves required in the army;[62] everyone knew that free men would not regularly work for another voluntarily; and everyone knew that there was an institution we call slavery. Hence, in my speculation, there was general acquiescence in the shift to slave labour. There was no jealousy of slaves, no competition with them, either in the early stages or in the peak periods;[63] on the contrary, the dream of the man who could not afford a slave was to be able to do so one day (Lysias 24.6). The free man was one who neither lived under the constraint of, nor was employed for the benefit of, another; who lived preferably on his ancestral plot of land, with its shrines and ancestral tombs. The creation of that type of free man in a low-technology, pre-industrial world led to the establishment of a slave society. There was no realistic alternative.

90

It will have been noticed that in this speculation I have said nothing about the absolute or relative profitability of slavery as a system of production. At no point has the modern historian's ideology been a more distorting influence – not one particular ideology, furthermore, but otherwise conflicting ideologies. Christian moral judgments, Adam Smith's faith in a free economy, and a mechanical application of the Marxist theory of surplus value have joined hands to substitute faith for demonstration. Thus, in a discussion headed 'Did Slavery Pay?', Michell concludes that 'except where it can be used in the simplest and least technical of tasks and in large numbers' it 'does not pay'.[64] Shtaerman agrees and goes so far as to say, incredibly, that 'no Roman who was known through his wealth achieved that from agriculture'.[65] One could rescue such false statements by introducing various qualifications but that would be a useless exercise. The significant points are, first, that Greeks and Romans for many centuries went on happily deriving income, often large income, from their slaves; secondly, that we have no basis for making comparisons of the efficiency, productivity or profitability of different types of labour in antiquity (nor, I may add, have we adequate data on the relative cheapness or costliness of slaves in general or in my particular period); thirdly, that the ancient themselves lacked the tools with which to make such comparisons, which for them would have been a purely academic exercise anyway.

The one certain conclusion that has emerged from the harsh debates among cliometricians is that they have been unable to come to any agreed conclusion on such questions as the relative efficiency or profitability of American slave labour or the economic significance of changing slave prices, despite the wealth of data and the sophisticated mathematical techniques applied to them;[66] but virtually everyone is now agreed that 'slavery was generally profitable to the individual planter' and that the society itself 'had come to recognise bondage as a way of making money as well as of making a living'.[67] The rare calculations by ancient writers are simply pathetic in their incompetence.[68] It is a mistake of modern historians to take seriously the occasional moralizing generalizations – Columella's assertion (1.7.5) that personal supervision always yields a greater return than supervision by a *vilicus* or than tenancy; the elder Pliny's endlessly quoted 'the *latifundia* have destroyed Italy' (*Natural History* 18.35) – on the assumption that they are based on systematic calculations. Similarly gloomy generalizations are attested from the United States in infinitely greater number; no historian of American slavery any longer accepts them as evidence, other than ideological, and I see no reason to give the ancient parallels higher credence. In short, considerations of efficiency, productivity, profitability, played little part if any in the creation of a slave society in Greece or Rome; comparative considerations none at all.

The story does not end there, of course. Once established, a slave society had its own dynamic: the conditions that led to its creation were not identical with the conditions that led to its maintenance, expansion or decline. Some of the latter were the consequences of the existence of the slave society, which we shall look at later.

Chapter 3

SLAVERY AND HUMANITY

In the preface to a synoptic study of the American laws relating to slavery, written in Philadelphia in 1827, we read: 'I speak of the case of slaves *generally*. Their condition will, no doubt, in a greater degree, take its complexion from the peculiar disposition of their respective masters, – a consideration which operates as much *against* as in *favour* of the slave'.[1]

Ancient historians might take that to heart. They can find it said by any number of ancient authors. In the considerable modern literature that is accumulating on the theme of ancient slavery and humanity, sometimes under that precise title, the dominant – indeed, the almost unanimous – concern is with the relations between individual slaves and individual masters, or with the views of individual Greek or Roman writers. Little result can be expected from such investigations other than confirmation of the commonplace that 'their condition will take its complexion from the peculiar disposition of their respective masters'. In the actual practice of historians, the consequence has often been less harmless than that: there is pressure to build up the dissenting view or the exceptional case, either against or in favour of the slave (or rather, the master) depending on the ideology of the historian himself.

Let me illustrate. One fundamental distinction through much of antiquity was that corporal punishment, public or private, was restricted to slaves. Demosthenes said with a rhetorical flourish (22.55) that the greatest difference between the slave and the free man is that the former 'is answerable with his body for all offences'. There were exceptions, as always, some easily explicable, as in the case of Roman soldiers in service or of free non-citizens suspected of espionage or treason; or in the Roman subjection of others besides slaves, for example Christians, to the crueler forms of capital punishment – crucifixion, burning

93

alive, wild beasts.[2] A second, analogous distinction was that slaves were permitted to give evidence only under torture. Again there were exceptions, not always amenable to explanation today because the evidence is too fragmentary.[3] Yet all the exceptions added together do not destroy the capital significance of the two generalizations about the slave's answerability with his body. No modern student denies them, but few seem to take them seriously enough. It is not easy to find a reasonably complete collection of the evidence in modern works.[4] Westermann manages some three sentences on two widely separated pages; Vogt misses the topic completely in a work built round the theme of slavery and humanity. Even Wallon fudges the issue on which he might have been expected to unloose a great burst of rhetoric: on Greece he restricts himself to the Athenian evidence,[5] on Rome he gives the whole subject little more than passing mention, and it is tempting to think that he found the edicts of Christian emperors on the subject too embarrassing.[6] Not so the older antiquarians: Pignoria, for example, devoted his second and third chapters to the topic.[7]

Silence is a kind of special pleading, which also takes more explicit forms, seizing first on the exceptions in practice and the qualifications in law, and then on the fact that in court advocates regularly argued, when it suited their purpose, that evidence under torture was worthless. Aristotle, as usual, summed up the rhetorical arguments on both sides in one paragraph (*Rhetoric* 1376b31–77a7). On such a weak foundation it is concluded by modern writers not only that the practice was 'irrational',[8] 'the one case in which real stupidity can be attributed to the Greeks',[9] but also that there is 'ground for supposing that torture was seldom actually used'.[10] There is in fact no ground for supposing anything one way or the other about the frequency of torture; there is only the free field for ideological play provided by the comic poets and orators. For Rome the evidence is too varied and overwhelming to permit much special pleading, other than silence or near-silence. The old Mommsen, writing nearly half a century after his fiery *Roman History*, could hardly bring himself to deal with the subject in his 1000-page work on criminal law: to torture criminals, let alone witnesses, is 'not only cruel but senseless (*sinnlos*)'.[11]

Irrational, stupid, *sinnlos* – today it is unnecessary to argue that this is no way to approach the use of torture in a society. Any doubts (which I believe were never justified) that we are faced with a normal, one might say 'routine', practice were finally removed by the discovery in Puteoli less than two decades ago of a Latin inscription dated, by letter forms, to the late Republic or the reign of Augustus. The text is the *lex locationis* laying down the terms under which the city invited bids for the post of funeral director, one of whose duties was to torture slaves when requested by either private individuals or magistrates. Two sections (II 8–14) contain the necessary details on torture, including specification of the instruments and of the charges.[12]

What was the rationale, then? It seems obvious to me where we must look. The potential or actual employment of naked force is of course an inescapable factor in the situation, but there is more to it than that. If a slave is a property with a soul, a non-person and yet indubitably a biological human being, institutional procedures are to be expected that will degrade and undermine his humanity and so distinguish him from human beings who are not property. Corporal punishment and torture constitute one such procedure. Hence it was an important symbol of the changing social structure and accompanying social psychology which set in by the second century A.D. that so-called *humiliores* were transferred by law to the 'slave category' in this particular respect.[13] This legal extension of corporal punishment and torture to the lower classes among the citizen population was not just another exception; it was a qualitative transformation in social values and behaviour.

No such explanation is needed for the third, qualitatively different and ubiquitous, manifestation of the answerability of slaves with their bodies, their unrestricted availability in sexual relations. This is treated as a commonplace in Graeco-Roman literature from Homer on; only modern writers have managed largely to ignore it, to the extent that the fundamental research remains to be done. Prostitution is only one aspect.[14] More interesting in the present context is the direct sexual exploitation of slaves by their masters and the latter's family and friends. Trimalchio may have been a character of fiction, but he reflected the real world in his reminiscences: 'For fourteen years I pleasured him; it is no disgrace to do what a master commands. I also gave my mistress satisfaction' (Petronius, *Satyricon* 75.11). And Horace was not being satirical when he recommended his own preference for household slaves, male or female: 'I like my sex easy and ready to hand' (*Satires* 1.2.116–19). The ethical position was summed up by the elder Seneca, with reference to the passive partner in buggery: 'Unchastity (*impudicitia*) is a crime in the freeborn, a necessity for a slave, a duty (*officium*) for the freedman.'[15]

Yet another dehumanizing device was the habit of addressing, or referring to, male slaves of any age as 'boy', *païs* in Greek, *puer* in Latin,[16] a practice familiar from other societies as well (and extended in non-slave societies to men performing domestic service). That this was common usage in everyday life, not merely a comic invention, is shown by the papyri from Ptolemaic Egypt and by the old Roman practice of naming slaves Marcipor or Lucipor. In the visual arts the same end was achieved by 'hierarchic scaling'.[17] We must rid our minds of the warm overtones of the word 'child' in this connection. Aristophanes (*Wasps* 1297–8, 1307) once invented an etymology of *païs* from *paiein*, 'to beat', and that was not the only one of his jokes to point to a hard reality.[18]

Yet the same slave who was called 'boy' and was perhaps beaten or sexually assaulted more or less regularly could once a year, during the Saturnalia (or the Greek Kronia), sit at table with, and even be waited on by, his master;[19] when he died, his grave was a *locus religiosus* under Roman law (*Digest* 11.7.2 pr), though not necessarily so among the Greeks. Such forms of 'tokenism within the framework of slavery' need not detain us,[20] but manumission must. No matter how many conditions were attached to a slave's liberation and how much authority his 'patron' may have retained by law, at a stroke he ceased to be a property. In juristic terms, he was 'transformed from an object to a subject of rights, the most complete metamorphosis one can imagine'.[21] He was now a human being unequivocally, in Rome even a citizen. *Potentially* he was also no longer kinless. That is to say, though his (or her) children born prior to the act of manumission might be, and often were, retained in slavery – a most significant qualification – any children born subsequently were free. That must be understood and registered in the fullest sense. Freedmen in the New World carried an external sign of their slave origin in their skin colour, even after many generations, with negative economic, social, political and psychological consequences of the gravest magnitude.[22] Ancient freedmen simply melted into the total population within one or at the most two generations.

Graeco-Roman manumission, in other words, reveals in the sharpest way the ambiguity inherent in slavery, in the reduction of human beings to the category of property. It also reveals, through the variations, the dialectics of that ambiguity. The Roman rule was that when a Roman citizen freed one of his slaves, barring certain circumstances the latter automatically acquired Roman citizenship himself. That astonishing rule – the only situation in which a private individual by a purely private act could in effect confer citizenship – was unintelligible to the Greeks, whose freedmen became 'metics' (roughly the equivalent of the Latin *peregrini*), free inhabitants who remained aliens in the political sphere. The difference has defied satisfactory explanation, but beneath it there lay a structural distinction between the Greek *polis* and the Roman.[23] In return, there is no 'problem' of freedmen in Greek literature: the word itself (*apeleutheros* or *exeleutheros*) rarely appears; whereas the Roman obsession with them, especially in the early Empire, requires no documentation. Yet for all the epithets which a Juvenal or a Tacitus could muster against 'orientals' and *Graeculi*,[24] their victims could successfully ignore them (unless they were caught up personally in the intrigues of the emperor's court). The poet Horace, whose freedman-father, a business

97

agent and broker (*coactor*), started him on a gentleman's career with a good education in Rome, inevitably received insults from time to time about his parentage. But that was because, as he himself boasted (*Satires* 1.6.17–18), he had moved into a world remote from that of the masses (*vulgus*).[25] So did tens of thousands of freedmen's sons like himself, and even the personal sneers would not have survived into the next generation. The contrast with the modern free Negro is evident.

It was scarcely, and perhaps not at all, possible to escape a measure of ambiguity in any action in which a slave was involved. Because he lacked juristic personality in principle, a slave's misdeeds were his master's responsibility, whether or not the latter initiated the offending action or even had any knowledge of it. So at an early date there arose what the Romans called noxal actions, suits against a master for injuries or damages committed by his slave, by his son *in potestate*, or by one of his animals.[26] That simple approach was, however, unworkable in many situations, in which the underlying principle clashed with other, equally basic conceptions. Noxal actions were private-law affairs, but what was the position when the action fell within the criminal law, a public-law affair? It was unthinkable for the state to punish a citizen who was in fact innocent of any crime or criminal intent; but to punish the offending slave meant damaging or destroying property, and protection of private property was a fundamental obligation of the ancient state. The Roman lawyers found an ingenious solution: they turned the slave over to the master for punishment (*servus sub poena vinculorum domino reddere*), which he accomplished by 'imprisoning' the slave in his *ergastulum* while continuing to exploit his labour.[27]

If, however, the safety of the state was endangered (or thought to be), that consideration overrode all others. After the final suppression in 71 B.C. of the revolt led by Spartacus, the road from Capua to Rome was lined with 6000 crucified slaves (Appian, *Civil War* 1.120). Concern for the property rights of their owners was drowned by the greater need of teaching the slave population as a whole an unforgettable lesson. *Raison d'état* could also provoke action in the opposite direction: war emergencies, both foreign and civil, sometimes compelled the recruitment of slaves into battle as combatants.[28] The Athenians did this for the first time at Marathon in 490 B.C., freeing the slaves beforehand. But they buried and memorialized the dead slaves (together with the Plataeans) separately from their own fallen. No surviving classical writer refers to the incident, not even Herodotus, who did not hesitate to mention helot soldiers. Were it not for Pausanias, writing more than 600 years later, we should not have known that slaves fought at Marathon.[29]

That exemplifies what I mean by ambiguity, and the Athenian performance was not less ambiguous because on other occasions they (and others) treated slaves killed in battle less equivocally.[30] Contemporary awareness of the ambiguity can be easily and widely documented from the ancient sources.[31] How could it have been otherwise? The Greeks may have coined the contemptuous word *andrapoda* (man-footed beings) for slaves collectively, on the model of *tetrapoda* (quadrupeds); slaves may have been branded like cattle; the Roman lawyers may have linked slaves and animals in noxal actions and in other property contexts; but no one could for a moment have forgotten that the differences were fundamental. Putting aside all psychological considerations, it was fundamental that a slave could think, could act deliberately, could make and respond to verbal suggestions, could flee, could join others in concerted actions, including rebellion, could carry out confidential or military assignments. However, I cannot discover that, apart from individual exceptions (and they are extremely rare in the available documentation), awareness of this ambiguity produced doubts or guilt-feelings in the master class. The three or four casual references in the Roman juristic literature to slavery being *contra naturem* provide proof enough:[32] they were a fleeting bow to an old primitivistic tradition of a Golden Age, without any implications for real life.[33] Slavery, the jurists quickly went on to say, was an institution of the *ius gentium* (law common to all peoples), and that, Gaius writes in his opening paragraph, comprised 'what natural reason prescribed for all men'.[34] No guilt-feelings were called for, only the endless complexities and refinements of juristic analysis arising from the ambiguity of the institution.

The contrast with the American South is striking in this respect, too, and I believe that there is a simple explanation. Slaves, we recall that Benjamin Franklin wrote, 'pejorate the families that use them; the white children become proud, disgusted with labour, and being educated in idleness, are rendered unfit to get a living by industry.'[35] That was a common complaint, recurring frequently, for example, in Tocqueville's *Journey to America*, notes taken on a visit he made in 1831/2. Such a complaint, about the effect of slavery not on the slaves but on the masters, was possible only in a capitalist society, in which getting a living by industry was an accepted virtue. In antiquity the only comparable worry, which was found among philosophers and moralists rather than among the kind of men Tocqueville talked to, was about the harmful effects of any 'excess' in human behaviour, a wide category in which ill-treatment of slaves was included but did not loom large – ill-treatment, I must stress, not the employment of slaves itself. No ancient moralist would have thought it harmful to be unfit for getting a living by industry; on the contrary, that was precisely the ideal for the truly free man.

In my view, the ambiguity inherent in slavery is an excellent starting-point from which to examine the theme of slavery and humanity. I shall therefore exemplify this ambiguity in various ways, at first by describing certain situations (or incidents) and asking questions about them, with little attempt to explain (though not without criticism of conventional modern judgments).

For my first example I return to Xenophon's 'fellow workers' (*Memorabilia* 2.3.3), and look at the final stages in the construction of the temple on the Athenian Acropolis known as the Erechtheum, at the end of the fifth century B.C. The state itself acted as the contractor, and in the accounts the daily or piece-work wage of each workman was recorded. In the surviving fragments of those accounts, the status of 86 of the workmen can be identified: 24 were Athenian citizens, 42 were non-citizens and 20 were slaves, the latter all skilled craftsmen.[36] Those on a daily wage were all paid the identical amount, regardless of status. Most of the slaves worked alongside their owners in the same trade on the same particular task, at least some of the time. Simias, a mason, had as many as five of his slaves with him on one occasion. These were 'fellow workers', it must be stressed, not slaves working for the profit of absentee master-rentiers. What, we are entitled to ask, went on in the mind of Simias while the day's work proceeded? Or in the minds of his slaves? And afterwards, when Simias ended up with all his own pay and a share of that of his slaves (however the actual pay-out was made)? We cannot answer, of course, but there is an important clue to be noted: in these final years of the construction, the most delicate work was being done – Simias and his five slaves, for example, were engaged in fluting one of the columns – and it would have been as impossible then as now to determine from the finished product which operations were performed by free men, which by slaves.

That this was not a unique situation in temple-building, at least in the Greek world, is certain despite the absence of comparably informative documentation. Temple-building was anyway a rare and 'abnormal' activity; masters and slaves as 'fellow workers' were far more commonly to be found in small workshops all over the ancient world. And on that situation the sources fail us: the literature ignores the questions I am immediately concerned with, while the figurative monuments are both very rare – far more so than one might think from some modern studies – and sometimes significantly distorted. On Greek painted pottery, upper-class ideology, often archaizing, prevails throughout, even when a potter-painter is depicting his own craft and his own workshop: the craftsman himself is denigrated in one way or another, and his slave still more, either by his physiognomy or by his 'slavish' posture.[37]

Whatever the mutual psychology in such workshops, a new dimension was added as the practice became increasingly common, notably in Rome and Italy from the late Republic on, of employing slaves as agents or of establishing them in a business or craft on their own, through the system the Romans called *peculium*. The extreme form, that of a slave-agent sent on missions abroad, need not detain us: it is highly probable that, at least while away, such slaves were in no meaningful sense looked upon as slaves by those with whom they transacted their business.[38] But what about the many who did not leave home, but who carried on their affairs precisely like any free man or freedman, who in many cases lived among, and shared a social life with, the free poor (and not in the master's house or in 'slave barracks')? Again there is a significant clue: the Roman law retained the fiction that the *peculium* was the property and the responsibility of the master while developing a complex and often confusing accumulation of rules around the *de facto* situation that it was the slave who possessed and managed the *peculium*, who accumulated debts and credits, not the master.[39] In particular, the cherished rule against the appearance of slaves in court proceedings (except under torture in restricted circumstances) had to be abandoned in a variety of cases, largely in the sphere we call commercial law.[40]

One incident, reported in some detail by Tacitus (*Annals* 14.42–5), highlights the ambiguity, indeed the conflicts, generated by the now confused social situation in the cities. In A.D. 61 the prefect of the city Pedanius Secundus, was murdered in his bed-chamber by one of his slaves, apparently out of a personal grievance. By 'ancestral custom' (*vetus mos*), all the slaves 'under the same roof' had to be executed in punishment, the women and children included. There were no fewer than four hundred, and opposition developed: the plebs demonstrated against the execution and the Senate held a formal debate. When the majority voted against any change in the law, there was a street riot in an attempt to block the executions; Nero intervened, brought out the troops, and the sentence was carried out. There are difficulties in the evidence about the precise legal position.[41] For a long time emperors and jurists continued to be exercised by such questions as, How widely or narrowly should the phrase 'under the same roof' be interpreted? Was a slave required to risk his own life in such a situation?[42] However, I am not now concerned with the legal aspect or with the attitudes expressed by Tacitus, who may not have favoured the strict interpretation, and by the 'humane' younger Pliny, who certainly approved.[43] What interests me here is a question that is almost ignored by modern commentators: Why did the urban plebs take such a strong stand (Tacitus even uses the word *seditio*)? Westermann, in a very brief statement, finds the explanation in a 'leveling process in the lower classes of labor' bringing about 'a growing sense of community of interest as between the poor free, the freedmen, and the slave populations'; to which a critic has replied that 'this explanation seems to be too narrowly rational. Only a deep sense of injustice could provoke the masses to such anger.'[44] But a 'deep sense of injustice' is an injection of a modern concept of justice into the situation, and is anyway hard to find in the first-century Roman masses (though they were capable of showing compassion at times[45]). Their favourite entertainment in the amphitheatre, fully shared by their betters, required the brutal killing of no less 'innocent' victims, after all, often in large numbers.[46] Westermann's 'community of interest' is surely overstated, but I believe that he was looking in the right place. The plebeian riots were aimed not at slavery as an institution, but at saving the lives of individuals with whom the plebs (many of them freedmen or descendants of freedmen, some of them presumably slaves themselves) associated daily in their work and their social life.

Pliny's account of another assassination, some time between the years 100 and 105 (*Letters* 3.14), raises a different issue. The victim, Larcius Macedo, a senator and son of a freedman, known to be a cruel master, was attacked in his bath by a number of his slaves, who made a botch of it. Larcius Macedo was left unconscious and was rescued by his 'more faithful' (*fideliores*) slaves and his concubines, though he died a few days later. The 'faithful slave' is a frequent enough theme among ancient writers, normally singled out as an exception and a model for which slaveowners were grateful in a situation in which they felt permanently exposed, in Pliny's words, to 'dangers, insults and outrages'. Something more than obedience was meant: obedience, after all, is the normal behaviour expected and commonly received by superiors in every hierarchical situation, whether in a work-force, slave or free, the army or a bureaucracy. Something more was meant, too, than merely responding to the promise of rewards, upgrading, eventual manumission. Seneca drew the distinction: so long, he wrote (*De beneficiis* 3.21), 'as he performs what is regularly demanded of a slave, that is a *ministerium* (a function exercised on behalf of a superior)', but 'when the programme of servile functions is exceeded, not by command but voluntarily', there is a *beneficium*.

That there were many 'faithful slaves' in antiquity is not to be doubted:[47] that is but one manifestation of a continuing human phenomenon, found even in the Nazi concentration camps.[48] Brutally deracinated human beings seeking new ties, new psychological attachments, not infrequently turn to those in whose power they find themselves, in the case of slaves to their masters and his family or to their overseers. This phenomenon occupies much attention in current discussions of New World slavery, which expose the intractability of the problem.[49] Not only are we compelled to deduce the psychology from the behaviour, but the latter is filled with ambiguities and contradictions. There is no reason to think that the picture was basically different or less complex in antiquity. One case which particularly earned Seneca's praise in a small collection of examples (*De beneficiis* 3.23–27) was of two slaves who betrayed the besieged city of Grumentum during the Social War of 91–89 B.C. and then rescued their mistress from the pillage and carnage that ensued. It is neither helpful nor meaningful to seize upon these passages in Seneca in order to comment, 'how great and enduring was the historical importance of such magnanimous actions done by slaves', and then to slide immediately into the Christian elevation of obedience as a virtue.[50] Were the slaves who fought and died with Spartacus less virtuous, less historically 'great and enduring' than the gladiators who hailed Caesar before going to their death in the amphitheatre?[51]

There remain to be considered two fields in which master-slave relations seem to draw modern commentators irresistibly into sentimentality and bathos because of the emotional nature inherent in such relationships. I refer to medicine and to the nursemaid-governess-*paedagogus* class among domestic servants.

The 'medical profession', we read, was perhaps the only one 'that required of its members almost the same obligations towards slaves as towards free men', because 'their professional ethics were truly humanitarian'.[52] That slaves – some slaves – received medical treatment can be taken for granted, without going to the trouble to dredge through the whole of ancient literary and epigraphical sources in search of a handful of texts that say so specifically.[53] Of itself that fact has no bearing on humanitarian ethics: one also attended to an injured cow and mended a damaged cart. The very phrase 'medical profession' is misleading. Anyone could (and did) 'practise' both privately (within the family) and publicly. The numbers of men qualified, in the Hippocratic sense, were few, and they were concentrated in the armies, in the gladiatorial schools or in the larger cities; they were so scarce, in fact, that cities competed in their efforts to procure the presence of physicians.[54]

Doctors, furthermore, whether genuine or quacks, were private practitioners, charging fees for their services and sometimes high fees: the catalogue of medical costs in Pliny's *Natural History* (29.6–22) is no doubt a caricature, as it was designed to argue a hostile case against physicians, but it is not a fiction. It follows that the great majority of the population never had access to a doctor (not surprisingly: that is still true in many parts of the world and was true, in my lifetime, even in Europe and America). 'I contemplate the great power of wealth', said the moneyless farmer in Euripides' *Electra* (427–9): 'you can entertain guests, and when your body is ill, you can save it by spending.' *A priori* we should assume that a disproportionately large percentage of the slave population were denied proper medical treatment, and confirmation is available from a statistical analysis of the cases recorded in the Hippocratic books called *Epidemics*.[55] Normally the decision would have been the master's. If paid, a doctor would presumably carry out his duties professionally. Some no doubt refused. Humanitarianism and ethics scarcely came into consideration; I cannot even find serious ambiguity. The sole contribution of the Hippocratic Oath, incidentally, is unambiguous enough in its way: 'In whatever house I enter, I shall not indulge in sexual activity with the bodies of women or of men, free or slave.'[56]

Two important distinctions between the Greek world and the Roman require notice. Among the Greeks a reputable medical profession developed from the sixth century B.C. and continued to the end of antiquity, attracting free men and winning the respect even of Plato. There were actually two sorts of doctors, Plato reports (*Laws* 4.720A–C), the free and their slave-assistants, and 'in most cases' it was the latter who treated slaves. That the slaves' fees were substantially less is a further implication from the way Plato develops the difference between the two 'kinds' of medical practice.[57] Whether or not there were also independent slave-doctors is a moot question: an unreliable Latin compiler, writing perhaps in the second century A.D. records that Athens prohibited slaves from becoming doctors (Hyginus, *Fabulae* 274.10), thereby implying that other cities allowed them. Be that as it may, slave-assistants to doctors certainly existed, and that is sufficient for our present purposes.

In contrast, the Romans effectively had no doctors until some Greeks were imported in the second century B.C., and the profession long remained in the hands of slaves and freedmen, chiefly from the Hellenistic East.[58] Egypt also provided slaves trained in the application of douches, enemas and massage;[59] the younger Pliny turned to one, a freedman named Harpocras from Memphis, at a time of grave illness and then asked the emperor to reward the man with Roman citizenship (*Letters* 10.5–7). Although free men, *peregrini* rather than freeborn Romans, later infiltrated the profession, medicine never attained the status in law of a 'liberal profession';[60] it remained what Cicero once defined it (*De officiis* 1.151) – one of the occupations (like teaching and architecture) 'respectable for those whose status they befit'; Justinian was still legislating about slave-physicians (*Code* 6.43.3.1). Members of the Roman élite, in sum, went to slaves and freedmen for medical treatment, and paid for it. Escape from payment was possible only if the doctor was one's own freedman or the freedman of a friend; then, the second-century jurist Julian held, services must be given free of charge, exactly as in the case of a pantomimist (*Digest* 38.1.27).

In broad outlines and on a descriptive level at least, the situation with respect to doctors is thus perceptible, whereas the case of nursemaids and female or male governesses (the common translation of *paedagogus* as 'tutor' is misleading) is befogged to a degree that may be beyond rescue. The evidence is anecdotal in the extreme, ranging from exemplary tales, moral discourses about the good old days (as in Tacitus, *Dialogus* 28–9), legacies or epitaphs for one's dear old nurse, to the persistent grumbling by moralists from Plato to Plutarch about the perniciousness of entrusting infants and children to illiterate, immoral and incompetent slaves and barbarians. What modern writers have made of this farrago is revealing of their own ideologies but not very illuminating about the subject itself. Barrow, for example, concentrates on the complaints of the moralists, whereas Vogt, in his pursuit of 'the humanitarian attitude typical of Roman society in particular' has 'no doubt as to which was the voice of real life', not Plato or Plutarch but the Graeco-Roman counterparts of the 'black mammy'.[61] I can make nothing of all this, at least not until the documentation is removed from anecdotage and converted to a form that lends itself to significant analysis, as was recently done with the Hippocratic *Epidemics*, to an indication, for example, of relative frequencies among contrasting and contradictory behaviour patterns, and of distinctions according to wealth or status.

In the end, I believe that there are narrow limits to the possibility of our understanding the implications of slave wet-nurses, governesses or doctors. To quote 'the Spanish proverb that "the hand that rules the cradle rules the world"'[62] contributes nothing, and I doubt that Plato's views about the importance of nurture in the infant years (or Freud's, for that matter) will help us discover the direct influence, let alone the 'permanent influence', of this class of slaves on society.[63] There are too many variables that we cannot control. Modern psychology has been unable to reach any agreement in this field, and I remain a complete sceptic about the easy generalizations and causal statements of historians writing about a society that has long been dead and cannot be observed directly. My scepticism extends beyond childhood influences to psychological motivation, feelings, personality structure. It embraces such seemingly axiomatic pronouncements as, 'Naturally, the first wish of a slave was to be free.'[64] The word 'naturally' reveals an old-fashioned belief in an immutable human nature, indifferent to social structure, values and status, which I find unacceptable. Given the difficulties historians are having in coming to agreement about American slaves, despite the substantial quantity of apparently relevant documentation (such as slave 'autobiographies') that is wholly lacking for antiquity, it is folly to hope that we can achieve much insight into the psychology of the ancient slave. However, one generalization, a commonplace one, is beyond doubt: the spectrum of individual personalities and modes of behaviour ranged from one extreme to its opposite, even under such 'abnormal' conditions of stress as civil war or slavery. That, at least, can be demonstrated for antiquity with respect to overt behaviour, and some superficial 'psychological' conclusions may then be permissible.

In a slave society it was inevitable that *raison d'état* would from time to time cause a state (or a faction) to invite or compel slaves to act as informers against their masters and the associates of the latter. Thus, on the discovery of the mutilation of the herms in 415 B.C., the Athenians by decree offered a reward and immunity to anyone who came forward with information about the affair, whether citizen, metic or slave (Thucydides 6.27.2). Some accepted the invitation, but the account we possess (chiefly in Andocides I), in which I have little confidence, does not seem to assign an important role to slaves and certainly permits no comparative judgment about the three categories, citizen, metic, slave. In Roman history, the slave informer was a recurrent theme in such periods of breakdown as the proscriptions of the first-century B.C. or the waves of imperial panic over plots and treason. Velleius Paterculus (2.67.2) said of the civil war following the assassination of Caesar that 'toward the proscribed, their wives showed the greatest loyalty, their freedmen not a little, their slaves some, their sons none'. That is obviously nothing more than a clever bon mot, not worth the effort to hunt among the anecdotes for 'a more favourable verdict on the behaviour of slaves than Velleius' remarks might lead one to expect'.[65]

As a manifestation of the conflict of values, the one really interesting aspect of the slave-informer pattern is the threat it imposed, or was thought to impose, to the very foundation of a slave-system, by breaching the slave's total subjection to his master. Caesar, we are told (Dio Cassius 41.38), refused a popular request to add to one of his laws an invitation to slave-informers, and he swore never to trust a slave's denunciation. That was only an individual reaction, but in the early Empire a clear pattern emerged: every pause in the treason panic was 'accompanied by rigorous action against slaves who had incriminated their masters'.[66] Lest there be any misunderstanding about the implications, Pliny spelled it out (*Panegyric* 42.3): 'You [Trajan] have delivered everyone from the domestic accuser, and under the single banner of the public safety you have suppressed what I might call a servile war. Thereby you have benefited slaves no less than masters, by giving security to us and virtue to them.' More than two centuries later Christian emperors ordered the execution by crucifixion or burning, without trial, of slaves who brought accusations against their masters, though treason charges were sometimes exempt from the ruling.[67]

In civil wars, the competing factions not uncommonly put their fears aside temporarily and sought to recruit slaves, their own and in particular those of their enemies. Instances are on record from the conflict in Corcyra in 427 B.C. (Thucydides

3.73) to the last century of the Roman Republic, when the total number of slaves drawn in, especially in the navies, approached six figures. In the *Res gestae* (25.1), Augustus treats his defeat of Sextus Pompey as the suppression of a slave rebellion: 'I captured about 30,000 slaves who had escaped from their masters and taken up arms against the republic, and I handed them over to their masters for punishment.' He neglected to mention the 6000 he had crucified or the 20,000 employed in his own navy; but that was merely the typical, disingenuous propaganda device of condemning the other side for involving slaves in the political conflicts of citizens.

How genuinely voluntary the participation of slaves was in these circumstances is an unanswerable question, but there is ground for much doubt. Insofar as they had a meaningful choice, the calculation would not have been an easy one. Rural slaves seem to have been more willing to be recruited than those in the cities, as was also the case in slave revolts: fundamental differences in their condition, style of life and expectations lay behind this divergence in response.[68] The political orientation of the competing factions was not an important factor: if the majority of the slaves of Corcyra sided with the *demos*, in the Roman civil wars large numbers of them joined one side or the other from time to time.[69] In so far as choice was involved, the only meaningful criterion was a guess about the eventual victor: neither faction had the slightest intention of challenging the institution of slavery. Nor did the slaves themselves: those who participated sought a personal escape from enslavement, vengeance and loot. A substantial number achieved those aims, many not so much by entering the more or less organized armies and navies of the contestants as by organizing themselves into small robber bands, either on their own or in the service of citizen freebooters.[70] Those who guessed wrong were savagely punished.

Yet even the swollen numbers of slaves involved in the war between Augustus and Sextus Pompey were a small fraction of the Italian slave population of the time. The painfully banal conclusion is that, even in such a period of social and political breakdown, the overwhelming majority of slaves took no action. Nor did they, obviously, in more stable, more quiet periods. What hostile steps could a slave in fact take against his master? He could pilfer and no doubt often did, but petty thievery is so common and widespread among certain sectors within virtually all known societies that the subject is not worth pursuing in detail in the present context (which the evidence prevents us from doing anyway). He could work slowly and badly, and no doubt often did that, too, but we have no basis for assessing labour efficiency or productivity in antiquity. He could actively sabotage, by arson, by destroying tools and equipment, and in other ways, but there is almost no reference to this in the sources and the silent evidence of the objects uncovered by archaeology, from pottery to temples, argues that sabotage was not common enough to be a worry.[71] He could run away, and that form of resistance requires somewhat fuller inquiry.

Fugitive slaves are almost an obsession in the sources,[72] and we have material remains of instruments devised to prevent flight, such as chains and metal collars. Slaveowners did not suffer such loss of property lightly. They sought help from friends and associates, they offered rewards by public advertisement, they consulted oracles, astrologers and dream interpreters, they appealed to the public authorities and they engaged professional 'slave-catchers' (*fugitivarii*), known in the Roman world, at any rate, from the late Republic.

It is impossible today to draw up any balance-sheet. We can do no more than enumerate the odds on both sides. Even without the visible stigma of skin colour, an obviously powerful advantage of the ancient slave over his New World counterpart, the difficulties (not to mention the risks) facing a fugitive are not to be underestimated. In a world in which the preservation of the institution was widely acknowledged to have the highest importance, especially within the élites who controlled the weapons of power, in a world without abolitionists to organize an 'underground railroad', where did a slave flee to? He might find a haven with another slaveowner who had 'corrupted' him, but that was not a flight from slavery, and anyway his new master was subject to a civil action.[73] The fate of those who took advantage of the special circumstances of a civil war depended heavily on the outcome of the conflict, as we have seen, and even those who accepted the invitation to freedom by the enemy in a foreign war had weak guarantees. There is good reason to believe, for example, that many of the 20,000 Athenian slaves who fled, at Spartan urging, in the final decade of the Pelopennesian War, ended up as Theban booty (*Hellenica Oxyrhynchia* 12.4). Once a war ended, furthermore, it was not uncommon for the peace treaty to provide for the mutual return of 'fugitives' and 'deserters'.[74]

And in time of peace, what haven could a runaway slave expect to find? In 46 B.C. Cicero's slave Dionysius stole valuable books from his master's library, somehow made his way to Illyricum and passed himself off as a freedman. Cicero brought two successive provincial governors into the hunt, Dionysius moved on and managed to disappear in Dalmatia, not yet under Roman rule and at the moment under invasion by the Romans.[75] He was obviously educated and resourceful, and presumably supplied with enough money; not all slaves, and few in particular from the countryside, could have managed to journey so far and then persuade inquirers that they had been manumitted. On the other hand, not all slaves were worth so much effort in the search nor were many slaveowners in the position of Cicero, able to command the aid of provincial governors. In the small, fragmented world of the city-states, there was neither the police nor the military machinery required.[76] Only in the large Hellenistic and Roman empires could the state presume to be at all effective in hunting down fugitives; at least they put up a considerable show on paper by increasingly ruthless rules of search and seizure.[77] But one may doubt their success in combing the urban underworlds: the professional slave-catchers operated through 'the keepers of less reputable inns, skippers engaged in contraband traffic, slave-dealers, actors, panders, gladiators and suchlike people', and were not themselves averse to turning a dishonest penny in their business.[78]

One course that was especially promising was also the one

that was far better suited to shepherds and farm workers than to city domestics, craftsmen and shopkeepers, namely, to take to the maquis and the life of an outlaw, more often than not in small bands of fugitives. Such bands were a normal feature of Graeco-Roman society, and they were of course not restricted to escaped slaves.[79] They are not easy for the historian to get at, partly because certain ancient writers used such words as *latrones* (bandits) freely and loosely for every kind of opposition group, and were quick to see 'slave revolts' everywhere; partly because of the large grey areas that in reality lay between outlaws and the hired thugs of 'respectable' civil-war leaders on the one hand, and on the other hand between bandits and more broadly motivated movements of violent social protest. The latter were inchoate enough and very vague in their aims in all historical periods, and to that extent there is a tempting parallel between ancient banditry and the widespread 'social banditry' of more modern peasant societies, of which Robin Hood is the paradigmatic figure.[80]

However, the participation of slaves seems to me to weaken the parallel or at least to complicate it markedly, as a unique Greek tale reveals. On the island of Chios, at a date that cannot be determined – so goes the third-century B.C. tale (Athenaeus 6.265C–266C) – a gang of fugitive slaves in the rugged, forested mountains, led by Drimacus, successfully resisted attempts to destroy them until finally the gang and the city came to a formal agreement: Drimacus would restrict his looting to fixed amounts according to need, and would otherwise help protect the bulk of the Chian property, and he would accept as recruits only those fugitive slaves who 'had suffered unbearably', returning the others to their masters. After his death Drimacus was heroized (in the technical Greek sense) as 'the gentle hero'.[81]

Doubts about this seemingly improbable story are weakened by a parallel among the 'maroons' of eighteenth-century Jamaica. *Marronage*, the desertion of bands of slaves who then managed to set up independent settlements in 'inaccessible, . . . inhospitable, out-of-the-way areas',[82] was common in the New World virtually from the introduction of slavery there. The most successful instances were in Brazil, Guiana and Jamaica, with the last-named achieving a 'perhaps unique record'.[83] More or less continuous military action was pursued for several decades in Jamaica from the late seventeenth century, until in 1739 the desperate governor signed a fifteen-point treaty with the maroon leaders headed by Captain Cudjoe.[84] Some of the provisions match those of the Chiot agreement with Drimacus almost textually. If enforced, the treaties involved the rebels in a consolidation of the slave system, not in a further threat to it. But the parallel disappears in the sequel: the maroons rebelled against Captain Cudjoe and sporadic conflict continued in Jamaica for another century, whereas Drimacus lived happily ever after and was 'heroized', if the account is to be believed in all its elements.

Outbreaks of slave violence have been numerous in every slave society. Normally they have also been minute in scale, shortlived and unanimously unsuccessful (apart from the success of a few slaves in escaping permanently from bondage). The typical maroon settlement counted its inhabitants in the low hundreds. Of the 250-odd outbreaks that have been identified in the history of the United States,[85] the greatest and most famous, Nat Turner's Rebellion of 1831, was a purely local affair involving a few hundred men for a few months, with the actual fighting restricted to three days. Most of the 'slave wars' of ancient authors were in the same class. Captain Cudjoe's maroons numbered some thousands, at a time when the rapidly rising slave population of Jamaica was about 100,000, the white population under ten thousand. What set the maroons apart was their ability to flee to jungles, swamps, mountains, suitable terrain for defensive guerilla warfare. They sought neither to overthrow the slave system nor even to make war on it, in most instances, if not themselves attacked.[86] Only Drimacus in Chios provides an ancient example, though others may have disappeared from the record. Neither Greece nor Italy nor Sicily, after all, was comparable to colonial Latin America or the Caribbean in this vital respect.

In the whole of history there have been only four slave revolts on the scale of a genuine war, with many thousands of men under arms on both sides, with battles between field armies, with the siege and occupation of cities: the three in Sicily and Italy in the period 140–70 B.C. and the great revolt in Haiti which coincided with, and must be viewed as a by-product of, the French Revolution. Only the latter, headed by free blacks and mulattoes, was successful.[87] A complete explanation of the three serious rebellions in antiquity may not be available, but key variables were certainly the general social and political crisis that had emerged in Roman society and the presence of very large numbers of newly enslaved men, many from the same regions in Syria and Asia Minor, and enough of them men of education and high social status to provide effective leadership. Without these components, slave outbreaks did not, and could not, be transformed into genuine rebellions, and the qualitative difference between the one and the other seems to me unbridgeable.

In particular, there is no warrant for the common argument that the absence of 'serious revolts of slaves' in classical Greece is 'a significant commentary upon the generally mild treatment of slaves during that time'.[88] Nor, I need hardly add, for hindsight arguments that the time was not ripe for a transformation of the socio-economic system. I do not underestimate the enormous difficulty involved in planning and carrying out a slave revolt of considerable scale and duration. Yet other categories of exploited peoples have revolted under no less difficult conditions persistently, with the aim of destroying the oppressive system, and not always without success: the Spartan helots, for example, the Libyan subjects of Carthage,[89] or colonial peoples all over the world in our own day, the latter in the face of far greater repressive force than was available to the Greeks or Romans.

Even the largest figures given for the major revolts in antiquity, which we cannot control but which were certainly not underestimates, amount to no more than a minority of the total slave populations of Sicily or Italy. And the participants in all the outlaw bands, flights and skirmishes were quantitatively negligible. My promised superficial 'psychological' conclusions therefore begin with the proposition that the vast majority of slaves in antiquity somehow accommodated themselves to their condition, whether passively and sullenly or positively, or perhaps most commonly, by a mixture of both. By 'positively' I refer to all those millions, chiefly to be found in the cities, who, in their behaviour, appear to have accepted the values of the free men – the full range, from serving as thugs, pimps, spies and intriguers to loyally performing services in the households, the workshops and the bureaux of their masters, with the hope of ultimate manumission, even at the price, not infrequently paid, of leaving their children behind as slaves.[90] These slaves had evidently learned the meaning and necessity of what Pliny called virtue, and they acted accordingly, each by his own lights.

How else could the slaves have survived except by compromise and accommodation? And how else, from the viewpoint of the slaveowners, could the whole system, and therefore society, have survived?[91] Rigid behavioural alternatives have never existed in the history of slavery, and the stress on them stultifies any inquiry. 'For every instance of physical cruelty on the one side an enterprising historian can find an instance of indulgence on the other.'[92] That critical remark made about the study of American slavery is, as we have seen, equally applicable to historians of ancient slavery. It is the objectors to Wallon who are the true sentimentalists, whether they are looking at the masters or considering the slaves. What, for example, may we legitimately imply about the psychology of the slaves who prayed and offered gifts to the gods of the Greeks and Romans or who joined the innumerable cult-associations, under the Roman Empire in particular those associated with ruler worship? Were there no pilferers among them, no saboteurs, no fugitives, actual or potential? Both are means of survival, hostile acts on the one hand, acceptance (even if only partial) of the ruling values of the society on the other hand, and both have often coexisted within the same individual and groups of individuals.[93] Of those values, religion was a major force for accommodation in antiquity as in the New World.[94] But there were no specifically slave divinities or cults – particular appeals and rites performed during the slave revolts were no different behaviourally from the prayers and sacrifices of the free citizens in times of war and crisis. Everyone, free and slave alike, simply accepted the ambiguity inherent in a property endowed with a soul. Societies, even civilized ones, have repeatedly demonstrated their capacity to survive for long periods with such tensions and contradictions.

In all this discussion I have sedulously avoided any reference to overt statements in ancient literature about the psychology of slaves, for the simple reason that they represent the views and hopes of the slaveowning class, not of the slaves themselves, and have no unequivocal standing as evidence, except about the ideology of the free. Some may be acutely attuned – I think in particular of Petronius, whose wealthy freedman-'hero' Trimalchio recalls without shame or apology his years as a deracinated slave, when he successfully played all the required roles in his master's establishment, and now repeats the latter's behaviour towards his own slaves.[95] But we lack the norms required in order to discriminate among the varied expressions of attitude and opinion. Ideological openness was facilitated by the nakedness of the oppression and exploitation: no 'false consciousness' was necessary or possible. Even the few writers who had a personal background of enslavement show no influence of that experience, emotional or intellectual, in their surviving works, nothing to distinguish them from writers who lacked that peculiar background. That is as true of the plays of Terence and the *Moral Discourses* of Epictetus – the one probably, the other certainly, an ex-slave – as of the poems of Horace, the freeborn son of a father who had been a slave.[96]

The only surviving ancient attempt at an analysis of slavery is in the first book of Aristotle's *Politics*. Attitudes and ideological overtones, in contrast, are revealed in thousands of passages throughout the literature. That they are not always the same needs no demonstration, but it is not sufficiently acknowledged that certain common elements are dominant. One is fear.[97] If all 400 slaves of Pedanius Secundus are not executed, asked the jurist Cassius Longinus in the debate in the Senate (Tacitus, *Annals* 14.43), who will be safe? A second element, a logical consequence of the slave-outsider equation, is racism, a term I insist on despite the absence of the skin-colour stigma; despite the variety of peoples who made up the ancient slave populations; despite the frequency of manumission and its peculiar consequences. The issue is not of a concept of 'race' acceptable to modern biologists or of a properly defined and consistently held concept, but of the view commonly taken in ordinary discourse, then as now. There were Greek slaves in Greece, Italian slaves in Rome, but they were unfortunate accidents; ideological expressions were invariably formulated around 'barbarians', outsiders, who made up the large majority in reality.

There is a tale in Herodotus (4.1–4) which is paradigmatic, not as history, since it is fictitious from beginning to end, but as ideology. The Scythians, so goes the tale, had invaded the land of the Medes in the course of the sixth century B.C., and remained there for twenty-eight years. The inevitable followed: a new generation of men grew up in Scythia, the progeny of the Scythian women who had been left behind and of their male slaves. When the Scythians finally returned from Media, the new generation, only too conscious of their dubious origin, resisted them with arms. Continual fighting, concentrated in the northeastern corner of the Crimea, produced no results, until one day a Scythian realized that they were employing the wrong tactics. We are merely getting ourselves killed he said, and at the same time we are killing our own slaves. Let us abandon our arms and each take a whip in his hand. 'So long as they see us with arms, they think themselves our equals and of equal birth. But once they see us with whips instead of arms, they will understand that they are our slaves, and, appreciating that, they will not resist.' And so it came to pass. At sight of the massed Scythians with their whips, the slaves promptly fled the battlefield.

We are not obligated to believe the story. But we are obligated, I think, to believe that it reflects a common viewpoint, an attitude, a frame of mind. With Aristotle that became a theory, developed in the first book of the *Politics*, that slavery is a natural institution and therefore 'good and just' (1254a18). Inevitably there has been a trend among contemporary classicists to argue this section of the *Politics* away; Aristotle was being tentative, it is said, and was himself dissatisfied and aware of the flaws in his demonstration. The apologia cannot be substantiated: it confuses Aristotle's acknowledgement of the obvious fact that some men are incorrectly, unjustly, enslaved with the naturalness of the institution itself, and it ignores the full integration of the doctrine into Aristotle's oeuvre, as in the discussion of *philia* in the *Nicomachean Ethics*.[98] Most Greeks and Romans, at any rate, were neither philosophers nor theorists, and they went on cheerfully believing, with Herodotus, that— barring the inevitable exceptions—slaves as a class were inferior beings, inferior in their psychology, by their nature. That is the implication, for example, underlying the commonplace in Roman Republican speeches that Jews, Syrians, Lydians, Medes, indeed all Asiatics, are 'born to slavery'.[99] Many relevant quotations are available (though perhaps none so elegant and pathetic as the Herodotus story), from antiquity as from modern slave societies.

None of this prevented writers in certain contexts from deploying slaves as instruments through which to discuss human behaviour and human nature, as they also deployed barbarians;[100] nor, in the case of playwrights, did it prevent their audiences from enjoying the game, and indeed, demanding it. What is surprising is that modern commentators, who do not normally accept such material as evidence about real Scythians or Persians or Egyptians, inconsistently accept it as valid information about the psychology of real slaves. Can anyone seriously suggest, because the slave-trickster of Aristophanes is an obedient agent without initiative of his own, whereas in Menander he has become a master-schemer, proud of his intellectual superiority and his ingenuity, solving for his owner problems which the latter cannot himself cope with,[101] that a significant change had occurred in the intervening decades in the nature of slaves and slavery? Or that the military language and metaphors so beloved of Plautus' slaves reflect anything of the talk or the thinking of Roman slaves about the year 200 b.c.?[102] And even the joking had to stop when certain boundaries were reached: there was no solidarity among the slaves themselves and never did the slave, for all his superiority as an intriguer, exceed his master in morality or provide him with moral exemplars.[103]

Only the moralists, addressing a small élite audience, dared match a slave against a master in virtue, and they did that by a fundamental twist that removed the sting.[104] Aristotle began his analysis on a polemical note that implied the existence of writings which denied that slavery was a natural institution. He did not name his opponents and they are hard to find in the surviving literature; a case has recently been made out that Euripides was one.[105] Plato was certainly not one: a theory of natural slavery is demonstrably implicit throughout his work and one may safely conclude that he would have agreed essentially with Aristotle's argument.[106] And after Aristotle? The simple answer is that he produced not only the first but also the last formal, systematic analysis of the subject in antiquity, so far as we know. Post-Aristotelian ethical philosophy was marked by a clean break between morality and society, by the location of virtue firmly within the individual soul, and by a consequent insistence on indifference to such externals as social status, including personal freedom in the legal sense. That was the fundamental twist to which I have just referred.

The most entertaining illustration of the new conception is the apocryphal tale that when Diogenes the Cynic was captured by pirates and placed on the auction-block, he pointed to a Corinthian in the crowd and said, 'Sell me to him, he needs a master' (Diogenes Laërtius 6.74). The most serious will be found in the numerous relevant fragments by, or supposedly derived from, the Stoic Chrysippus in the mid-third century b.c. But the whole subject of slavery, like ethics in general, was soon abandoned by those who could still legitimately be called philosophers, and left to sermonizers and moralizers. It is

among the latter, notably Seneca, Epictetus and Dio Chrysostom, that the well known disquisitions on slavery, which loom so
large in modern accounts, are to be found, and they are marked
by 'a total disinterest in any political or social issues'.[107] No
doubt they were decent in intention, but the rhetoric against
excess and brutality, directed to the masters, *preached obedience to
the slaves*. That was equally true of the early Christians, from the
Gospels to St Augustine. Apart from the injection of original
sin into the concept of natural slavery, and their concern with
such peculiar problems as the legality of the ownership of
Christian slaves by Jewish masters, neither the New Testament
nor the Church Fathers added anything significant to the
rhetoric of the Roman Stoics.

This is not the usual reading of either Roman Stoics or
Church Fathers. In what has quickly become the standard
essay on Seneca and slavery, Richter writes that Seneca,
especially in the 47th *Moral Epistle*, was a 'co-founder of our
value-system', the man who 'enriched' the discussion by introducing 'the truly human as an active impulse', who was 'the
first and essentially the only literary spokesman' of the 'interpretation of legal principles' through 'social conscience'.
Echoes, Richter continues, with justification, can be found in the
letters of the younger Pliny (notably 8.16).[108] But the Pliny who
was proud of his *humanitas* also defended the law that held the
whole *familia* responsible when a master was killed by his slave.
'There is no one', he wrote to a friend in reporting the Larcius
Macedo case (3.14.5), 'who can be safe because he is kind and
tolerant; masters are murdered out of wickedness, not out of
reason (*iudicio*).' There is no contradiction: on the contrary, the
two aspects must be taken together, as they usually are not by
modern commentators. The *humanitas* of Seneca and Pliny, like
the occasional piece of imperial legislation ameliorating this or
that brutality with respect to slaves, which no doubt helped
individual slaves in their personal relations (in so far as the laws
were enforceable and enforced), served to reinforce the institution itself, not to weaken it. Plato had understood that long
before (*Laws* 6.777D–E).[109] And everyone was agreed that the

institution must be preserved. On two separate occasions the emperor Constantine issued rulings protecting masters who, in the exercise of their 'domestic authority', had beaten their slaves to death (*Theodosian Code* 9.12.1,2): they 'shall be free from blame if by correcting the wickedest actions they wanted to obtain better conduct of their servants. It is our wish that in such actions . . . there shall be no inquiry . . . into whether the punishment appears to have been with the intention of killing the man or simply as punishment.'

And so we have come full circle: I close as I began by insisting on a sharp distinction between more or less humane treatment of individual slaves by individual masters and the inhumanity of slavery as an institution. Vogt set out to 'show in what ways slaves themselves were able to enter the moral world' and found one in the soliloquies of the Plautine 'good slave'. 'Even,' he writes, 'if the motives for these sentiments appear to be fear of punishment or the hope that freedom may be granted, we are still left with the impression that this is an honourable and decent servant.'[110] The ghost of Wilhelm von Humboldt is all too visible, and behind him the ghosts of Seneca and St Paul, demanding accommodation and obedience in the name of some higher value. Not everyone will rank the creation of honourable and decent servants as one of the higher moral goals of humanity, or accommodation to enslavement as a moral virtue. My topic, slavery and humanity, is thus plunged into the centre of *modern* moral and ideological controversy, as much a field for the philosopher and the theologian as for the historian.

Chapter 4

THE DECLINE OF
ANCIENT SLAVERY

In the year 404, the noble Roman lady Melania (the younger),
supposedly a descendant of the ancient *gens* of the Valerii,
finally persuaded her equally noble husband Pinianus to shed
their worldly goods and live a saintly Christian life. It was not
easy. Their estates, scattered throughout Italy, Sicily, Spain,
Britain and northern Africa, brought in an annual income of
1600 Roman pounds of gold. Not even the self-styled Empress
Serena was able to raise the price of their town house in Rome.
The barbarian threats made buyers of land hesitant in some
districts; the properties in Spain were in fact not sold until
many years later, when Melania was settled in a life of poverty
in Palestine. But they succeeded, and the vast sums obtained
were disposed of in a variety of charitable and holy works. Of her
slaves, furthermore, she manumitted 8000, according to the
contemporary bishop Palladius. That number included only
those who were willing to accept freedom; she had countless
more: her Latin biographer says that one domain near Rome
alone included 60 hamlets, each with about 400 slaves engaged
in agriculture, a total of some 24,000.[1]

We need not believe any of these figures, but we must accept
that very large numbers of slaves were credible to writers in the
fifth century and even later. In the combative last years of the
Goth ruler Alaric, A.D. 408–410, precisely when Melania was
busy divesting herself of her slaves, the emperors were trying to
prevent the enslavement in Illyria of peasants fleeing from the
barbarians, of captives who had been ransomed from them, and
even of the barbarian tribe known as the Scirians who had been
forcibly settled within the empire as *coloni*.[2] A generation
earlier, Roman officers holding the line against the same Goths
were so busily engaged in slave-dealing with the enemy that

Roman defences were neglected.³ Subsequently, when the Visigoths settled in Spain, they took over into their vulgar version of the Roman law many provisions pertaining to slavery, though that institution had been unimportant in their own society during the period of migrations. In the code of King Erwig, who reigned as late as 680–687, there were twenty-one provisions in Book IX laying down ferocious penalties for harbouring fugitive slaves, and another provision requiring each slave-owner to supply one out of every ten of his slaves to the army, then desperately short of recruits. Somewhat later, the 16th Council of Toledo ruled that there was no entitlement to a priest in a 'very poor' parish, defined as one possessing fewer than ten slaves.

These examples – and many more can be cited – are sufficient to explain why Marc Bloch opened his posthumously published essay, 'How and Why Ancient Slavery Came to an End', by writing, against the still common view: 'In the Roman world of the first centuries [A.D.] the slave was everywhere. . . . In the era of the [Germanic] invasions and in the first period of the barbarian kingdoms, there were still many slaves in all of Europe, more of them, it appears, than in the early Empire.'⁴ However, there is an acute terminological difficulty, which Bloch acknowledged but did not perhaps take seriously enough. Were the *servi* of the Germanic codes all chattel slaves? The Visigothic laws, for example, ignore *coloni*, yet we know that they certainly existed, and were important, in the Visigothic kingdom. Are we to assume that *coloni* were included under *servi*? It is notorious that the drafters of the imperial constitutions in the late empire were 'unable' to 'define' a *colonus* in a way that would have been acceptable to the elegant classical jurists. Consider such a law as Constantine's, that *coloni* who seek to flee 'should be put in irons like slaves, so that they may be compelled by a servile penalty to perform the duties appropriate to them as free men'; or of Valentinian I, that *coloni* and *inquilini* shall be 'slaves of the land, not by tie of the tax, under the name and title of *coloni*'.⁵ Fourth-century emperors were concerned with imperial finance; 'they did not have it in mind to draw up the rules of the colonate'.[6]

Law codes and hagiographies, it turns out unhappily, provide the largest body of our evidence about slavery in the later Roman Empire, and the fact raises difficult questions of method. Contemporary parallels suggest that the bare bones of legal enactment often give a false picture of what is actually being done in society. It is therefore not unreasonable to wonder, for example, how easily or frequently slaves were in practice able to obtain redress under the 'humanitarian' rulings that are cited so enthusiastically by modern historians.[7] Likewise, twenty-one provisions about fugitives in a Visigothic code suggest that the law was being violated regularly. In other situations, a rapid series of inconsistent, even contradictory, enactments may conceal an underlying conflict about something other than the subject ostensibly being regulated: Title 12 of Book IV of the *Theodosian Code*, on the *senatus consultum Claudianum*, gives the impression that fourth-century emperors were floundering to find the correct line on marriages between free women and slaves, whereas it is a surface expression of the final stage in the ideological struggle between pagans and Christians.[8] Furthermore, most of the enactments in the codes were addressed in the first instance to local officials in response to local situations. The fact that they were then enshrined in codifications tells us something about the psychology of the imperial chanceries, but not necessarily anything about general conditions throughout the empire.[9]

Laymen were of course no more precise. The late fifth-century North African bishop Victor Vitensis complained, in three different and unconnected passages, about the horrible treatment meted out to Catholic bishops in Africa under the Vandals: they were reduced to being *servi Vandalorum* (1.14), they were compelled to perform *labores rusticani* inappropriate to *viri ingenui* (2.10), they were *relegati colonatus iure* (3.20). That Victor meant the same thing by each phrase is not to be doubted. A century earlier, Libanius of Antioch, writing in Greek at the other end of the empire, referred in his 47th oration to *georgoi, hoi ergazomenoi, oiketai, somata, douloi* and *ergatai* — terms which I believe to be synonymous, all referring to Syrian peasants whose status is not definable by any single modern word, who were subject to a master (*despotes*) and yet were not chattel slaves (despite the appearance of the word *douloi* in the text).[10] This oration is famous for its unclarity — the abundant literature on the subject bears ample witness to that[11] — but we must ask, was it equally unclear to contemporaries? Occasionally we need to remind ourselves that neither Victor nor Libanius was seeking to provide source material for twentieth-century historians and students of Roman law, and that proconsuls and other recipients of imperial rulings were not troubled by the language: they knew well enough how to interpret the rulings even if they could not write a learned disquisition on the distinctions between slaves, *coloni* and the rest.

A generation ago Paul Collinet argued that the profusion of technical terms in the juristic documents is no mere confusion, but a reflection of the social realities of the late Empire, of regional variations, for example, or of different statuses with different origins that may or may not have converged.[12] This is a serious argument, yet, to my knowledge, no one has tested it by a systematic study of the terminology. The practice of drawing inferences and even broad generalizations from single texts or a number of scattered texts has not advanced our understanding much, and is not likely to be more fruitful in the future. Everyone has his favourite passage in the *Theodosian Code*, just as, for an earlier period, one can quote either Columella (1.7.6–7) on the unreliability of slave labour or the younger Pliny (9.37.2–3) on the unreliability of free tenants, according to taste or predisposition.

What appears to us as confusion is in fact central to the whole question of the decline of slavery in antiquity. 'Decline' is a dangerous word. Slavery is not a moral category, comparable to good manners or honesty; it is an institution performing various functions, in particular that of providing an important part of the labour supply. So long as that labour is needed, slavery cannot decline *tout court*; it has to be replaced. I believe the impression to be correct that the Roman Empire eventually saw a slow, quantitative decline in slaves, though recent research shows that the amount of the drop was far less than used to be thought (and is still too often repeated). If so, a changeover was presumably taking place in the status and organization of labour. But where? in which sector or sectors of the labour force? 'Location' is as central to the decline of slavery as it was to its establishment.

The lack of statistics, a serious impediment to the analysis, is compounded by a shortage of appropriate comparative material Three fundamental differences block comparison with the slave societies of the New World. First, New World slavery existed within the larger context of a European society based on free wage labour and growing industrialization, whereas ancient slavery existed in a pre-industrial context and co-existed with other types of dependent labour, not with free wage-labour. Secondly, New World slavery did not decline over a long period of time; it was abolished, most spectacularly in the American Civil War. And thirdly, following on the other two, modern slavery was replaced by free labour, not (except marginally) by other forms of dependent labour.

We are therefore compelled to seek our answer without much help from elsewhere. Several conventional explanations are available. The first can be dismissed quickly – I refer to the humanitarian argument, whether the moral agents are thought to be Stoics or Christians or both – as I have dealt with that previously. Neither exhortations nor the rare legal enactments to treat slaves decently were anti-slavery measures in intention or effect. After Constantine ruled in 315 that slaves condemned to work in the mines or to fight in the arena were to be branded on the hands or legs, not on the face (*Theodosian Code* 9.40.2), prudent slaveowners who in the past had branded fugitives turned to inscribed bronze collars instead – thirty-five such collars have been found so far, one from Sardinia naming the slaveowner as Felix the archdeacon.[13] Little trace of abolitionism can be detected there, any more than in the series of papal and conciliar rulings, from the early fifth century, restricting and even forbidding the manumission of slaves who were the property of the church or of clerics.[14] Church property, it was said repeatedly, must be preserved. The saintly Melanias are of course irrelevant in this context: they were laymen divesting themselves, as individuals, of wealth, not just of slaves, and no one has tried to argue that early Christianity was responsible for, or even striving for, the abolition of private property.

The second kind of explanation rests on the 'conquest theory' of slavery examined in my second chapter. Rome, so goes the argument, had to pay the price of her successful expansion; as more and more of the world was incorporated into the empire, more and more tribes and nations were thereby rendered immune from enslavement; Rome's eastern conquests threw hundreds of thousands of men, women and children on to the slave market while the conquests were proceeding, but not after the final settlements, first in Greece, then in Asia Minor and Syria; likewise with Caesar in Gaul, and so on. There is an apparent plausibility in such reasoning, but it is too flawed to provide a sufficient explanation for the decline of slavery.

Most of the conquering was completed by the death of Augustus in A.D. 14; why did the supposed supply deficiency not begin to bite within a generation?[15] First of all, the gap between the formal legal rules and the practice was a large one here, too. A century ago Mommsen noticed that, almost without exception, the individual slaves whose origins are specified in literary or epigraphical sources were either from Italy or from provinces *within* the empire. Subsequent inquiry has confirmed that observation.[16] Many of these 'internal' slaves came on to the market through breeding or through the accepted practice of 'exposing' unwanted infants,[17] but many also through the illegal activities, such as kidnapping or the purchase of freeborn children, that helped keep the slave dealers in business. Secondly, although the massive aggression of the previous centuries had come to an end with Augustus, war did not, and war captives continued to be sold into slavery as regularly as before – under the Julio-Claudians, the Antonines, the Severi and thereafter. Finally, the slave traders had free access to all the territories outside Roman rule, the Germanic world in particular. Historians somehow forget this, presumably because of the tacit and unsupported assumption that Germans were unsatisfactory as slaves. Yet large-scale trading in Germans can be documented from the third, fourth and fifth centuries, and I do not understand why modern historians should think that they were an inferior source to the other 'barbarian' peoples who had proved perfectly adequate for centuries, among the Greeks as among the Romans. Verlinden saw the difficulty, and got round it with the argument that by this time the colonate 'had become solidly entrenched'.[18] But that begs the question.

One by-product of the 'conquest theory' unfortunately requires a brief consideration. A pseudo-statistical argument by A. H. M. Jones that slave prices multiplied some eightfold between the fourth century B.C. and the second century A.D. has entrenched itself despite the obvious flaws and errors in the calculation: it is so convenient to have a simple formula – the end of Roman expansion dried up the supply of slaves, followed by an increase in the cost of slaves that made them unprofitable and therefore drove the employers of labour to other sources.[19] The argument is frankly worthless. It is folly to draw trends over six centuries from a handful of individual prices (some of them patently fictitious) mentioned by Athenian court pleaders, Greek and Roman poets, comic or serious, and the *Satyricon* of Petronius. Slave prices, in particular, were subject to enormous individual variation.[20] It is untenable, furthermore, to relate increasing prices automatically to a decrease in supply. The general price trend in the United States from the inception of slavery to its end was always upward, with a spectacular leap in the decade of the 1850s, and the complexity of the underlying factors has led to some of the most virulent of the debates among historians today. Ancient historians cannot join in that debate because the data are lacking, but I cannot resist calling attention to one series that at least has the merit of coherence: the price paid for manumission in Delphi rose steadily and significantly in the last two centuries B.C., precisely the period of the greatest supply (approaching a glut) thanks to Roman conquests and the subsidiary slave-raiding activity.[21] Or I could note that in Diocletian's edict of maximum prices (A.D. 301), the most expensive slave, a 40-year old male, cost no more than three years' wages of a stone mason or a carpenter working 200 days a year.[22] But I have no confidence in these 'calculations' either, and prefer to conclude with Shtaerman: 'It is not possible to affirm that a reduction had taken place in their number. The thesis of an increase in their price has not been confirmed.'[23]

When Europeans in North America, the Caribbean and Brazil discovered that native Indians were an unsatisfactory labour supply, they turned to Africa — through trade, not conquest. Then, at the beginning of the nineteenth century, when the slave trade was formally prohibited, they met their needs by illegal trading and by more or less systematic slave-breeding, though only in the United States did the existing slave population reproduce itself (and more). Many slaves were being bred in the Roman world, too. We must take seriously the report that Cicero's friend Atticus restricted his *familia urbana* to slaves bred and reared in the house, even though the source is the unreliable Cornelius Nepos (*Atticus* 13.4); or the assertion of Columella (1.8.19) that it was his practice to reward the slave mother of three children with exemption from work, with freedom if she produced still more; or the statement of Appian (*Civil War* 1.7) that slave-owners in the Italian countryside made substantial subsidiary profits from the multitude of slave progeny, whether one believes he is accurately referring to the second century B.C. or is rather reflecting his own time.

Nevertheless, it appears to be the case that in the later Empire, on the whole, the employers of labour were not successful in maintaining a sufficient complement of slave labour. The comparative evidence suggests that adequate steps were hypothetically possible; therefore, it follows that the cause of the failure lay within the society itself, that the explanation for it must be a structural one. I hasten to say that I do not use the label 'structural' in a Lévi-Straussian or any other special sense, but in a traditional way, in the sense that Weberians or Marxists offer a structural account.

Let us be quite clear about the extraordinary difficulty of the enterprise. The ancient slave system was fully developed and stabilized as a system by the second century B.C. Thereafter there was some geographical extension of slave employment, as additional territories were incorporated into the Roman empire. There was also fuller utilization of the flexibility inherent in the system, notably through the *peculium* device and manumission, with some attendant betterment in the personal relations between masters and slaves, modifications which, I have argued, helped to strengthen the system. But when did the 'decline', the replacement, of the system occur? No one can answer. The replacement was not a total one before perhaps the time of Charlemagne (as Marc Bloch argued); no contemporary was sensitive to the transformation: a nice symbol is the retention in Justinian's sixth-century codification of the body of the classical Roman law pertaining to slavery. Obviously, therefore, no one recorded the process or tried to explain it. We ourselves lack the data to *chart* changes as they were occurring; we can only observe the existence of certain phenomena at time A and of other phenomena at time B.

Let us accept, for the sake of the argument, Shtaerman's date, the second century A.D., for the *beginning* of the 'crisis', and another century or two for that 'crisis' to express itself in significant changes. We must not fall into the habit of foreshortening time that is seductive to prehistorians and historians of societies of the distant past. A fundamental socio-economic transformation that took as long to complete itself as the history of modern industrial capitalism is not elucidated by the injection of the notion of crisis, so favoured by some Marxist historians, and I avoid it (now as before). Strictly speaking, we should now embark on a history not of slavery but of Graeco-Roman society itself in its final centuries, as I said in closing my first chapter. This is impracticable, but at the least we must look again at the conditions which, I suggested, were necessary for the development of slavery. The three were private ownership of land, with sufficient concentration to require a permanent work-force; a sufficient development of commodity production and of markets; and the unavailability of an alternative, 'internal' labour supply. If I am right, then we should expect to find changes in one or more of those conditions in order for slavery to have declined. We must also bear in mind two further propositions from the earlier analysis, namely, the need always to keep analytically distinct the urban and rural sectors, and the continued dominance outside the 'classical heartland' of non-slave forms of dependent labour (alongside small peasant land-owners).

As always, the starting-point is the land. That private ownership continued right through the Roman Empire requires no demonstration, nor that there was a continuing trend of greater and greater accumulation of holdings by the wealthiest sector of the population, with the emperor and the imperial family at the top of the pyramid.[24] Once the incorporation of new territories had ceased and the settlement of underdeveloped acquisitions had been more or less completed, all further accumulation had necessarily to be at the expense of the less successful or less powerful owners. Some of that process had a political foundation, in the confiscations and redistributions during the treason-mania of the first century A.D., for example, or in the frequent bequests to the emperor and to high-ranking individuals. Most of the accumulation, however, had a simple economic basis, and the survival of numerous middle-sized holdings throughout the empire implies that smallholders were the main victims. But this land-ownership trend, towards more middle-sized and large estates at the expense of free small-holders, cannot *of itself* explain what was happening to the rural labour pattern, the apparent decline in the predominance of slave labour in the regions where it was firmly established, and a strengthening of the existing regime in the many areas where other forms of dependent labour prevailed.

The latter point requires underscoring. Wherever one looks in the provinces outside the old Graeco-Roman heartland, one finds an underlying population of cultivators who, usually in a tradition going back long before Roman times, were neither slave nor free, whether called *laoi* or *paroikoi* or whatever native word the Romans sometimes translated into *clientes* (e.g. Caesar, *Gallic War* 1.4.2). This was true in Asia Minor, Syria and Egypt, in North Africa, and in the underdeveloped countries conquered from Celts, Dacians, Scythians and Germans.[25] It was true not only on the imperial estates, but also on the large private domains, whether those of local magnates or those taken over by Roman migrants, on lands held by the cities and on private land administratively incorporated into city territory. There were regional variations in the details, as in the status of this population, which we can rarely catch exactly, but all shared a common quality that set them apart from slaves on the one hand and from free peasant proprietors on the other.

It may be objected that I have passed over in silence the hypothesis that increasing concentration of land ownership stimulated a shift away from slave labour in the search for greater productivity and profitability. That hypothesis can be falsified for the Roman Empire, I believe, but first it is necessary to eliminate a confusion that is widespread. Concentration of ownership does not automatically entail an increase in the size of the units of exploitation, and only the latter are relevant to a consideration of possible economic improvement and growth. Much of the increasing accumulation of land in single hands was a mere aggregation, leaving the units of exploitation, the individual farms, within the aggregate unaffected. Two of Cicero's clients provide late Republican examples: Aulus Caecina owned numerous farms, including two adjacent ones, treated as separate units; Sextus Roscius of Amerina owned thirteen distinct units all in the Tiber Valley.[26] Moving to the first and second centuries A.D., there is the younger Pliny, who owned several *praedia* in the Como district and one in Umbria, to which he later added a second, adjacent one, with several villas on his estates, another in the city of Rome, and yet another in Ostia;[27] or there is Herodes Atticus, with properties in several districts in Attica, another in Euboea, others in Corinth, on the

Appian Way near Rome, and in Egypt.[28] For the later Empire it is enough to cite the saintly Melania, or Symmachus (who had no legendary aura), possessor of at least a dozen villas in different parts of Italy as well as land in Samnium, Apulia, Sicily and Mauretania.[29]

There is reason to think that the holdings of Herodes Atticus in the Marathon district formed a single territorial block.[30] Some other examples of physical consolidation indicate still more extensive tracts. In North Africa, according to the sober Frontinus writing at the end of the first century A.D., some private domains were larger than the territories of cities, each with a work force large enough to inhabit hamlets (*vici*) ringing the villa like ramparts.[31] A few Gallic estates reached great size: the one at Montmaurin near Toulouse, for example, had possibly 1000 hectares of farmed land.[32] Or there was the so-called *massa Calvisiana* in southern Sicily, an early third-century establishment that extended for more than fifteen kilometres on the eastern side of the Gela River.[33]

This listing of instances (and the number can be multiplied) tells us much about the land hunger and wealth of the élites in the later Empire, but next to nothing about our problem, that of the labour regime. Two questions require answer. 1) Which pattern was more common, territorial consolidation of landed properties or mere aggregation of scattered units in the hands of single owners? 2) Were the large tracts exploited as single units, that is, were they farmed as one or broken down into multiple units?

The answer to the first question must be impressionistic: I believe that the dispersed holdings – of a Pliny, a Herodes Atticus or a Symmachus – represented the usual pattern. On the second question, the evidence is decisive that exploitation of large tracts was normally in smaller sub-divisions. That is certain for North Africa, clear for Sicily and Italy from the ease with which *massa* were sold or otherwise alienated piecemeal when the occasion arose, increasingly probable for Gaul.[34] Even Horace's Sabine farm, a gift from Maecenas which enabled him to live in Rome properly, though modestly, was divided into one sector exploited directly by a *vilicus* and eight slaves, and another that was further subdivided and leased to five tenants.[35] What all this means is that, granting the possibility of savings in marketing the produce, for example, the tillage and pasturage continued to be based on the typical units exploited by the large, but more modest, landowners of the past, those, say, for and about whom Columella was writing in the first century A.D.

The unit of exploitation is the central consideration, and it is a simple notion, yet it is continually confused by modern writers with other types of classification. Rostovtzeff, for instance, distinguished three types: 1) 'a combination of a fair, sometimes even luxurious, summer residence and of a real *villa rustica* with rooms appropriate for the agricultural exploitation of a rather large estate'; 2) 'a real farmhouse . . . built for the use of a well-to-do farmer who probably lived in his villa all the year round'; 3) 'an agricultural factory run by slaves and visited from time to time by the owner'.[36] These he called three 'economic types', and I must demur: they refer to owner-residence, not to the method of organization and exploitation. No doubt the latter may have varied *in individual cases* according to whether or not the owner was an absentee, but it certainly need not have, and I know no evidence that it often did. Pliny's organization of his holdings did not differ between those that included a villa he sometimes visited and those that did not.

A similar flaw is present in the four 'forms of property' that underlie Shtaerman's account of what she calls 'the crisis in the slave-owning system in the western Roman Empire'[37] — the most serious full-scale structural investigation of the problem we have, it should be acknowledged. Her forms constitute a juridical-political classification: 1) the slave form, 2) the 'community form', property in the hands of village or tribal communities not within city territory, 3) the 'extraterritorial' *latifundia* (*saltus*), and 4) state or imperial holdings. In one fundamental respect all the owners of these 'forms' of property had a common interest, the income they could squeeze from their estates, in the end a cash income if they were private owners (whether directly in cash rents or indirectly from the sale of produce). Is there any reason to believe that Shtaerman's 'forms' are also economic types, to revert to Rostovtzeff's language? She insists that they are, but, apart from some unsupportable assertions, she makes no effort to demonstrate that there were basically different methods of organization and employment for each type, as indeed she could not.[38] Nor does tenancy have anything to contribute to this particular question. Either tenants leased units small enough to be exploited on a family basis, as with peasant holdings, or they leased units large enough to require slave labour. There was only a shift in direct control from owner to tenant, not a change in the mode of exploitation or production.

We do not know what the ancients considered to be an optimum unit of exploitation, which would of course vary greatly, depending on the terrain or on its use, as between pasturage and mixed farming, for example. However, there are hints in the writings of the Roman agronomists and land-surveyors that they believed 200 *jugera* (about 50 hectares) to be what a single bailiff could manage. Holdings of that size or somewhat larger were widespread everywhere, even in the later Empire: it is not only among the wealthiest landowners that we should look in studying the employment of slaves in the countryside. I am not suggesting that there were no differences between a 50- and a 25,000-hectare holding. But I am arguing that for purposes of our discussion 'large holdings' included a very considerable proportion of all the landed properties in the Roman empire as early as the first century A.D. (and even the first century B.C.): we are not restricted to the small senatorial stratum, let alone to the extremes of a Herodes Atticus or a Symmachus.[39]

However, it is among the latter in particular that significant economies of scale, and therefore 'economic' stimuli to changes in the labour pattern, were hypothetically possible. What can we discover about that? One of Pliny's letters (3.19) is immediately relevant. An estate adjoining one of his in Umbria was up for sale at a bargain price, and he was thinking of buying it. The primary advantage, he writes, would be one of amenity

(*pulchritudo*). There are also practical advantages; two properties could be visited in one journey, both could be put under a
single procurator (agent) and perhaps even under one *actor*
(bailiff), only one country-house need be kept up to the standards appropriate for an occasional sojourn by a senator. On the
debit side, he adds, are the risks in putting two holdings under
the same 'hazards of fortune' (*incerta fortunae*), the weather for
example. There is calculation here, to be sure, but to apply such
terms as 'maximization of profits' or 'economy of scale' would
be ludicrous. I once characterized Cato's approach to farm
management as 'cheese-paring',[40] and I see nothing significantly more sophisticated here. This is said not in criticism of
men who knew how to enrich themselves from the land, but in
an attempt to underscore the limits of Roman calculation and
planning. They lacked both the techniques and the practical
possibilities necessary for maximization of profits in a meaningful sense, beyond squeezing labour, cheese-paring and adding
new holdings to the old. Weber and Mickwitz have said what
needs to be said on the subject,[41] and I am unaware that any of
the historians who seem to disagree have answered them; they
have simply been ignored.

How, after all, could an ancient landowner (or any landowner, for that matter) have increased the productivity of his
holdings, once he had achieved the optimum unit of exploitation
and the best possible crop-mix, had found ways to keep his
slaves occupied the year round at maximum intensity of labour,
and had made all possible savings by specialization or cheese-
paring? The only answer known to me is technological advance.
And in agriculture, only when new technology is available is it
possible and necessary to enlarge substantially the units of
exploitation in order to take advantage of the innovations.
Otherwise consolidation of holdings is irrelevant, except for
reasons of amenity.

In recent years a number of scholars have gone to great
lengths to hunt out technological improvements in antiquity,
especially during the Roman Empire.[42] We may cheerfully
accept that there was no 'simple terminal halt to technique. . . .

But at the same time, no major cluster of inventions ever occurred to propel the ancient economy forward to qualitatively new forces of production.'[43] The latter is of course the critical conclusion, and my stress on it is not an anachronistic reading back into antiquity of modern technological values. So simple an advance as the introduction of the three-field system, hardly a technical invention, was made in the Middle Ages about the time of Charlemagne.[44] And the water-mill, though an ancient invention, 'is medieval with respect to the era of its real expansion' – 'there must be no mistake about that'.[45] As against a handful that have been tracked down for the whole of the duration of the Roman Empire, more than 5600 are listed in the English *Domesday Book* of 1086.[46]

This is not the place to discuss the complex issue of the limits on ancient technology, and of the links, clearly indirect, between slave labour and the relatively static technology.[47] We must, however, look at a corollary not infrequently stated in the modern literature, namely, that productivity increased with the shift from slaves to *coloni*. Shtaerman, for example, writes that, though we have no substantiating evidence, 'we must nevertheless assume that even the *coloni* employed better methods on their holdings' because they 'were more interested than the slaves in the results of their labour'.[48] Let us concede the interest; the proposition remains mere dogma resting on the same moral judgment we encountered earlier in the attitudes of Franklin, Millar and Adam Smith.[49] Note her words, 'we must assume'. We must in fact assume nothing of the kind, as is shown not only by the continuing stagnation in technology and the decline in metal tools down to the time of Charlemagne, but also by agricultural yield figures. Columella, writing in the first century A.D., asserts (3.3.4) that in much of Italy the crop-seed ratio for wheat had dropped below fourfold, which was presumably the target at the time for good Italian grain land (by no means the best in the Empire). Yet in medieval England and France one has to come down to the fourteenth century before that figure was regularly exceeded; until then, yields under threefold were common, under twofold not unknown. Admittedly, Columella's is a single, rather equivocal figure, medieval Italian figures are not available, and yield ratios do not of themselves necessarily reveal the level of productivity.[50] Nevertheless, fragile though they may be as evidence, they in common with technology – the only bases we have for comparison – point away from the argument that inefficiency was an element in the decline of ancient slavery.

At last, we are in a position to turn to the second of the three conditions to be examined, namely, the level of commodity production and of markets, specifically as it affected the employers of labour, on the land above all. I assume that the rigidity of the market, taking the Roman empire as a whole, requires no detailed argument. A society in which the great majority were depressed peasants, tenants (free or bound) and slaves had little resilience in purchasing power. Markets in antiquity were regularly 'expanded' only by conquest and the incorporation of new territories, and that opportunity was to all intents and purposes closed with Augustus, except for the internal settlement of the new acquisitions that followed rapidly. I assume, too, that no one wishes to dispute the continuation of commodity production on both the large and the middle-sized estates: the large cash incomes that are attested to the end of antiquity in a sufficient variety of sources are evidence enough. I assume, finally, that there is no doubt about very considerable regional variations, often among nearby districts, in all aspects of agricultural production and marketing.

The question then is whether, *over the empire as a whole*, there was a significant decline in commodity production. I believe that the answer is in the affirmative and that the reasons are to be found in two separate, though not unrelated, developments. One was the continued expansion, probably at an accelerated pace, of the practice of payments in kind to (and by) the state. A measure of taxation in kind, of compulsory billeting of troops and compulsory purchases at prices fixed by the state, of compulsory (and unpaid) transport service had existed, and grown, in the Roman provinces from late in the third century B.C. We cannot quantify the ratio between cash payments and goods or services contributed in kind, nor do we know what percentage of levies in kind were in fact commuted to money payments. Nevertheless, we may conclude that during the third and fourth centuries the army was largely fed, transported and equipped by levies of goods in kind; soldiers, and soon the bureaucracy too, were often paid in kind; the manufacture of arms and uniforms was transformed into a monopolistic state activity. In other words, the market, especially for the products of the land, was reduced by the increasing withdrawal of much the largest consumer. A neat illustration of the consequences that could ensue is provided by the rapid decline of Lyons when the centre of supply for the armies of the Rhine was shifted to Arles and Trier.[51] Furthermore, there was no local correlation between agricultural production and army requirements: the disproportionately large armies kept in Britain took a proportionately larger bite out of local production.[52] And, from the time of Diocletian, the armies became larger, not smaller.

The other development was a still later one, not setting in before the fourth and fifth centuries. In the year 527 the emperor wrote to an official in southern Italy, in a communication drafted by Cassiodorus (*Variae* 8.31), ordering all *possessores* and *curiales* to return to the cities and leave the countryside to their *coloni*.[53] A flight from the cities by the wealthier (and wealthiest) sectors of the population was widespread in the last centuries of the western Empire, notably but not exclusively in the regions most subject to the Germanic invasions.[54] A corollary was a general decline in the urban population. There was extensive geographic variation, as there was in the impact of the armies, but there can be no question about the over-all pattern – in general, not in detail, because research into the phenomenon is still almost nonexistent: it is absent, for example, from Jones's monumental *Later Roman Empire*.[55] Ancient writers, such as Cassiodorus or St Ambrose before him (writing about Aemilia), deplored the effect on civilization and culture. My interest is another one: when wealthy absentee landowners withdrew to their estates, they tended to convert their new bases not only into fortified centres but also into self-sufficient communities, supplying as much of their own needs as possible, in food and clothing, in woodwork and even metalwork. These men of course continued as commodity producers, as I have already indicated, but they appear to have reduced the market as a whole by their change in residence, which amounted to a change in way of life.

Did this development induce a change in crop patterns, and then in the organization of the large estates, including the labour system? Some historians have suggested a correlation, for the early Empire, between crops and labour; viticulture, it is argued, was eminently suited for slave labour, cereal production not.[56] Was there in fact such a correlation, and were there others under the changing conditions of the later Empire? The possibility cannot be dismissed; neither can it be accepted in the absence of the necessary research. Neither Columella nor the two Plinys nor the *agrimensores* nor the later moralists, pagan or Christian, provide the answers. Complex archaeological investigation is required, and by that I do not mean aerial photography or the study of centuriation and cadasters, valuable as those types of research have proved to be in other respects. John Bradford, the great pioneer of the employment of aerial photography in the study of antiquity, made the decisive comment twenty years ago: 'topographical archaeology', he wrote, 'cannot distinguish the status of *centuriae* simply by their outlines'.[57] We require accurate maps showing the relationship of farm-buildings to each other, to road-systems, to market centres and to army camps; we need complete inventories of the equipment found on agricultural sites, and of the organic remains.

Let us move from this area of ignorance to a subject about which we do know something, and that is my third basic condition, the availability of an 'internal' labour supply. Earlier I argued that a necessary condition for the emergence of a slave society was the absence of an internal supply of free labour because of the political, military and social-psychological nexus. I shall now argue that the fundamental change in the political-military structure which occurred in the course of Roman imperial history was perhaps the decisive factor in the gradual replacement of slaves by other types of labour. I imply no naive cause-and-effect development but a dialectical one. Nor do I suggest a deliberate, thought-out change in policy with respect to labour in general or slavery in particular. On the contrary, there was only a slow process of shifting practices, locality by locality, in response to the continuing need on a large scale for labour on the land.[58] Changes in the practice were made possible by the new political and juridical developments, and in turn stimulated and reinforced the latter. Only later, centuries later, did it become evident that the labour regime had been undergoing a basic transformation, specifically in those central regions that had long been genuine slave societies.

The key was handed to us by Fustel de Coulanges almost a century ago, though hardly anyone noticed.[59] He made two fundamental observations in his inquiry into the origins of the colonate. The first was that the Roman law was always one-sided in dealing with relations between superiors and inferiors, specifically in the laws of debt and tenancy. Max Weber, writing independently of Fustel, so far as I can tell, commented that these 'draconic' laws would have been unacceptable to a class 'socially more important and more self-conscious' than their actual victims, the economically and politically weak sector comprising small landowners and dispossessed peasants.[60] Fustel's other observation was that practice, not legislation, created and advanced the colonate, and that the practice was only occasionally registered after the fact in imperial enactments. The demonstration is so elegant that it deserves repetition. In Justinian's *Code* there are twenty-six regulations collected under the single rubric *De agricolis censitis vel colonis* (11.42), creating the illusion of a coherent legislative programme. However, in the earlier *Theodosian Code*, promulgated in A.D. 438, these rulings are scattered among several titles and under different rubrics, and that demonstrates that the legislation was in fact *ad hoc* and piecemeal, nothing more than govermental response to particular problems or disputes arising out of local practice. In none of these regulations, furthermore, is anything laid down about the obligations of the *colonus* to the landowner, though rules of considerable detail and complexity certainly existed.[61] Fustel might have added that the traditional Roman tenancy contract, *locatio conductio rei*, disappeared from the sources after Diocletian without any comment by a jurist or emperor.[62]

The pressure on the little men that continued and mounted all through the Empire was already present in the Republic. Debt-bondage in its formal sense may have long since been abolished, but defaulting debtors were always subject to *addictio*, which in effect meant compulsory labour.[63] Strictly speaking, the authority of a magistrate was required, but who is prepared to argue that due process of law had been applied to all the bondsmen involved in the conspiracy of Catiline (Sallust, *Catiline* 33), to the *obaerati* (or *obaerarii*) of Varro (*De re rustica* 1.17.2), or to the citizens tied by debt (*nexi*) with whom, Columella reports disapprovingly (1.3.12), some wealthy landowners staffed their holdings? Or that the *coloni* of Ahenobarbus who joined his private fleet along with his slaves and freedmen (Caesar, *Civil War* 1.34.2, 56.3) went along as willing volunteers who shared their landlord's political views? Why, in a different context, did the younger Pliny's tenants stay on after they had failed to pay their rents and had had their possessions sold up (3.19)? The jurists tell us that a tenant was free to leave at the end of his contract, normally five years (*Digest* 19.2.25). Yet Hadrian found it necessary to condemn the 'inhuman practice (*mos*)' of retaining tenants on public land against their will;[64] a century later, in 244, an emperor ruled that 'neither unwilling tenants nor their heirs are to be retained after the completion of the period of the lease' (*Justinian Code* 4.65.11), and added three ominous words, *saepe rescriptum est* (it has often been laid down in rescripts).

This kind of evidence, these hints, if one prefers, convince me that there was a gradual erosion in the capacity of the lower classes to resist working for the benefit of others under conditions of less than full 'freedom of contract'. Significantly, much of the evidence comes from Italy during precisely the centuries when it was the centre, the heart, of the ancient slave society, and it comes from the agricultural sector, the critical sector.

The process was not initiated by the state, but it was also not interfered with, and in certain respects it was soon abetted by the state. Once upon a time the peasant had been incorporated into the community as a full member, with all the far-flung consequences we considered earlier. In Rome, to be sure, he never achieved quite the status of his Athenian counterpart, but his citizenship, and especially his indispensable military contribution, counted for much. From the time of Augustus on, everything changed, and changed with some rapidity. Citizenship lost its old meaning: the political rights that it embraced soon disappeared completely, and for some three centuries conscription was replaced by voluntary enlistment, relieving men of military age of a burden but at the same time removing from them an important weapon, indeed for most men the only one they possessed with respect to the state. The change is neatly symbolized by the appearance, early in the second century A.D., of a formal distinction between *honestiores* and *humiliores*, which can be roughly rendered as 'upper classes' and 'lower classes'. Inequality before the law, never eliminated in the realities of life, was now officially introduced into the criminal law, and the *humiliores* were liable to what had heretofore been considered 'slavish' forms of cruel punishment.[65]

The emperor was still *pater patriae*, of course. At the end of the second century the tenants from one section of the Carthaginian *tractus* appealed to the emperor Commodus against excessive demands being made upon them by the tenants-in-chief, abetted by the imperial procurator who not only had ignored their petitions for redress 'for many years' but had also sent in soldiers to fetter, beat and torture the protesters, some of whom were Roman citizens.[66] The emperor solemnly instructed his African officials to restore the peasants to their lawful condition. We may doubt that he made much impact even momentarily in Carthage, let alone on the vast imperial domains elsewhere. In four eloquent pages, Rostovtzeff long ago pointed out that the elaborately detailed regulations for the African domains provided the sole defence of the tenants against *conductores* and procurators, on the one hand, but that on the other hand, it was these regulations which delivered the peasants into the power of the very same officials.[67] Appeal to the emperor was always possible in principle, but if even municipal councillors 'were further from their imperial protector than was safe', what hope was there for *coloni*? Roman emperors on the whole did not positively favour injustice, but neither did justice for the humble rank very high on their scale of values, certainly not high enough either to draw them into a serious quarrel with the ruling class or to jeopardize the imperial treasury. 'It has often been laid down in rescripts' is a phrase that reveals their unwillingness or inability to take effective action in this area. The ultimate powerlessness of the emperors is illustrated by Julian's total failure, in the face of upper-class opposition, to help the poor in the Antioch famine of 363.[69] Or by the futile resistance to *patrocinium*, finally abandoned in 415: 'the government realized', it has been well said, 'that it was more important to collect its revenue than to collect it from any particular set of people.'[70]

If, however, the state no longer permitted the peasant to vote or needed his fighting power, it continued to need his money, in increasing quantities. The bulk of the taxation fell on the land, in some form. Although appeals for tax reduction are attested as early as the reign of Tiberius (Tacitus, *Annals* 2.42), and although the first known increase in the land-tax is attributed to Vespasian (Suetonius, *Vespasian* 16.2), the burden did not begin to mount seriously until the third century. Thereafter it grew steadily until, on one possibly exaggerated estimate, by Justinian's reign the state took between one fourth and one third of the gross yield of the land of the empire.[71] To that must be added the substantial sums that never reached the treasury, having been diverted by a horde of tax-collectors and officials, partly as legal perquisites (known as *sportulae*), partly as illegal exactions. Along the way, finally, Italy by the beginning of the fourth century lost its age-old privilege of exemption from land-taxes.

The increasing fiscal requirements can be attributed in the

first instance to that iron law of absolutist bureaucracy that it grows both in numbers and in cost. From the imperial court down, there were, decade by decade, more men to support from public funds, at a steadily growing standard of luxury. Secondly, an external feature came on the scene near the end of the second century, namely, serious outside aggression against the empire for the first time in more than two hundred years. It has become unfashionable to stress the 'barbarian invasions' in a discussion such as the present one, but that does not diminish the extent of the financial and material damage inflicted by fifty years of continuous civil war in the third century and by the persistent assaults thereafter of Germans, of Persians in the east, and of miscellaneous groups elsewhere.

The social distribution of these burdens was, as usual, uneven. Land taxes lay most heavily, directly or indirectly, on those who actually worked the land, peasants and tenants. Some also fell on the owners of slave-worked estates, which could not be passed on, but the wealthiest among them were the most adept at tax evasion. The emperor Julian, we are told, refused the traditional remission of tax arrears on the express ground that 'this profited only the wealthy', while the poor had to pay on the dot.[72] For many peasants, the double burden of taxation and war led either to outlawry or to the one available source of protection, a powerful local individual. That was what the institution known as *patrocinium* was about: in return for protection and a measure of relief, the peasant accepted the personal authority of a landlord (or landlord's agent) over himself and his holding, hence the loss of what remained of his independence.[73] The six rulings (dated between 340 and 415) in Book IX, Title 24, *De patrociniis vicorum*, of the *Theodosian Code*, are explicit about this. That was the same period in which Libanius complained, in his 47th oration, that protection of *his* peasants was being taken over by others, and not even the family of the much more influential Quintus Aurelius Symmachus was immune from such interference.[74]

By now, I trust, it is evident why I began with the complexity of the terminology, which, I suggested, was an index of the new social reality. In large areas of the empire, the labour on the land remained primarily of the traditional dependent kinds, carried over into the Roman Empire from earlier times. Slavery, too, survived on a considerable quantitative scale, with continuous recruitment, through trade and war, through breeding, and, in smaller measure, through such illegal and quasi-legal procedures as self-sale, sale of freeborn children and the pre-arranged abandonment of freeborn infants known in Greek as *threptoi* (foundlings). But a significant new element had been added, as the status of many once free rural people – peasants, tenants, agricultural labourers – was steadily being depressed into one of dependency, of 'unfreedom'. The history of the word *colonus* is the symbol: originally *colonus* meant simply 'someone who farms', then it acquired a second meaning, 'tenant-farmer', and by the early fourth century a third, in the words of the emperor Valentinian I, 'slave of the land'. As the Empire moved into its late, post-Diocletianic phase, the formal distinctions among the various categories of rural dependents tended to disappear *de facto* and even *de iure*. 'We may speak', wrote a distinguished Romanist, 'of a regression from contract to status, a reversal of the well-known phrase of Sir Henry Maine.'[75] Again word-history provides a symbol: *servus* eventually came to mean 'serf', so that a new word was required for its old meaning, 'slave'. That became the case as much in what I have repeatedly called the classical heartland of the slave society as elsewhere in the empire.

In the cities, two of the factors I enumerated in connection with markets – the state factories and the growing industrial production on the *latifundia* – helped to destroy such larger manufacturing establishments as had once existed in ancient cities, and contributed to an altogether paradoxical transformation in the urban crafts. The *plebs urbana* of the later Empire have been remarkably neglected in modern histories, except when they rioted.[76] Yet no one doubts that they were present in large numbers or that they still counted among the free men – as late as 432 an imperial instruction referred to the *ordo plebeiorum*[77] – unlike *coloni* and slaves. What did they do when they were not rioting? The answer is that, like the Paris 'mob' in the French Revolution, they included not only the unskilled and the *Lumpenproletariat* but also the urban artisan class engaged in petty trade and petty commodity production – highly specialized, hard working and mostly very poor.[78] It was the urban slaves who were now a parasitical element. We can judge only from impressions, but it is striking that in all the sources from the late Empire, when productive slaves appear they are working in the rural sector, as farmers or craftsmen, whereas the still numerous urban slaves appear with equal regularity as domestics and adminstrators, as a luxury for the conspicuous consumption not only of the wealthy but also of the more modest rhetors and teachers.[79]

The workers in the imperial factories formed a group apart, a group whose status has resisted attempts at conventional definition. The only collective terms applied to them in the texts, *collegiati, corporati*, are not helpful. It has been argued that because the certainly servile labels – *mancipi* or *ex familia* – are attested only for the weavers, dyers and collectors of purple dye, they alone were genuine slaves.[80] But work in the imperial factories had been added to the list of severe punishments, like the older condemnation to the mines, and that makes one pause a bit. We then notice that the mint employees, a more esteemed group, were not only branded but were regarded as slaves under the terms of the *senatus consultum Claudianum*. An edict of 380 forbade any woman of higher rank from cohabiting with a *monetarius* under penalty of losing her freedom under that ancient law.[81] The old Roman juristic categories had lost their validity.

The availability of an 'internal' labour supply, in sum, rendered it unnecessary for the *possessores* to do more than they did in recruiting a complement of slave labour. I am unable to discover any considerations, or consciousness, of relative productivity in the long slow process I have tried to pin down, no searching for an 'increase of production' on the part of 'clear-sighted social groups'.[82] Late antique moralists complained about the idleness and shiftlessness of the city population, both slave and free, in contrast to the hard-working rustic population,[83] but their predecessors grumbled in the same way about slaves and tenants alike: witness Columella or the younger Pliny. Ideologically significant though they may be, such texts are no more revealing of the facts of economic behaviour than the similar grumbles of American slave-owners or of letters to *The Times* about the idleness and indiscipline of English workingmen. None of the grumblers suffered in their purses.

On the 'location' test, the world of late antiquity was no longer a slave society, despite the continued presence of slaves in large numbers. Slaves no longer dominated large-scale production in the countryside; large-scale production in the cities had been reduced to the state factories; slaves no longer provided the bulk of the property revenues of the élites. Only in the domestic sphere did they remain predominant, and the top of that pyramid was now occupied by the court eunuchs.[84] A structural transformation had clearly occurred, in which slaves were gradually replaced in the towns by men who remained juridically free but were no longer the free citizens of the classical world, and in the countryside by men who were neither juridically nor politically free in the old sense. However, the *organization* of the rural economy does not appear to have been transformed. I am unable to fit late antiquity into any neat series of stages. Although rudiments of a manorial (or seigneurial) system have been detected on the imperial estates of North Africa and in one or two other places, that system and its feudal superstructure were not to emerge before the time of Charlemagne, as Marc Bloch correctly insisted. Slave society did not immediately give way to feudal society.

NOTES

Chapter 1

1. Davis (1974) 11.
2. Temperley (1977) 97.
3. Heeren (1826) 234.
4. Marx-Engels, *Werke* 20 (Berlin 1962), p. 168.
5. Lauffer (1960) 71.
6. Westermann (1955) 152. My reason for singling him out among contemporary historians, along with Vogt, will become apparent later in this chapter.
7. Vogt (1974) 172–4. (In view of Vogt's habit of reprinting his articles on this subject, often several times, with casual minor revisions, I shall regularly cite the English translation, which is the latest version.) Backhaus (1975) 543–4 has carried the misconception of the place of Wallon in the historiography of ancient slavery to a *reductio ad absurdum*. As further examples of the interference of the 'abolitionist cliché' and other extraneous ideological considerations into the history of slavery, he mentions the valueless books by Tourmagne (1880) and Letourneau (1897), as well as Ingram (1895) and Nieboer (1900), none of which properly exemplifies his objections. In so far as Tourmagne and Letourneau had contemporary interests, they were in a vague socialism. Ingram, one of the genuine pan-sophists of the second half of the nineteenth century, who held the chairs of oratory and Greek in sequence at Trinity College, Dublin, was most creative as a statistician and economist, and was accordingly invited to write the article on slavery and serfdom for the 1887 edition of the *Encyclopaedia Britannica*. His book, an unpretentious long essay, was a by-product of that article and it naturally closed the story with an account of current anti-slavery efforts. Ingram's philosophical position was basically Comtean. Nieboer, finally, wrote the first serious anthropological study of slavery (his subtitle is 'Ethnological Researches'), and he said explicitly in his preface that he was concerned with neither the historical

study of the subject nor the 'philanthropic' (i.e. 'to further the suppression of the African slave-trade') but with a search for 'sociological laws' in the evidence from 'savages'. Backhaus is repeated almost word for word by Mazza (1977) xlii–xliii. Neither seems aware of Abignente (1890), published, as the title-page indicates, on the occasion of an anti-slavery congress in Brussels, yet Abignente's is probably the best account (in its second half) of medieval slavery before Verlinden's recent work.

8. See, for instance, the glowing assessment of Wallon's contribution by J. Marquardt, *Das Privatleben der Römer* (2 vols., 2nd ed., 1866; repr. Darmstadt 1964) I 135n1; cf. L. Mitteis, *Reichsrecht und Volksrecht* (Leipzig 1891), p. 357n1. The main exception to the twentieth-century trend has been in the Soviet Union: Wallon's *Histoire* was translated into Russian in 1941.

9. F. Overbeck, *Studien zur Geschichte der alten Kirche* (Schloss-Chemnitz 1875), ch. 3. This study was apparently unknown to Westermann and it is not listed in Brockmeyer (1971).

10. Millar (1771) 222–5.

11. *The Social Teaching of the Christian Churches*, trans. Olive Wyon (2 vols., London and New York 1931) I 132. He goes on to write: 'Thus the Christians changed nothing whatever in the laws affecting slaves. . . . This forms a most typical illustration of the attitude of Christians towards the world; they renounced the world, and yet they compromised with it, and they did not, and could not, dream of making any change in the social system.'

12. An account of the competition is complicated by several circumstances: (1) The eight entries were anonymous, and Michelet's report to the Académie, *Mémoires* 3 (1840) 655–71, identifies each only by a number. (2) The winning entry was a joint effort by Wallon and J. Yanoski, as the former explains in his preface: Wallon wrote the ancient sections, Yanoski the medieval, beginning with the Germanic codes. (3) What was eventually published differed, to a greater or lesser extent, from the manuscripts submitted to the Académie. Biot, awarded a gold medal, published his *De l'abolition de l'esclavage ancien en Occident* the following year, and, if Michelet's page references in his report are anything to go by, the printed book

(449 pp.) was much longer than the original submission. Wallon worked for the better part of a decade before bringing out his enormous three volumes. Yanoski turned immediately to other historical studies and died in 1851. In 1860 his original manuscript was published, with some additions by Wallon, under the title *De l'abolition de l'esclavage ancien au moyen âge et sa transformation en servitude de glèbe*. When I return to a consideration of this affair, I shall for convenience refer to three prize-winners.

13. Vogt (1974) 145.
14. 'The failure of the Humanists to achieve anything in the struggle for human rights' is another typical illustration: Vogt (1974) 203.
15. See Vidal-Naquet (1972).
16. See J. G. A. Pocock, *The Ancient Constitution and the Feudal Law* (Cambridge 1957); cf. Finley (1975) ch. 2: 'The Ancestral Constitution'.
17. Thus, in a powerful, late anti-abolitionist work, *An Essay on Liberty and Slavery*, by A. T. Bledsoe, Professor of Mathematics in the University of Virginia (1856; repr., Freeport, N.Y., 1971), much the longest chapter, 'The Argument from the Scriptures' (pp. 138–225), includes a typical, brief bow to Aristotle. For nineteenth-century abolitionists, in contrast, the defence of slavery by the great Artistotle was a rather serious nuisance: see e.g. L. Schiller, *Die Lehre des Aristoteles von der Sklaverei* (*Jahresbericht von der K. Studienanstalt zu Erlangen* 1847), who called the abolitionist movement a 'holy war' (p. 3).
18. See Jameson (1911) 82–103.
19. Cassirer (1951) 182.
20. On this distinction, see G. H. Nadel, 'Philosophy of History before Historicism', *History and Theory* 3 (1954) 291–315, esp. pp. 292–304.
21. Cassirer (1951) 209–210.
22. See P. Vidal-Naquet, 'Tradition de la démocratie grecque', published as an introduction to M. I. Finley, *Démocratie antique et démocratie moderne*, trans. M. Alexandre (Paris 1976), pp. 7–44; N. Loraux and Vidal-Naquet, 'La formation de l'Athènes bourgeoise. Essai d'historiographie 1750–1850', in *Classical Influences on Western Thought A.D. 1650–1870*, ed. R. R. Bolgar (Cambridge 1978), pp. 169–222.

23. See the admirable summary by Davis (1966) ch. 13-14; cf. Jameson (1911); E. D. Seeber, *Anti-Slavery Opinion during the Second Half of the Eighteenth Century* (Baltimore 1937); M. Duchet, *Anthropologie et histoire au siècle des lumières* (Paris 1971), esp. pp. 137-93.

24. A minute inquiry into the sources of Montesquieu's Book XV appears in Jameson (1911) 260-87.

25. In contrast, in *Rome au siècle d'Auguste*, an erudite and popular work modelled on Barthélemy's *Anacharsis*, as the subtitle indicates, *Voyage d'un Gaulois à Rome* (4 vols., Paris 1835; rev. ed., 1846-7), L. C. Dezobry devotes one bitter 'letter' (no. 10) to slavery and returns to the subject elsewhere, notably in the lengthy no. 88 on the villas. One sentence will illustrate his position sufficiently: 'The citizens among whom the light of philosophy seemingly ought to foster sentiments of humanity are as pitiless as the others' (I 100-1). See further below on this contrast between Greek and Roman 'antiquities'.

26. Stier (1945) 23 praises his opposition to the 'wholly unclear fanaticism of his contemporaries for freedom'.

27. Momigliano (1966) 42, 49.

28. Yet Gibbon possessed copies of most of the main antiquarian and demographic studies mentioned below: Geoffrey Keynes, *The Library of Edward Gibbon* (London 1940).

29. *A History of Greece* (new ed., London 1862) II 59.

30. Momigliano (1966) 7.

31. The list in Brockmeyer (1971) is neither complete nor wholly accurate.

32. The still valuable classified list in Blair (1833) 131-41, set out in two columns, Latin and English, is, in his own words, 'drawn chiefly' from Popma and Pignoria, who 'have left little for us to do'. It is worth noting that these are the only three works specifically devoted to ancient slavery that are included in J. R. McCulloch's classic (1845).

33. See Momigliano (1966) ch. 4: 'Friedrich Creuzer and Greek Historiography'.

34. McCulloch (1845) 356 commented: 'Had the author's knowledge of modern science borne any proportion to his knowledge of antiquity, the book would have been all that had been desired.'

35. G. C. Lewis appended this study to his translation of the

Staatshaushaltung (2 vols., London 1828) II 415–94, and then demolished Böckh's calculations in two pages.

36. Vogt (1974) 171.

37. Momigliano (1966) 21.

38. *Quarterly Review* 50 (1834) 399–412.

39. In his *Deutsche Schriften* 4 (Leipzig and Berlin 1836), pp. 1–74.

40. This seems to me to be a conscious rejection of the rapidly growing neo-humanism (or classical humanism) of the time, about which I shall have more to say later.

41. It is worth mentioning that in two notes (7 and 11) he accepted both Grotius' argument that slavery was at least a mitigation of the barbarian practice of killing war captives, and the view that Christianity was ultimately responsible for the decline of ancient slavery. I am struck by the reminiscences here (and in one or two other places) of the review of Blair (cited above, n. 38) which he knew. He had been unable to obtain a copy of Blair's book.

42. Again I must note a remarkable exception. That great pioneer of modern classical study, Christian Gottlob Heyne, who was sometimes stimulated to pursue an historical inquiry by a contemporary issue or event, such as the American War of Independence or the early penal settlements in Australia, chose a ceremonial academic occasion in 1789 to deliver a Latin oration on the sources of slave supply of the Greeks and Romans, opening with several pages on the current debate over modern slavery and citing Millar's *Distinction of Ranks*: *Opuscula* 4 (Göttingen 1796), pp. 120–39. It is tempting to suggest that Heyne owed his knowledge of Millar and some of his more general ideas on the subject to his pupil, J. F. Reitemeier, on whom see below.

43. Later we shall consider the new conception that human society had progressed through distinct stages marked by different modes of subsistence.

44. Franklin, 'Observations concerning the Increase of Mankind', in *The Papers of Benjamin Franklin*, ed. L. W. Labaree, 4 (New Haven 1961), pp. 225–34, at pp. 229–30; Millar (1771) 199–203; Smith, *Wealth of Nations*, Bk. I, ch. 8. It should be stressed that no one in this period suggested that slave labour was unprofitable: the illegitimate shift from expensive or inefficient to unprofitable has been made by some twentieth-century

ancient historians. It should also be said that the older negative judgment of slavery, dubious at best, was based solely on assumptions about the virtues of economic freedom: see Temperley (1977) 106–9.

45. Hume (1752) 384.

46. McCulloch (1845) 257. It is not unlikely that McCulloch deliberately chose the phrase 'political economy' from the title of the English version of Böckh's *Staatshaushaltung*, in the light of his comment on the latter, quoted above in in n. 34.

47. Beloch (1886) 35.

48. Wallace (1753).

49. See the long survey of the modern literature on Greek slavery in Part I of Lencman (1966).

50. E.g. Millar (1771) 233–5; for eighteenth-century France, the compendious but uncritical summaries in J. J. Spengler, *French Predecessors of Malthus* (Durham, N.C., 1942), French trans. by G. Lecarpentier and A. Fage (Paris 1954), Index, svv. Hume, Slavery.

51. De Sainte Croix, 'Recherches sur la population d'Attique', read to the Académie des Inscriptions in 1785 but not published in the *Mémoires* until vol. 48 (1808) 147–75; Letronne, 'Mémoire sur la population d'Attique', *Mémoires* 6 (1822) 165–220; Dureau de la Malle (1840) bk. II, the fruit of twenty years' work, some of it published earlier in vols. 9 and 12 of the *Mémoires* of the Académie.

52. They also reveal the basis of that otherwise puzzling remark by Büchsenschütz I mentioned earlier, that slavery was bad not only morally and economically but also demographically.

53. Much of the literature is summarized at excruciating length by Sargent (1924) ch. 1; see more briefly and recently Lencman (1966) pt. I.

54. *Op. cit.* in n. 12, pp. 660–1.

55. Biot (1840) 125–6, 140–1; cf. Yanoski (1860) 55–6.

56. Michelet, *op. cit.* in n. 12, pp. 664–5.

57. The references can easily be found in the detailed index in the final volume of the Deutsche Taschenbuch Verlag edition of the *Römische Geschichte* (8 vols., Munich 1976), which also gives the pagination of the 'standard' (6th) edition of 1874. A very brief appreciation of the uniqueness of Mommsen's treatment of slavery will be found in Karl Christ's essay in vol. 8, pp. 34–5.

58. See Finley (1977b) 129–35.

59. For example, W. Richter's 168-page monograph, *Die Sklaverei im griechischen Altertum. Ein Kulturbild* (Breslau 1886), was a pointless 'sequel' to the work of Wallon and Büchsenschütz, both of which he knew and cited. There was even less point to A. Schneider, *Zur Geschichte der Sclaverei im alten Rom*, a 52-page essay published by the Zurich Staatswissenschaftliche Fakultät (1892) as a Festschrift for Ihering.

60. After months of search, I succeeded in obtaining a photocopy through the courtesy of the Rare Books Department of the Cornell University Library. A promised sequel on Roman slavery was never produced. Heyne's approval is explicit in the oration cited above, n. 42.

61. The one-sentence summary in Vogt (1974) 170–1 also misses the essential argument. He locates the book in the wrong (Enlightenment) context when he writes (having overlooked the actual date of composition), 'In 1789, the first year of the French Revolution, Johann Friedrich Reitemeier . . . published an essay. . . .'

62. The extent of his originality becomes evident in a comparison with Christoph Meiners, *Geschichte der Luxus der Atheniensier* (Lemgo 1782), winner in the 1781 prize competition of the Hessen-Casselschen Gesellschaft der Alterthümer. I have not seen Reitemeier's own monograph on the subject, which may have been stimulated by the same competition.

63. The stress on the economic importance of luxuries also merits attention, in the light of the similar emphasis later on among students of medieval and modern economic history, e.g. Roscher (1871) ch. 7, 'Ueber den Luxus'; Werner Sombart, *Luxus und Kapitalismus* (Munich and Leipzig 1913), the first of his *Studien zur Entwicklungsgeschichte des modernen Kapitalismus*, preparatory studies for the 2nd ed. of *Der modern Kapitalismus*.

64. An excellent survey, with bibliography, is provided by B. Bravo, *Philologie, histoire, philosophie de l'histoire, étude sur J. G. Droysen* . . . (Polish Acad. of Sciences 1968), ch. 1.

65. I ignore the fairly considerable quantity of nineteenth-century publication, without value, by dilettantes of various kinds, e.g. J. A. St. John, *The History of the Manners and Customs of Ancient Greece* (3 vols., London 1842) III 1–67, Tourmagne (1880),

Letourneau (1897); or, more recently, Joël Schmidt, *Vie et mort des esclaves dans la Rome antique* (Paris 1973).

66. 'Ueber das Verhältniss der Nationalökonomik zum klassischen Alterthums', in Roscher (1871) ch. 1. More important was the work of Rodbertus, but as Bücher (1922) 2 rightly remarked, 'the imposing scientific achievement of that rare man . . . would have slept on in its paper grave, volumes IV, V and VII of Hildebrand's *Jahrbücher*', had Bücher not revived the ideas a generation later and been assaulted for them by Eduard Meyer. I therefore prefer to postpone consideration of the issues they raised until we come to the Bücher-Meyer controversy.

67. Marx (1973). The comments on antiquity are concentrated in the section (pp. 471–514) headed 'Forms which precede capitalist production', published separately as Marx (1964).

68. The importance of the property regime is correctly stressed by Welskopf (1957), esp. ch. 5, 9. This book remains the safest guide to Marx's thinking on the subject. Although the aim, stated in a sub-title that was deleted before publication, was specifically to present the views of Marx, Engels, Lenin and Stalin, the author never confuses the four men, and the reader has no difficulty in differentiating among them. That cannot be said of Backhaus (1974), discussed in the closing pages of the present chapter.

69. Carandini (1976) 226–7, repeated almost gnomically in his brief contribution to *Marxismo, mondo antico et terzo mondo*, ed. E. Flores (Naples 1979), p. 99.

70. Hobsbawm (1964) 38–43; contra F. Tökei, *Zur Theorie der Gesellschaftsformen* (Budapest 1977), pp. 95–7.

71. On this passage see Mintz (1977) 258–61. For parallel statements in Marx's other writings, see Welskopf (1957) 460–6.

72. See Welskopf, *ibid.*, Shtaerman (1969) 15–20. Backhaus fails to notice the essential passage in the *Grundrisse* (so far as I can discover, given his appalling method of citation), and that makes it easier for him to read Marx a lesson on his supposed failure to have learned from Cairnes the fundamental differences between ancient and American slavery. In concluding his article on Cairnes, Backhaus (1975) seems to contradict himself, when he speaks of the 'structural similarities (on the economic side fundamental)' between slavery in the United States and in the Roman Empire.

73. The 1899 Turin publication was preceded by a partial publication in 1897; it was followed by a translation into French in 1909, into Spanish and German in 1910, and by a second edition in Italian in 1940, with notes by C. Barbagallo and a new preface written by Ciccotti himself before his death in 1939.

74. Lange (1899) 761–70. The same assessment was made by Karl Kautsky in a review of the German translation in *Die neue Zeit* for 1910/11.

75. Vogt (1974) 177 misses the essential, Marxist theory underlying Ciccotti's book when he writes that, 'as the title suggests, Ciccotti's main interest was in the process by which slavery was superseded'. He ends his page on Ciccotti with the following: 'But there remains the service which Ciccotti performed of showing that economic phenomena are an essential to an understanding of the problem of slavery as a whole.' Who, one cannot avoid asking, required that to be demonstrated? Mazza (1977) xlv repeats this judgment and goes on to the even more astonishing notion that prior credit for the discovery should be given to Eduard Meyer.

76. On the complex question of the relation of Bücher and Weber to each other and to Marx, see briefly Finley (1977a) 314–24, and the references there.

77. Hence I do not find sufficient the explanation given by Mazza (1977) xix, xlii, that Ciccotti's weaknesses are those of the 'Marxism of the Second International'.

78. Bücher (1922) 2. He refers the reader to Bücher (1906) 98–103; cf. pp. 162, 310–11, 331–4. It is worth noting that Bücher starts this discussion from Popma's list of 146 servile 'functional labels'.

79. Salvioli (1906) 119–21, 133–57, respectively. It is beside the point that, at the end of his life, Salvioli appears to have rejected all such periodization based on the economy: 'La città antica e la sua economia a proposito delli grandi epoche della storia economica', *Atti della R. Accademia di scienze morali e politiche, Napoli* 45 (1923) 196–226.

80. Weber (1896) 293. For the discussion of Eduard Meyer below, it is important to note that the foundation for this argument had been developed five years earlier, in the final forty pages of Weber (1891).

81. Pöhlmann, in *Historische Zeitschrift*, n.F. 46 (1899) 109–10;

Francotte, in *Bull. bibliographique et pédagogique de Musée Belge* 3 (1910) 245–9. Francotte (1900–1) had already discussed Ciccotti's views, e.g. II 27–8. Extracts from reviews and comments in books are conveniently assembled in Ciccotti (1977) 31–9.

82. The German translation was published by a Socialist publishing house and was reviewed at length by Karl Kautsky in *Die neue Zeit* for 1910/11, under the title, 'Sklaverei und Kapitalismus'. Kautsky was also responsible for the German translation of Salvioli.

83. See Lepore (1970) 3–17.

84. Karl Christ, *Von Gibbon zu Rostovtzeff* (Darmstadt 1972), p. 293; cf. pp. 308–11.

85. Vogt (1974) 178–9.

86. Westermann (1935) 894. This sentence was dropped in Westermann (1955) but the first footnote cites Meyer alone.

87. See e.g. Meyer (1902) 46. Cf. the ecstatic paean to this view of Meyer's in Stier (1945) 45–53.

88. J. Hasebroek, *Griechische Wirtschafts- und Gesellschaftsgeschichte bis zur Perserzeit* (Tübingen 1931), p. vi. Stier (1945), an idolator of Meyer's, shares this assessment (p. 52) with Hasebroek, the leading anti-modernist of his day.

89. Meyer (1898) 174n2, (1895) 118–19 and 141, *Geschichte des Altertums* (1901) III 550, respectively.

90. Meyer (1895) 83 and (1898) 195, respectively.

91. Meyer (1899) 186 and (1895) 83n1, respectively.

92. In the *Zeitschrift für Social- und Wirtschaftsgeschichte*, which he edited, 4 (1896) 153–7, preceded by a review of Bücher (1906) by the co-editor, Stephan Bauer.

93. Among the increasingly voluminous works on Meyer's political views and activities, see e.g. L. Canfora, *Intellettuali in Germania* (Bari 1979), passim, with particular reference to the period 1914–1919.

94. It is a sign of Meyer's standing that Max Weber thought it worth the trouble to demolish his essay on the theory and method of history, in an article first published in the *Archiv für Sozialwissenschaft und Sozialpolitik* for 1905, available in English in Weber, *Methodology of the Social Sciences*, trans. and ed. by E. A. Shils and H. A. Finch (Glencoe, Ill., 1949), pp. 113–63. It is characteristic of Meyer that when he reprinted his essay in his

Kleine Schriften he took only trivial notice (21n1, 44n2, 55n2) of what he called Weber's 'very penetrating, very praiseworthy criticism'.

95. Pöhlmann (1925), originally published in 1893–1901 under the title, *Geschichte der antiken Kommunismus und Sozialismus*. In the 2nd ed. (1912), Pöhlmann changed the title (though not the substance), because of criticism.

96. Pöhlmann (1925), esp. I 173–9; Oertel (1925) II 542–53.

97. Pöhlmann (1925) I 174 and 176, respectively; Oertel (1925) II 550 and 542, respectively.

98. *Ueber Finanzen und Monopole im alten Griechenland* (Berlin 1907).

99. 'Zur Frage der attischen Grossindustrie', *Rheinisches Museum* 79 (1930) 230–52, reprinted in Oertel (1975) 184–202. A different evaluation of Oertel as an economic historian will be found in Braunert's brief introduction to the volume.

100. Calderini (1908).

101. Will (1954).

102. *La propriété foncière en Grèce jusqu'à la conquête romaine* (Paris 1893), p. 636. In contrast, nearly half his 200-page *La main d'oeuvre industrielle dans l'ancienne Grèce* (Paris 1900) is devoted to slaves and freedmen, but in three flat-footed antiquarian chapters that were by then wholly retrograde. Subsequently, he wrote a book (Paris 1896) about his teacher and friend, Fustel de Coulanges, without mentioning the latter's great study of the colonate.

103. *Le travail dans le monde romain* (Paris 1912), pp. 8, 26, 326, respectively; trans. by E. D. F. Wareing as *Ancient Rome at Work* (London and New York 1927), pp. 2, 16, 242. (I have had to correct the translator, who writes 'the colony system' for the colonate.)

104. *Le travail dans la Grèce ancienne* (Paris 1920), pp. 249, 455–6, respectively; trans. by M. R. Dobie as *Ancient Greece at Work* (London and New York 1926), pp. 206–7, 380–1.

105. The neglect is all the more surprising as Francotte was able to summarize his book in German (Francotte 1916).

106. Westermann (1955) ix.

107. That is evident in his 'The Economic Basis of the Decline of Ancient Culture', *American Historical Review* 20 (1915) 723–43, written long before he was commissioned to prepare the Pauly-Wissowa article.

108. Westermann (1955) 140.

109. He once referred to his 'innate dislike for any "theorization" of history', and he promptly proceeded to demonstrate how 'dislike' leads to confusion and incomprehension: 'The Decay of the Ancient World in Its Economic Explanation', *Economic History Review* 2 (1930) 197–214. The extraordinary paean to Weber (1909) in the preface to Rostowzew (1910) is an anomaly I cannot explain.

110. Rostovtzeff (1941) 1258. Although this work, unlike the earlier one on the Roman Empire, was not available to Westermann when he wrote the Pauly-Wissowa article, he was able to make full use of it in preparing the subsequent book.

111. Rostovtzeff (1941) ch. 2.

112. In a review in the *Zeitschrift für die gesammte Staatswissenschaften* 92 (1932) 334–5.

113. Rostovtzeff (1941) 690.

114. This is implied in the two sentences in Westermann (1955) 2nn8, 9, on slaves in Homer, and 4, respectively.

115. I restrict myself to citing three reviews: P. A. Brunt, in *Journal of Roman Studies* 48 (1958) 164–70; G.E.M. de Ste Croix, in *Classical Review*, n.s. 7 (1957) 54–9; H. J. Wolff, in *Iura* 7 (1956) 308–15.

116. *Zeitschrift für Sozialforschung* 5 (1936) 442.

117. See the nuanced account of M. Fuhrmann, 'Die "Querelle des Anciens et des Modernes", der Nationalismus und die deutsche Klassik', in *Classical Influences on Western Thought A.D. 1650–1870*, ed. R. R. Bolgar (Cambridge 1978), pp. 107–29.

118. 'Premesse per una discussione su Wilamowitz', *Rivista storica italiana* 84 (1972) 746–55, at pp. 752–3; cf. W. Rehm, *Griechentum und Goethezeit* (Leipzig 1936), p. 241 on Humboldt's Hellenism: 'it virtually touched the religious'. The position is fully expressed in Schwartz's salute to Wilamowitz on his eightieth birthday, *Die Antike* 5 (1929) 1–5, reprinted in Schwartz (1938) 362–7.

119. Schwartz (1938) 98; Stier (1945) 1; Jaeger, *Humanistische Reden und Vorträge* (Berlin and Leipzig 1937), p. 182, respectively.

120. W. von Humboldt, *Gesammelte Schriften* I, ed. A. Leitzmann (Berlin 1903), p. 271.

121. Schwartz (1938) 364.

122. Wilamowitz (1910) 36, 32, 93, respectively. In the 2nd ed.

(1923) the Roman section was replaced but Wilamowitz's remained unchanged. I cannot resist noting that Burckhardt (1898–1902), dismissed by Wilamowitz in a notorious but influential denunciation, considered slavery to be deserving of a chapter in the section entitled 'The Polis in its Historical Development' (I 141–58).

123. See Raskolnikoff (1975); briefly Lencman (1966) 38–62; M. Mazza, in his introduction to Shtaerman/Trofimova (1975).

124. 'La teoria marxista-lenininista e la ricerca storica concreta', trans. F. Venturi, *Rivista storica italiana* 75 (1963) 588–603, at p. 596 (originally published earlier in the year in *Voprosy Istorii*).

125. Vogt himself had edited a volume designed to answer the question whether the great struggle between Rome and Carthage was determined by the 'blood-inheritance' (*Bluterbe*) of the two nations: *Rom und Karthago* (Leipzig 1943), p. 7.

126. Vogt (1974) 170–2, 206–8, has managed to erect a myth about one platitudinous paragraph by Humboldt, from which I have already quoted at n. 121. The fact is that the whole essay, a fragment, was circulated to a few friends in 1793 but was not published until 1893, and has nothing to say about slavery apart from that single paragraph.

127. Vogt (1974) 25. In the final sentence, the echo of Heeren (1826), quoted above at n. 3, is striking. Vogt does not mention Heeren, whose very considerable influence was not within the 'humanist' stream.

128. Vogt (1974) 208–10.

129. Vogt (1974) 179, 103, 184, respectively.

130. In a review of Lencman (1966) in *Revue des études anciennes* 69 (1967) 289.

131. R. Mandrou, 'A côté du Congrès: Une mise en accusation du matérialisme historique', *Annales, E.S.C.* 16 (1961) 518–20.

132. I refer specifically to the articles by Lencman, Amusin and Kazakevich which appeared in the *Vestnik Drevnei Istorii* precisely within the period (1946–59) Vittinghoff claims to have surveyed; on those articles, see Lencman (1966) 56–8.

133. Vittinghoff (1960) 94n36. Vogt (1974) 184, a member of the editorial board of *Saeculum*, called Vittinghoff's essay 'a critical appreciation of the problems and aims of Soviet scholarship'.

134. Vittinghoff (1961).

135. Finley (1959) 161.

136. Kiechle (1969) 1.
137. I have quoted the opening sentence of Kiechle's 'Technical Progress in the Main Period of Ancient Slavery', in the *Proceedings* of the 4th Intl. Conference of Economic History, Bloomington 1968 (Paris and The Hague 1973), pp. 335–46, which is marginally blunter than the comparable sentence in his book.
138. See further below, ch. 4 nn. 41 and 46.
139. Backhaus (1974) 8–9.
140. For the record, A. Mehl, 'Die antike Sklavenhaltergesellschaft und der Begriff der Volksmassen in neurer marxistischen Literatur zur Alten Geschichte', *Gymnasium* 84 (1977) 444–66, is nothing but Vittinghoff *redivivus*.
141. Vogt (1974) 185. It will not have escaped the attentive reader that Vogt is not wholly consistent in his programmatic statements.
142. P. Bourdieu, in *Actes de la recherche en sciences sociales* 17/18 (1977) 3.
143. *More Letters of Charles Darwin*, ed. F. Darwin and A. C. Seward (2 vols., London 1903) I 195.
144. M. Hesse, 'Theory and Value in the Social Sciences', in *Action and Interpretation*, ed. C. Hookway and P. Pettit (Cambridge 1978), pp. 1–16, at p. 2.
145. Buckland (1908) v.

Chapter 2

1. Fustel de Coulanges (1885) 3.
2. Anderson (1974a) 21.
3. On the modern varieties, see the thirteen case-studies in W. Kloosterboer, *Involuntary Labour after the Abolition of Slavery* (Leiden 1960).
4. See J-P. Vernant, *Mythe et pensée chez les Grecs* (Paris 1965) pt. 4. Cf. Y. Garlan, in Garnsey (1980), on the relatively late emergence of both hired labour and the free peasant-owner in Greek history.
5. For the present I treat the slave as an ideal type. We shall see later in the chapter how much differentiation there was in reality within the slave population.
6. Meillassoux (1975) 20.
7. Lauffer (1960) 81.

8. Anderson (1974b) 486.

9. A complete example is provided by S. Miers and I. Kopytoff, in the introduction to *Slavery in Africa: Historical and Anthropological Perspectives* (Madison 1977), esp. pp. 5–6, 11, 76–8. For a correct approach, see J. Bazin, 'Guerre et servitude à Ségou', in Meillassoux (1975), not shared by all the contributors to the volume; P. Hill, 'From Slavery to Freedom: The Case of Farm-Slavery in Nigerian Hausaland', *Comparative Studies in Society and History* 18 (1976) 395–426.

10. M. Bloch, *The Historians Craft*, trans. P. Putnam (Manchester 1954), pp. 175–6.

11. Anderson (1974b) 484.

12. Diakonoff (1974) 63, 64, 78, respectively; cf. A. Jähne, 'Zwei Tendenzen gesellschaftlicher Entwicklung im Hellenismus', *Klio* 60 (1978) 137–50, at p. 140, and the reply by H. Kreissig, pp. 217–19. Diakonoff, whose pages on Greece and Rome reveal inadequate knowledge, surprisingly continues the equation Marxist=Soviet. His use of the term 'social formation' is significantly different from that of Anderson (1974a) 22n6, and his fundamental conception had been effectively demolished in advance by e.g. Hahn (1971), and earlier by K. Zelin, 'Principes de classification morphologique des formes de dépendance', in Annequin (1978) 45–77, originally published in Russian in *Vestnik Drevnei Istorii* (1967) no. 2, pp. 7–30.

13. Meillassoux (1975) 20.

14. See Finley (1960) (1964) (1965a) for a detailed account of what follows immediately, with the necessary documentation.

15. Ducat (1978) has denied all this in a lengthy and perverse article, replete with misstatements (particularly of the views of others) and omissions. Thus he writes (p. 22) that the chattel slaves and the helots differed 'only in the fact that instead of belonging to an individual the latter belonged to a collectivity'. To reach that conclusion, he fails to mention the self-reproduction of the helots or to consider the implications of their right to a formally defined share of the produce.

16. Ducat (1978) 23 and Annequin (1975) 9, respectively.

17. Cf. 'those explanations which try to reduce Marxist social theory to three factors in all (individual, community, means of production), in my opinion, cannot be anything else than fatal simplifications almost resembling cabbalistic number

mysticism': G. Komoróczy, 'Landed Property in Ancient Mesopotamia and the Theory of the So-called Asiatic Mode of Production', *Oikumene* 2 (1978) 9–26, at 10*n*3.

18. See Patterson (1977b) 431–2.

19. See Capogrossi (1978).

20. *Digest* 1.5.4.1.; for other texts, see Buckland (1908) ch. 2. Cf. the definition in Article 1 of the Slavery Convention of the League of Nations (1926): 'Slavery is a status or condition of a person over whom any or all the powers attaching to the rights of ownership are exercised' (quoted from C. W. W. Greenidge, *Slavery*, London 1958, p. 224).

21. Capogrossi (1978) 725–6. Cf. the inclusion of enslaved captives in the 'tithe' of war-spoils dedicated to a god: Bömer (1957–63) III 252–5.

22. Meyer (1898) 211.

23. Patterson (1977b) 431. He offers as a 'working definition' of slavery 'that condition in which there is an institutionalized alienation from the rights of labor and kinship'.

24. I follow in essence the analysis of this text, and of the related *Justinian Code* 3.38.11, by Puglisi (1977).

25. See Buckland (1908) 77–8.

26. K. R. Bradley, 'The Age at Time of Sale of Female Slaves', *Arethusa* 11 (1978) 243–52; cf. Hopkins (1978) 164–5 on the Delphic manumissions.

27. David (1976) 110–11.

28. On flexibility in American slavery, see Degler (1976) 8–10.

29. Vidal-Naquet (1968).

30. This has been well stressed by P. Garnsey and J. E. Skydsgaard, in Garnsey (1980).

31. Pippidi (1973) is now fundamental.

32. See Kreissig (1978) pt. II, with bibliography; E. S. Golubcova, in Blavatskaya (1972). The contrary view has been maintained by I. S. Svencickaya, without meeting the arguments on the other side; most recently, 'Some Problems of Agrarian Relations in the Province of Asia', *Eirene* 15 (1977) 27–54. Although I should not lay heavy stress on the point, it may be important that Isocrates, in a letter to Philip II (*Epistles* 3.5), chose to say 'helots', not 'slaves', in anticipating the fate of the people to be conquered in Asia.

33. By debt–bondsmen I mean the *obaerati* (or *obaeraii*) of Varro,

De re rustica 1.17.2, and the men tied by *nexum* who are mentioned by Columella (1.3.12); on tenants in debt, see Finley (1976) 112–17.

34. Contrast C. R. Whittaker, 'Rural Labour in Three Provinces of Rome', in Garnsey (1980), with A. Daubigney and F. Favory, 'L'esclavage en Narbonnaise et Lyonnaise', in *Colloque (1972)* 315–88. On Visigothic Spain, see below at the beginning of ch. 4.

35. I. Wallerstein, 'A World-System Perspective on the Social Sciences', *British Journal of Sociology* 27 (1976) 343–52. Cf. Anderson (1974a) 22: The Ancient World as a whole was never continuously or ubiquitously marked by the predominance of slave-labour. But its great *classical* epochs . . . were those in which slavery was massive and general, amidst other labour systems.'

36. See the table in Hopkins (1978) 101; cf. Degler (1959).

37. See Jameson (1977–8).

38. Demosthenes 27.9–11, Lysias 12.19, Tacitus, *Annals* 14.43, Frontinus 96–118, respectively.

39. Cf. Philochorus 328F97, ap. Macrobius, *Saturnalia* 1.10.22.

40. The possibility that the situation changed in the later Roman Empire will be considered in ch. 4.

41. I make no assessment of the relative income from these various sources; see Finley (1973) ch. 2.

42. This is equally true, despite profound differences in other respects, of Meyer (1898) and Hopkins (1978) 8–15, 102–6; contra Westermann (1955) 70; P. Ducrey, *Le traitement des prisonniers de la guerre dans la Grèce antique* . . . (Paris 1968), pp. 74–5; and in a different context, F. De Martino, 'Interno all' origine della schiavitù a Roma', *Labeo* 20 (1974) 163–93, at pp. 179–93.

43. The evidence is presented by Volkmann (1961) 227–8.

44. Diodorus 23.9.1, Polybius 1.19.15.

45. The references are Livy 7.16.7; 10.13.14; 10.23.13; 10.47.4. See G. Tibiletti, 'Il *possesso* dell' *ager publicus* e le norme *de modo agrorum* sino ai Gracchi', *Athenaeum*, n.s. 26 (1948) 173–235; 27 (1949) 2–41.

46. M. Gelzer, *The Roman Nobility*, trans. R. Seager (Oxford 1969), p. 21. Gelzer's pages 18–22 (originally published in 1912) lay out the evidence neatly.

47. E.g. E. Maróti, 'The Vilicus and the Villa-System in Ancient Italy', *Oikumene* 1 (1976) 109–24.

48. P. A. Brunt, *Social Conflicts in the Roman Republic* (London 1971), pp. 18–19.

49. The evidence is collected by J. M. Libourel, 'Galley Slaves in the Second Punic War', *Classical Philology* 68 (1973) 116–19.

50. Hahn (1971) 35 and Mintz (1977) 257, respectively.

51. See Pippidi (1973) 65.

52. The fullest account is still A. Plassart, 'Les archers d'Athènes', *Revue des études grecques* 26 (1913) 151–213. Cf. O. Jacob, *Les esclaves publics à Athènes* (*Bibl. de la Fac. de Philosophie et Lettres à l'Univ. de Liège* 35, 1928), ch. 2.

53. See M. I. Finley, *Aspects of Antiquity* (2nd ed., Harmondsworth and New York 1977), ch. 12; 'The Black Sea and Danubian Regions and the Slave Trade in Antiquity', *Klio* 40 (1962) 51–9. The primacy of trade over conquest was argued briefly, but neatly, by Burckhardt (1898–1902) I 142.

54. For what follows, I am heavily indebted to Hahn (1971).

55. On what follows I restrict references to two points: on population growth, see the preliminary analysis in A. M. Snodgrass, *Archaeology and the Rise of the Greek State* (Cambridge Inaug. 1977), pp. 10–16; on private property in land, M. I. Finley, 'The Alienability of Land in Ancient Greece: A Point of View', *Eirene* 7 (1968) 25–32), reprinted in French, *Annales, E.S.C.* 25 (1970) 1271–7.

56. See J. Servais, in *Thorikos 1965* (Brussels 1967), pp. 22–24, and J. Bingen in *Thorikos 1964* (Brussels 1967), pp. 29–30, respectively.

57. As evidence of commodity production in other Greek *poleis* I note (1) the carriage of wine, olive and pottery to Naucratis in the Egyptian Delta by traders from a number of cities in Asia Minor and the Aegean islands, beginning before 600 B.C.: M. M. Austin, *Greece and Egypt in the Archaic Age* (*Proceedings of the Cambridge Philological Society*, Supp. 2, 1970), pp. 22–7, 36–40; (2) several Thasian regulations controlling the sale of local grapes and wine and the import of foreign wine; the earliest clear text, *Inscriptiones Graecae* XII Supp., no. 347, originally published with a useful commentary by G. Daux, in *Bulletin de correspondance hellénique* 50 (1926) 214–26, dates from the final decades of the fifth century B.C., but there can be no doubt that

regulation began much earlier, as shown by the fragmentary early fifth-century inscription, *Supplementum Epigraphicum Graecum* XVIII 347.

58. In this context, taxes and liturgies need not be distinguished.

59. Hopkins (1978) 102 correctly stresses the point: 'We have to explain not only the importation of slaves, but the extrusion of citizens.' However, as I have already indicated, I link that not with the establishment of the slave society but with its expansion. On Athens, I believe I was the first to challenge the prevailing view of a sharply declining peasantry in fourth-century Athens: *Studies in Land and Credit in Ancient Athens 500–200 B.C.* (New Brunswick, N.J., 1952), pp. 79–87; 'Land, Debt, and the Man of Property in Classical Athens', *Political Science Quarterly* 68 (1953) 249–68. My arguments have been generally accepted, e.g. by Cl. Mossé, 'La vie économique d'Athènes au IVe siècle: Crise ou renouveau?', *Praelectiones Pataviniae* (1972) 135–44; V. N. Andreyev, 'Some Aspects of Agrarian Conditions in Attica in the Fifth to Third Centuries B.C.', *Eirene* 12 (1974) 5–46, at pp. 18–25; G. Audring, 'Zur wirtschaftlichen und sozialen Lage der attischen Bauern im ausgehenden 5. und im 4. Jahrhundert v. u. Z.', *Jahrbuch für Wirtschaftsgeschichte* (Sonderband 1977) 9–86, at pp. 35–43. The role of 'free' land in the rise of New World slavery is still contested: see the negative views of S. L. Engerman, 'Some Considerations relating to Property Rights in Man', *Journal of Economic History* 33 (1973) 43–65, and Patterson (1977a), with an important qualification by Mintz (1977).

60. Jameson (1977–8).

61. Meyer (1898) 193–8.

62. Mintz (1977) 257 includes 'police power adequate to the legal-military containment of a free population' among the conditions adverse to the introduction of modern slavery.

63. The only statement known from the whole of antiquity that has been taken to imply slave-free competition is a brief fragment of the lost work of the third-century B.C. historian Timaeus (566F11a, ap. Athenaeus 6.264D), reporting that the acquisition of 1000 slaves in backward Locris by 'Aristotle's friend' Mnason stirred great resentment because it deprived 'the young' of their customary livelihood earned by 'serving the elders domestically'. Even if true, and that is by no means

certain, the anecdote is irrelevant in an account of slavery *as a labour-force*. Heitland (1921) 441*n*4 curtly dismissed it as referring 'solely to domestic and personal attendance'; cf. the more nuanced but equally dismissive analysis of Vidal-Naquet (1968) 105–6. Recently G. Nenci, while acknowledging the uniqueness of the text, has made an ingenious effort to squeeze greater significance from it but I am not persuaded: 'Il problema della concorrenza fra mandopera libera e servile nella Grecia classica', *Annali della Scuola Normale di Pisa, Classe di Lettere e Filosofia*, 3rd ser., 8 (1978) 1287–1300.

64. H. Michell, *The Economics of Ancient Greece* (2nd ed., Cambridge 1957), p. 166.

65. Shtaerman (1969) 13 and 19, respectively.

66. It is enough to cite R. W. Fogel and S. L. Engerman, *Time on the Cross* (2 vols., Boston 1974), the critique by David (1976), and the review of the latter by D. Macleod in the *Times Literary Supplement* for June 23, 1978. The older discussions can be conveniently studied in *Did Slavery Pay?*, ed. H. G. J. Aitken (Boston 1971).

67. Degler (1976) 8.

68. Mickwitz (1937) and (1939) remain fundamental; cf. G.E.M. de Ste. Croix, 'Greek and Roman Accounting', in *Studies in the History of Accounting*, ed. A. C. Littleton and B. S. Yamey (London 1956), pp. 14–74; Duncan-Jones (1974) ch. 2.

Chapter 3

1. Stroud (1856) 5.

2. 'Crueler' is, to be sure, a most subjective assessment in this context: see e.g. I. Barkan, *Capital Punishment in Ancient Athens* (diss. Chicago 1936), esp. pp. 63–72 on *apotympanismos*; or the refutation of the standard modern view about execution by hemlock, by C. Gill, 'The Death of Socrates', *Classical Quarterly* 23 (1973) 25–8.

3. See e.g. the discussion in Biezunska-Malowist (1974–7) I 121–6 of two third-century B.C. Ptolemaic legal texts, *P. Halle* 1, pertaining to Alexandria, and *P. Lille* 29, probably from either Naucratis or Ptolemais (both also Greek cities).

4. G. Glotz, 'Les esclaves et la peine du fouet en droit grec', *Comptes rendus de l'Acad. des Inscriptions* (1908) 571–87, on which

Morrow (1939) 66–71 is based; Thür (1977), replacing all previous accounts of torture in Athenian law courts; Buckland (1908) 86–97.

5. Wallon (1879) I 306–29.

6. The evidence on the Christian emperors will be found in Buckland (1908) 86–97.

7. Cf. Blair (1833) 106–13 and end-notes 59–65.

8. A. R. W. Harrison, *The Law of Athens* II (Oxford 1971), p. 147.

9. Mahaffy, quoted with evident approval by Morrow (1939) 80.

10. Ehrenberg (1951) 187; cf. Barrow (1925) 31–5. Thür (1977) 314–15 converts the Athenian court practice into a charade: on the one hand, there was a 'blind faith' in torture, but on the other hand it was never actually employed, in the fourth century B.C. at any rate, despite the frequent challenges to the opponent to do so.

11. Mommsen (1961) 416n1.

12. The inscription is published by L. Bove in *Labeo* 13 (1967) 43–8; see further F. De Martino, *ibid.* 21 (1975) 210–14. On private torture of slaves in Athens, see Thür (1977) 43–8; on instruments employed, J. Vergote, 'Folterwerkzeuge', in *Reallexikon der Antike und Christentum* 8 (1972) 112–41.

13. See Garnsey (1970) ch. 4.

14. I have been unable to find any reasonable account of slaves among ancient prostitutes, or, for that matter, of prostitution itself. Significantly, the word 'prostitution' does not appear in the index of Vogt (1974).

15. *Controversies* IV praef. 10, a quotation I owe to P. Veyne, 'La famille et l'amour sous le Haut-Empire romain', *Annales, E.S.C.* 38 (1978) 35–63, an article with valuable scattered hints and aperçus on the subject of slaves and sex. I note that in K. J. Dover, *Greek Homosexuality* (London 1978), the most important scholarly work on the subject, slavery is ignored apart from an interesting but irrelevant half-page (97) on the 'tendency in comedy to treat masturbation as behaviour characteristic of slaves'.

16. I know of no full study of either slave-appellation other than Biezunska-Malowist (1974–7) I 11–18 on the Ptolemaic period, II 10–12 on the Roman period, following J. A. Straus, 'La terminologie de l'esclavage dans les papyrus grecs d'époque

romaine trouvés en Egypt', in *Colloque* (*1973*) 333–7. (In the Roman period the word *païs* largely disappeared from the papyri.) On *puer*, the interesting analysis by J. Maurin of the *puer-dominus* link as a sort of substitute kinship seems to me to miss the element of degradation: 'Remarques sur la notion de "puer" à l'époque classique', *Bulletin de l'Assn. Guillaume Budé* (1975) 221–30.

17. The evidence will be found in Himmelmann (1971).

18. See Klees (1975) 30n123, who cites Epicrates ap. Athenaeus 6.262D as evidence of slave irritation with the eternal call of 'païi, païi'.

19. See Bömer (1957–63) III 173–95.

20. The phrase is that of Barrington Moore Jr., *Social Origins of Dictatorship and Democracy* (Penguin ed., 1969), p. 132 n. 47.

21. E. Levy, 'Libertas und Civitas', ZRG 78 (1961) 142–72, at p. 145.

22. See e.g. D. W. Cohen and J. P. Greene, ed., *Neither Slave nor Free: The Freedman of African Descent in the Slave Societies of the New World* (Baltimore and London 1972); Ira Berlin, *Slaves without Masters: The Free Negro in the Antebellum South* (New York 1974); K. M. Stampp, *The Era of Reconstruction* (London 1965), esp. ch. 7.

23. See P. Gauthier, '"Générosité" romaine et "avarice" grecque: sur l'octroi du droit de cité', in *Mélanges . . . offerts à William Seston* (Paris 1974), pp. 7–15.

24. They are paraded throughout A. M. Duff, *Freedmen in the Early Roman Empire* (repr., Cambridge 1958), who shares the views of his sources.

25. All the references in Horace's poems to slavery are examined by Highet (1973), with moral condemnation and over-confident psychological insight (see further below, n. 96). Highet misses the significance of the critical lines I have cited from the 'autobiographical' satire.

26. The fundamental study remains F. De Visscher, *Le régime romain de la noxalité* (Brussels 1947); cf. his later restatement, 'Il sistema romano della nossalità', *Iura* 11 (1960) 1–68.

27. See M. Kaser, 'Zur Kriminalgerichtsbarkeit gegen Sklaven', *Studia et documenta historiae et iuris* 6 (1940) 357–68, with further discussion by T. Mayer-Maly, *ibid.* 23 (1957) 323–34.

28. Garlan (1972), with sequel in *Colloque (1972)* 15–28; at inter-

minable length, Welwei (1974–77); N. Rouland, *Les esclaves romains en temps de guerre* (Brussels 1977).

29. Pausanias 1.32.3; 7.15.7.

30. See briefly Bömer (1957–63) IV 149–52.

31. See e.g. Capogrossi (1978) 725–30, and his interesting suggestion that *mancipium* came to be an early synonym for *servus* because a slave is the only *res mancipi* that is not a 'natural' object, unlike land, a house or an ox. See also Calabi (1979) on Aristotle.

32. For the references and a brief analysis, which I accept, see Milani (1972) 225–33; cf. L. Capogrossi Colonesi, in *Colloque (1973)* 379–81; E. Levy, 'Natural Law in Roman Thought', *Studia et documenta historiae et iuris* 15 (1949) 1–23. For a different analysis, abstract and formal, based on a classification derived from ancient rhetoric, see J. Modrzejewski, '*Aut nascuntur aut fiunt*: Les schémas antiques des sources de l'esclavage', *Bulletino del Istituto di diritto romano* 79 (1976) 1–25.

33. This point is well developed in R.W. and A. J. Carlyle, *A History of Mediaeval Political Theory in the West* I (New York and Edinburgh 1903), pp. 33–44.

34. Cf. Cicero, *De officiis* 3.5.23.

35. See above, ch. 1 before n. 46.

36. The data are conveniently set out in R. H. Randall, Jr., 'The Erechtheum Workmen', *American Journal of Archaeology* 57 (1953) 199–210.

37. See Himmelmann (1971) 36–8. It need hardly be said that neither Greek nor Roman craftsmen similarly denigrated themselves on their tombstones or other personal monuments (e.g. dedications), as distinct from objects they produced for sale.

38. See E. Kazakevich, 'Slave Agents in Athens', *Vestnik Drevnei Istorii* (1961) no. 3, pp. 3–21; cf. her 'Were *hoi choris oikountes* Slaves?', *ibid.* (1963) no. 3, pp. 23–42 (both in Russian). The articles by E. Perotti, in *Colloque (1972)* 47–56 and *Colloque (1973)* 179–91, add nothing. The Roman situation is indicated clearly enough in a gloss by Gaius (*Digest* 40.9.10): 'Men often think their assets are greater than they really are. This frequently happens to people who have overseas interests in distant regions, run by slaves and freedmen; often the business declines over a long period without their knowing it. . . .'

39. See Buckland (1908) ch. 8–9.

40. A. Biscardi, 'La capacità processuale dello schiavo', *Labeo* 21 (1975) 143–71; on Athens, briefly Gernet (1955) 159–64.

41. See Kajanto (1969) 44–7, and the commentary by A. N. Sherwin-White (Oxford 1966) to the two letters of Pliny (3.14; 8.14) on comparable cases forty-odd years later. The account by Barrow (1928) 55–9 is written, appropriately enough, in the style of a novel. He begins by finding the law 'almost unintelligible', though both Tacitus (14.43) and Pliny (3.14) make the reason brutally clear, and he ends with the absurd conclusion that Hadrian brought about a 'reconciliation between the interests of the master and the slave' on the subject. The basic rule in fact remained in force throughout the Empire and was reaffirmed by Justinian in A.D. 532 (*Code* 6.35.12).

42. The bulk of the available juristic texts are assembled in one chapter of the *Digest* (29.5); see the brief summary in Mommsen (1961) 630–2.

43. Kajanto (1969) 48–59 argues that Tacitus approved. The account by Z. Yavetz, *Plebs and Princeps* (Oxford 1969), pp. 29–37, lacks incisiveness.

44. Westermann (1955) 114 and Kajanto (1969) 59, respectively.

45. Evidence is provided in the purely lexical study of R. F. Newbold, 'The Vulgus in Tacitus', *Rheinisches Museum* 119 (1976) 85–92.

46. The best account remains that of L. Friedlaender, *Darstellung aus der Sittengeschichte Roms*, 10th ed. by G. Wissowa (4 vols., Leipzig 1921–3) II 50–112.

47. See Vogt (1974) ch. 7.

48. The concentration-camp analogy is drawn by Elkins (1959), a flawed work that is nonetheless important for having introduced the issue of the psychology of the slave into the debate: Patterson (1977b) 415; cf. J. W. Blassingame, *The Slave Community* (New York 1972). esp. ch. 7 and Appendix.

49. Genovese (1974) is currently the pivotal work round which the debate concentrates: see esp. pp. 3–112.

50. Vogt (1974) 140–5.

51. I choose this particular contrast only because of Vogt's 'Lo schiavo morente. Immagine di compiuta umanità', *Studi romani* 20 (1972) 317–28, summarized in Vogt (1978) 41–2.

52. Vogt (1974) 14–15.

53. E.g. Kudlien (1968), who sets out in his 46-page monograph to prove the correctness of Vogt's statement, which I have just quoted, and does so by quoting a few such texts and by distorting or brushing aside the important passages that argue for the opposite, traditional view. Joly (1969/70) has effectively demolished his argument. The attempted defence by Gil, based exclusively on passages from comedy and comic fragments, is a failure: 'Ärztlicher Beistand und attische Komödie. Zur Frage der *demosieuontes* und Sklaven-Ärzte', *Sudhoffs Archiv* 57 (1973) 255–74.

54. See L. Cohn-Haft, *The Public Physicians of Ancient Greece* (*Smith College Studies in History* 42, 1956), esp. ch. 4.

55. Joly (1969/70) 6–10.

56. My sole reason for mentioning this document, which in antiquity lacked the ideological standing given to it by the modern medical profession, is that Kudlien (1968) begins his argument by twisting the sentence I have quoted into medical *treatment* of all patients regardless of sex or status, following the lead of Vogt (1974) 14.

57. The 'humanitarians' have struggled to get rid of this clearly factual statement. E.g. Vogt (1974) shifts from the false 'Plato's suggestion that the medical profession *ought* to employ slave physicians' (p. 15) to the even more false 'Plato describes the *possibility in some ideal future society*' (p. 115, my italics in both quotations). Again Joly (1969/70) provides the effective reply, ignored by Vogt.

58. See K.-H. Below, *Der Arzt im römischen Recht* (*Münchener Beiträge zur Papyrusforschung und antiken Rechtsgeschichte* 37, 1953), pp. 7–21.

59. A second-century B.C. papyrus seems to refer to a special school in Alexandria for such slaves: R. Remondon, 'Problèmes du bilinguisme dans l'Egypte lagide (U.P.Z. I, 148)', *Chronique d'Egypte* 39 (1964) 126–46.

60. K. Visky, 'La qualifica della medicina e dell' architettura nel fonti del diritto romano', *Iura* 10 (1959) 24–66, is decisive.

61. Barrow (1928) 35–43; Vogt (1974) 132, 109, respectively. It would be pointless to pile up further references.

62. Vogt (1974) 109.

63. Vogt (1978) 40.

64. E. M. Shtaerman, 'Zur Methodologie der Erforschung der

Weltanschauung ausgebeuteter Klassen Roms', *Klio* 57 (1975) 5–13, at p. 6 (cf. Bellen (1971) 129). This brief article seems to offer more support for my pessimism than for her cautious optimism. It is revealing that the chapter entitled 'The Ideology of the Slave' in Shtaerman (1969) is restricted to cult.

65. Vogt (1974) 51.

66. R. A. Bauman, *Impietas in Principem (Münchener Beitr. z. Papyrusforschung u. antike Rechtsgesch.* 67, 1974), p. 56.

67. *Theodosian Code* 9.5.6.

68. See e.g. Sartori (1973) 158–60.

69. The evidence is fully laid out by Kühne (1962); on individual occasions, see Sartori (1973); K. R. Bradley, 'Slaves and the Conspiracy of Catiline', *Classical Philology* 73 (1978) 329–36; J. Annequin, 'Esclaves et affranchis dans la Conjuration de Catilina', in *Colloque (1971)* 193–238.

70. See e.g. J. Annequin and M. Létroublon, 'Une approche des discours de Cicéron: les niveaux d'intervention des esclaves dans la violence', in *Colloque (1972)* 211–47.

71. The only study known to me is a short article by J. Češka, 'Über die Vernichtung von Arbeitsgeräten durch die antiken Sklaven' (in Slovak), summarized in *Bibliotheca Classica Orientalis* 2 (1957) 201–2.

72. The only full study, Bellen (1971), is restricted to the Roman Empire. Shtaerman (1969) 238–43 collects miscellaneous information for the late Republic. I know no special study of fugitive slaves in either Greece or the Hellenistic world outside Egypt: I. Biezunska-Malowist, 'Les esclaves fugitifs dans l'Egypte gréco-romaine', in *Studi . . . Edoardo Volterra* 6 (1969), pp. 77–90, summarized in Biezunska-Malowist (1974–7) I 103–5.

73. A central thesis of Bellen (1971), esp. 126–8, is that a change in his 'place of work' was the predominant aim of flight in the Roman Empire. That conclusion rests on the two civil-law actions available against third parties (p. 133) and overlooks all the instances in which there was no third party involved.

74. Some documentation will be found in Garlan (1972) 29–35.

75. See, in chronological order, *Letters to His Friends* 13.77.3; 5.9.2; 5.11.3; 5.10.1.

76. Lysias, *Oration* 23, provides evidence for Athens about 400 B.C.

77. See especially Bellen (1971) pt. I.

78. D. Daube, 'Slave-catching', *Juridical Review* 64 (1952) 12–28.

79. Evidence for the Roman Empire is collected by R. Mac-Mullen, *Enemies of the Roman Order* (Cambridge, Mass., 1966), App. B; cf. Bellen (1971) 92–115. The lengthy article by P. Briant, ' "Brigandage", dissidence et conquête en Asie aché-ménide et hellénistique', *Dialogues d'histoire ancienne* 2 (1976) 163–258, is not concerned with this aspect of brigandage.

80. E. J. Hobsbawm, *Bandits* (London 1969). The one attempt to examine the ancient phenomenon in the light of modern study of social banditry fails to take slaves into sufficient consideration: F. Flam-Zuckermann, 'A propos d'une inscription de Suisse (*CIL*, XIII, 5010): étude du phénomène du brigandage dans l'Empire romain', *Latomus* 29 (1970) 451–73.

81. See Vogt (1974) 79–81. A. Fuks has made an attempt to find a genuine slave revolt, but his account fails on too many essential details and on his acceptance of Beloch's impossible estimate of a population of 30,000 free men and 100,000 slaves on the island: 'Slave War and Slave Troubles in Chios in the Third Century B.C.', *Athenaeum*, n.s. 46 (1968) 102–111; see J. Vogt, 'Zum Experiment des Drimakos: Sklavenhaltung und Räuberstand', *Saeculum* 24 (1973) 213–19.

82. Price (1973) 5.

83. Patterson (1970) 275.

84. The text is given by Bryan Edwards, *The History . . . of the West Indies* (London 1807) I App. 2, reprinted in Price (1973) 237–9; cf. Patterson (1970) 265–75.

85. H. Aptheker, *American Negro Slave Revolts* (repr. New York 1963).

86. This important distinction is stressed by Degler (1970) 351–2.

87. See C. L. R. James, *The Black Jacobins: Toussaint L'Ouverture and the San Domingo Revolution* (2nd ed., New York 1963).

88. Westermann (1955) 18.

89. See C. R. Whittaker, 'Land and Labour in North Africa', *Klio* 60 (1978) 331–62, at pp. 338–9.

90. Hopkins (1978) 155–8, 165–6.

91. Of the large and rapidly growing body of literature on this question in the New World, I cite (in addition to works already mentioned), because it deals with an urban industrial situation, C. B. Drew, 'Disciplining Slave Ironworkers in the Antebellum South: Coercion, Conciliation and Accommodation', *American Historical Review* 79 (1973) 393–418.

92. Frederickson/Lasch (1967) 119.

93. *Ibid.* 127–8. They draw the distinction between *intransigeance*, 'a personal strategy of survival', and *resistance*, 'a political concept'.

94. The massive ancient evidence is now available in Bömer (1957–63), the American in Genovese (1974).

95. P. Veyne, 'Vie de Trimalcion', *Annales, E.S.C.* 16 (1961) 213–47; the critique of F. Dupont, *Le plaisir et la loi* (Paris 1977), pp. 9–16, seems to me wholly misdirected.

96. Repeated attempts to find evidence of Terence's slave-origin in his plays have been laid to rest by Spranger (1960), esp. 90–8. Highet (1973) 269 thinks that Horace 'naturally' wrote 'a good deal about slaves and slavery' because the 'subject haunted him' and finds it 'surprising' that the poet's tone 'is seldom sympathetic, and often downright cruel'. These judgments merely reflect Highet's own moral judgment of slavery and his puritanical views of sex: apart from the reference in one poem to his servile paternity (see above, n. 25), I find nothing to differentiate Horace on slavery from any number of Greek and Roman writers, and I doubt that anyone would have suggested otherwise if his ancestry were not known. The same is true of the comments on Epictetus scattered in the extraordinary essay by Mazzarino (1966) II 2, 131–99, entitled 'The "Famous Slaves" and the Contradictions of the Imperial Age', which is largely about Plutarch, Appian and other second-century intellectuals. Mazzarino's title is taken from a work by a grammarian, an ex-slave, named Hermippus (of Berytus), who is recorded as having written a monograph on famous slaves in the field of culture. 'At first sight,' Mazzarino writes (p. 177), 'we should be tempted to relegate the monograph . . . to the limbo of works of curious erudition. But we should be wrong.' The flaw in the ingenious and learned speculation that follows is that we know precisely nothing about the monograph.

97. A sufficient sample is given by Burckhardt (1898–1902) I 149.

98. Milani (1972) 104–39. I was not firm enough myself about this in 'Aristotle and Economic Analysis', *Past & Present* 47 (1970) 3–25, reprinted in Finley (1978) ch. 2.

99. Livy 35.49.8; 36.17.5; Cicero, explicitly in *On the Consular*

Provinces 10, implicitly in *For Flaccus* 65. Cf. Himmelmann (1971) on Greek pictorial representations.

100. See e.g. H. H. Bacon, *Barbarians in Greek Tragedy* (New Haven 1961).

101. Leo Salingar, *Shakespeare and the Tradition of Comedy* (Cambridge 1961), ch. 3.

102. Spranger (1960) 40–2.

103. Spranger (1960) 32–5, 112–13, respectively.

104. On what follows, the best account is the neglected book by Milani (1972).

105. K. Synodinou, *On the Concept of Slavery in Euripides* (Ioannina 1977), with full discussion of the copious bibliography.

106. See Vlastos (1941); cf. Morrow (1939) on the severity of Plato's *Laws* with respect to slaves.

107. Milani (1972) 221.

108. Richter (1958) 198, 212, 216, respectively. It is noteworthy that Richter avoids many of the extreme claims for Seneca's influence on Roman legislation or policy. M. T. Griffin, *Seneca, a Philosopher in Politics* (Oxford 1976), virtually denies any influence – 'Seneca's views on slavery found little expression in his work as an imperial adviser' (p. 284) – and notes particularly (pp. 280–1) the improbability that Seneca intervened on the 'humane' side in the Senate debate following the assassination of Pedanius Secundus. Nevertheless, her chapter 8, 'Seneca on Slavery', is built round the judgment, 'Seneca's pronouncements on slavery are justly admired' (p. 275).

109. I cannot follow Richter (1958) 212*n*47 that there is a fundamental difference between Plato and Seneca here.

110. Vogt (1974) 129, 131.

Chapter 4

1. The data have to be assembled from the Greek and Latin lives of Melania and from Palladius, *Lausiac History*. There is a good modern edition of the Greek life by D. Gorce (Paris 1962).

2. *Theodosian Code* 10.10.25; 5.7.2; 5.6.3, respectively.

3. Themistius, *Orations* 10.136B; cf. P. D. King, *Law and Society in the Visigothic Kingdom* (Cambridge 1972), pp. 159–80, for other references and for what follows immediately in the text; also

Nehlsen (1972) ch. 4; D. Claude, 'Soziale Spannungen im Westgotenreich', *Klio* 60 (1978) 311–25; Verlinden (1955) 59–102.

4. Originally published in *Annales E.S.C.* 2 (1947) 30–44, 161–70, the article is reprinted in Finley (1968) 204–28.

5. *Theodosian Code* 5.17.1 and *Justinian Code* 11.53.1, respectively.

6. Fustel de Coulanges (1885) 92.

7. On New World slavery, see the bitter comments on precisely this question that run through Stroud (1856). His pessimism is shared by e.g. Degler (1970) 345–8, and, rather reluctantly, by Genovese (1974) 25–49. I shall return to the question below, in connection with *coloni*.

8. R. Andreotti, 'L'applicazione del "Senatus Consultum Claudianum" nel Basso impero', in *Neue Beiträge zur Geschichte der alten Welt*, ed. E. C. Welskopf, 2 (Berlin 1965), pp. 3–12.

9. See e.g. G. I. Luzzatto, 'Ricerche sull' applicazione dalle costituzioni imperiali nelle Provincie', in *Studi . . . in onore di C. Ferrini*, ed. G. G. Archi (Milan 1946), pp. 263–93.

10. By this time *dominus* was being employed without its strict, classical property connotation, for example as a synonym for *patronus*: see Seyfarth (1963) 87–9.

11. See L. Harmand, *Libanius, Discours sur les patronages* (Paris 1955), to be used with caution.

12. P. Collinet, 'Le colonat dans l'Empire romain', in *Recueils . . . Jean Bodin* 2 (1937) 85–122.

13. G. Sotgiu, 'Un collare di schiavo rinvenuto in Sardegna', *Archeologia classica* 25/26 (1973/4) 688–97; cf. Bellen (1971) 23–29.

14. See F. Fabbrini, *La manumissio in ecclesia* (Milan 1965), pp. 227–43.

15. With all due reserve, I offer the totals of known manumission inscriptions from Thessaly in north-central Greece, analysed by Babacos in 1966: 2nd century B.C. — 119; 1st century B.C. — 91; reigns of Augustus and Tiberius — 238; 1st century after A.D. 37 (the death of Tiberius) — 82; 2nd and 3rd centuries A.D. — 127: A. M. Babacos, *Actes d'aliénation en commun . . . de la Thessalie antique* (Thessaloniki 1966), App. A.

16. T. Mommsen, 'Bürgerliches und peregrinisches Freiheitsschutz im römischen Staat', in his *Juristische Schriften* 3 (Berlin 1907) 1–20 (originally published in 1885). The observation was then

checked and confirmed by M. Bang, 'Die Herkunft der römischen Sklaven', *Römische Mitteilungen* 25 (1910) 223–51; 27 (1912) 189–221. Bang's analysis has been rightly challenged, not only on details but also on basic statistical principles, particularly on the reliability and randomness of his sample: on the latter, see F. G. Maier, 'Römische Bevölkerungsgeschichte und Inschriftenstatistik', *Historia* 2 (1953–4) 318–51, at pp. 344–7; on details, e.g. A. Bodor, 'Dacian Slaves and Freedmen in the Roman Empire and the Fate of the Dacian Prisoners of War', *Acta Antiqua Philippopolitana* (1963) 45–52. Nevertheless, there seems to me no possible doubt about the correctness of the one implication which I have drawn from his documentation.

17. 'Foundlings' have so far resisted any even quasi-quantitative assessment, essential for an evaluation of their importance as a source of slaves in antiquity. On perhaps the best evidence, from Roman Egypt, see Biezunska-Malowist (1974–7) II 21–6, with bibliography for other periods and regions.

18. Verlinden (1955) 47–9.

19. A. H. M. Jones, 'Slavery in the Ancient World', *Economic History Review*, 2nd ser., 9 (1956) 185–99, at pp. 191–4, reprinted in Finley (1968) 1–15. Anderson (1974a), for example, accepts the Jones arithmetic fully (pp. 76–7) and builds on it further by arguing in contrary directions (p. 93): 'the price-curve of slaves – which, as we have seen, sloped steeply upwards in the first two hundred years of the Principate, *because of supply shortages* – started to flatten out and fall in the 3rd century, *a sure sign of contracting demand*' (my italics).

20. See the table of prices from Roman Egypt in Biezunska-Malowist (1974–7) II 165–7. Jones dismisses this (for him) inconvenient evidence with the unconvincing argument that Egypt was 'economically segregated from the rest of the empire and followed its own rules'.

21. Hopkins (1978) 158–63.

22. In the latest edition of the edict, by M. Giacchero (2 vols., Genoa 1974), the wages appear in sect. 7, the slave prices in sect. 29. Improved readings of both sections, based on new finds, are published by M. Crawford and J. Reynolds in the *Zeitschrift für Papyrologie und Epigraphik* 26 (1977) 125–51 and 34 (1979) 163–210, but my 'calculation' is unaffected. Two

qualifications should be mentioned: (1) day-labourers are to be paid maintenance in addition to their wages; (2) the edict allows buyer and seller to negotiate a higher price, up to double the one fixed, if the slave is specially qualified.

23. Shtaerman/Trofimova (1975) 27; cf. Shtaerman (1969) 25–6, 55–6.

24. See Finley (1973) ch. 4.

25. See e.g. C. R. Whittaker, in Garnsey (1980); Kreissig (1978) pt. II; Pippidi (1973); A. Grenier, in Frank (1933–40) III 406–10; Rostowzew (1910).

26. Cicero, *Oration for Aulus Caecina* 11, 21, 94; *Oration for Sextus Roscius* 20.

27. See Duncan-Jones (1974) ch. 1.

28. See generally P. Graindor, *Un milliardaire antique, Hérode Atticus et sa famille* (Cairo 1930); briefly on the evidence, John Day, *An Economic History of Athens under Roman Domination* (New York 1932), pp. 235–6.

29. The evidence is cited in Jones (1964) III 250n32.

30. U. Kahrstedt, *Die wirtschaftliche Gesicht Griechenlands in der Kaiserzeit* (Bern 1954), pp. 47–8.

31. Gromatici veteres, ed. C. Lachmann (Berlin 1848), p. 53.

32. G. Fouet, *La villa gallo-romaine de Montmaurin* (*Gallia*, Supp. 20, 1969).

33. M. I. Finley, *Ancient Sicily to the Arab Conquest* (rev. ed., London 1979), pp. 158–62.

34. For Gaul we depend entirely on archaeology, and until recently archaeologists have not been very sensitive to the problem of units of exploitation, admittedly a difficult one for them. But see now e.g. M. Lutz, 'Le domaine gallo-romain de Saint-Ulrich (Moselle)', *Gallia* 29 (1971) 17–44, at pp. 22–5.

35. Horace, *Satires* 2.7.118 and *Epistles* 1.14.1–3.

36. Rostovtzeff (1957) 564.

37. Shtaerman (1964) 26.

38. See Anderson (1974a) 61n9, 86n43; Zelin, in Annequin (1978) 51–7. In her later books, Shtaerman (1968) and (1975) has modified her views in important ways but has held fast to her central villa-*saltus* distinction.

39. Shtaerman (1969) and (1975) repeatedly and rightly insists that the medium-sized estates were centres of slave exploitation in Italy. Unfortunately, she also holds that the big consoli-

dated tracts, the genuine *latifundia*, had to avoid slave labour because of their size. She never asks herself why (if true) the smaller units of exploitation into which the *latifundia* were regularly subdivided could not all have been worked by slaves, as some are known to have been.

40. Finley (1965b) 40.
41. Weber (1909), esp. 8–10, 31–3, 142–5; Mickwitz (1937) and (1939).
42. Kiechle (1969) provides the fullest information, though it is often antiquated, especially in his major section, on 'Arretine' pottery, and it rapidly turns into pure speculation (and sometimes fiction) when he moves from descriptive detail about material objects to division of labour, organization of production and the like.
43. Anderson (1947a) 26.
44. White (1964) 69–76.
45. Marc Bloch, 'Avènement et conquêtes du moulin à eau', *Annales d'histoire économique et sociale* 7 (1935) 538–63 (a model study), at p. 545.
46. White (1964) 84. The most recent account of the diffusion of the water-mill in antiquity is E. Maróti, 'Über die Verbreitung der Wassermühlen in Europa', *Acta Antiqua* 23 (1975) 255–80.
47. See Finley (1965b), and for a similar analysis made independently, H. W. Pleket, 'Technology and Society in the Graeco-Roman World', *Acta Historiae Neerlandica* 2 (1967) 1–22. Kiechle (1969) ignored the former and dismissed the latter in a contemptuous sentence (173n16), to which Pleket replied effectively in 'Technology in the Greco-Roman World: A General Report', *Talanta* 5 (1973) 6–47, at pp. 28–30. That article is the 'elaborated text' of Pleket's report to the 4th Intl. Economic History Conference in Bloomington in 1968, finally published, in its shorter original version, in the Conference *Proceedings* (Paris and The Hague 1973), pp. 303–34, followed immediately by Kiechle's 'Technical Progress in the Main Period of Ancient Slavery' (pp. 335–46), a bare summary of his book (cited as forthcoming four years after its publication), without any reference to Pleket's preceding report.
48. Shtaerman (1964) 90–1.
49. See ch. 1 at n. 44.
50. On the last point, see e.g. P. F. Brandon, 'Cereal Yields of the

Sussex Estate of Battle Abbey during the Later Middle Ages', *Economic History Review*, 2nd ser., 25 (1972) 403–20.

51. L. Cracco Ruggini, 'Les structures de la société et de l'économie lyonnaises au IIe siècle . . .', in *Les martyrs de Lyon* (*177*) (CNRS, Paris 1978), pp. 65–91, at pp. 82–3. On the effects of the military *annona* in the Danubian provinces, see Erik Gren, *Kleinasien und der Ostbalkan in der wirtschaftlichen Entwicklung der römischen Kaiserzeit* (Uppsala Univ. Årsskrift 1941:9), pp. 138–50, the only such investigation known to me.

52. Rivet (1969) 189–98.

53. See L. Cracco Ruggini and G. Cracco, 'Changing Fortunes of the Italian City from Late Antiquity to Early Middle Ages', *Rivista di filologia classica* 105 (1977) 448–75.

54. In the Danubian provinces there was no recovery from the widespread destruction of cities in the third century; see e.g. A. Mócsy, 'Pannonia', in *RE*, Supp. 9 (1962) 516–776, at cols. 697–8.

55. A notable older exception is C. Jullian, *Histoire de la Gaule*, vol. 8 (Pan's 1926), ch. 4.

56. Yeo (1952), esp. 468–71.

57. John Bradford, *Ancient Landscapes* (London 1957), p. 214.

58. I have elsewhere developed my objection to the thesis that an absolute manpower shortage was the key to the political and economic history of the later Empire: see my review in the *Journal of Roman Studies* 48 (1958) 156–64, of A. E. R. Boak, *Manpower Shortage and the Decline of the Roman Empire in the West* (Ann Arbor 1955). One of Boak's main props, the supposedly widespread abandonment of arable in Italy and elsewhere, has been removed by C. R. Whittaker, in Finley (1976) ch. 8: '*Agri deserti*'.

59. Fustel de Coulanges (1885) 15–24; cf. Finley (1976) 115–17. One of the few who did notice and gave his enthusiastic support was A. Schulten, *Die römischen Grundherrschaften* (Weimar 1896), pp. 93–8.

60. Weber (1891) 232.

61. Fustel de Coulanges (1885) 119; cf. Heitland (1921) 378–84.

62. Levy (1948) 17–25.

63. F. v. Woess, 'Personalexekution und cessio bonorum im römischen Reichsrecht', *ZRG* 43 (1922) 485–529, remains fundamental.

64. *Digest* 49.14.3.6; cf. 39.4.9.1.
65. See generally Garnsey (1970).
66. *Corpus inscriptionum latinarum* VIII 10570; text and translation are given in Frank (1933–40) IV 96–8.
67. Rostowzew (1910) 370–3.
68. Garnsey (1970) 274.
69. See J. H. W. G. Liebeschuetz, *Antioch . . . in the Later Roman Empire* (Oxford 1972), pp. 126–32.
70. E. R. Hardy, *The Large Estates of Byzantine Egypt* (New York 1931), pp. 22–3.
71. Jones (1964) 469; cf. his 'Over-Taxation and the Decline of the Roman Empire', *Antiquity* 33 (1959) 39–43, reprinted in his *The Roman Economy*, ed. P. A. Brunt (Oxford 1974), ch. 4.
72. Ammianus 16.5.15; cf. Salvian, *On the Government of God* 4.30–31; 5.35.
73. See above all I. Hahn, 'Das bäuerliche Patrocinium in Ost und West', *Klio* 50 (1968) 261–76; more generally, for the eastern provinces, Patlagean (1977) 271–301.
74. Symmachus, *Letters* 1.74; 4.68.
75. Levy (1948) 21n89.
76. Both the availability and the neglect of untapped sources of information were documented by Seyfarth (1963) 104–27 and Hahn (1961), and we finally have the massive inquiry of Patlagean (1977) ch. 2, 3 and 5 into the eastern provinces.
77. *Theodosian Code* 9.45.5 *ad fin.*
78. See Patlagean (1977) ch. 2, 3 and 5; briefly, the documentation in A. F. Norman, 'Gradations in Later Municipal Society', *Journal of Roman Studies* 48 (1958) 79–85.
79. See Hahn (1961), (1976) 460–6.
80. N. Charbonnel, 'La condition des ouvriers dans les ateliers impériaux au IVe et Ve siècles', *Travaux et recherches de la Fac. de droit de Paris, Série Sciences Historiques* 1 (1964) 61–93, at pp. 67–70. The best account of the imperial factories remains that of A. W. Persson, *Staat und Manufaktur im römischen Reiche* (Lund 1923), pp. 67–75, apparently unknown to Charbonnel; but see Hahn (1961) 32–3.
81. *Theodosian Code* 10.20.10.
82. Hahn (1976) 469.
83. Hahn (1976).
84. See Hopkins (1978) ch. 4.

BIBLIOGRAPHY

Note: Works cited only once are not normally repeated here.

Abbreviations: *Abh. Mainz* = Akad. d. Wissenschaften u. d. Literatur, Mainz, *Abhandlungen der geistes- u. sozialwiss. Klasse*
RE = G. Wissowa, W. Kroll, et al., ed., *Paulys Real-Enzyklopädie der klassischen Altertumswissenschaft,* 1894–. Stuttgart
ZRG = *Zeitschrift der Savigny-Stiftung für Rechtsgeschichte, Romanistische Abteilung*

Abignente, G. (1890). *La schiavitù nei suoi rapporti colla chiesa e col laicato.* Turin

Anderson, P. (1974a). *Passages from Antiquity to Feudalism.* London

Anderson, P. (1974b). *Lineages of the Absolute State.* London

Annequin, J., et al., ed. (1975). *Formes d'exploitation du travail et rapports sociaux dans l'antiquité classique (Recherches internationales à la lumière du marxisme* 84). Paris

Backhaus, W. (1974). *Marx, Engels und die Sklaverei.* Düsseldorf

Backhaus, W. (1975). 'John Elliott Cairnes und die Erforschung der antiken Sklaverei', *Historische Zeitschrift* CCXX 543–67

Barrow, R. H. (1925). *Slavery in the Roman Empire.* London

Bellen, H. (1971). *Studien zur Sklavenflucht im römischen Kaiserreich.* Wiesbaden

Beloch, J. (1886). *Die Bevölkerung der griechisch-römischen Welt.* Leipzig

Biezunska-Malowist, I. (1974–7). *L'esclavage dans l'Egypte gréco-romaine,* 2 vols. (Polish Academy of Science)

Biot, Ed. (1840). *De l'abolition de l'esclavage ancien en Occident.* Paris

Blair, W. (1833). *An Inquiry into the State of Slavery amongst the Romans.* Edinburgh

Blavatskaya, T. V., et al. (1972). *Die Sklaverei in hellenistischen Staaten im 3–1. Jh. v. Chr.,* trans. M. Bräuer-Pospelova et al. Wiesbaden

Böckh, A. (1817). *Die Staatshaushaltung der Athener,* 2 vols. (3rd ed. by Max Fränkel, 1886). Berlin

Bömer, F. (1957–63). *Untersuchungen über die Religion der Sklaven in*

̸and und Rom, in *Abh. Mainz* 1957 no. 7, 1960 no. 1, 1961
1963 no. 10

̸er, N. (1971). *Bibliographie zur antiken Sklaverei*, ed J. Vogt.
̸hum

̸, K. (1904). *Die Entstehung der Volkswirtschaft*, 5th ed. (1st ed.
1893). Tübingen

Bücher, K. (1922). *Beiträge zur Wirtschaftsgeschichte*. Tübingen

Büchsenschütz, B. (1869). *Besitz und Erwerb im griechischen Altenthume*.
Halle

Buckland, W. W. (1908). *The Roman Law of Slavery*. Cambridge

Burckhardt, J. (1898–1902). *Griechische Kulturgeschichte*, 4 vols., cited
from reprint (1956), Darmstadt

Calabi, F. (1979). '"Despotes" e "technites". Definizioni essenziali e
definizioni funzionali nella "Politica" di Aristotele', *Quaderni di
storia* IX 109–34

Calderini, A. (1908). *La manomissione e la condizione dei liberti in
Grecia*. Milan

Capogrossi, L. (1978). 'Il campo semantico della schiavitù nella
cultura latina del terzo e del secondo secolo a. C.', *Studi storici*
XVIII 716–33

Carandini, A. (1976). 'Le forme di produzione dell' economica
e le forme di circolazione dell' antropologia economica',
Quaderni di Critica marxista 215–34, reprinted in his *Archeologia e
cultura materiale* (2nd ed., Bari 1979) 354–84

Cassirer, E. (1951). *The Philosophy of the Enlightenment*, trans. F. C. A.
Koelln and J. C. Pettegrove. Boston

Ciccotti, E. (1899). *Il tramonto della schiavitù nel mondo antico*, cited in
the 1977 ed. Turin

Ciccotti, E. (1977). *Il tramonto della schiavitù nel mondo antico*, 2 vols.
(first ed. 1899). Bari

Colloque (1971). *Actes du Colloque 1971 sur l'esclavage* (*Annales littér-
aires de l'Univ. de Besançon* 140, 1972)

Colloque (1972). *Ibid.* 163, 1974

Colloque (1973). *Ibid.* 182, 1976

David, P. A., et al. (1976). *Reckoning with Slavery*. New York

Davis, D. B. (1966). *The Problem of Slavery in Western Culture*. Ithaca

Davis, D. B. (1974). 'Slavery and the Post-World War II. Historians',
Daedalus CIII 1–16

Degler, C. N. (1959). 'Starr on Slavery', *Journal of Economic History*
XIX 271–7

Degler, C. N. (1970). 'Slavery in Brazil and the United States. A Comparison', *American Historical Review* LXXV 1004–28; reprinted in (and cited from) Weinstein/Gatell (1973) 342–73

Degler, C. N. (1976). 'The Irony of American Slavery', in *Perspectives and Irony in American Slavery*, ed. H. P. Owens, pp. 3–25. Jackson, Miss.

Diakonoff, I. M. (1974). 'Slaves, Helots and Serfs in Early Antiquity' *Acta Antiqua* XXII 45–78

Ducat, J. (1978). 'Aspects de l'hilotisme', *Ancient Society* IX 5–46

Duncan-Jones, R. (1974). *The Economy of the Roman Empire*. Cambridge

Dureau de la Malle, A.J.C.A. (1840). *Economie politique des Romains*, 2 vols. Paris

Ehrenberg, V. (1951). *The People of Aristophanes*, 2nd ed. Oxford

Elkins, S. M. (1959). *Slavery*. Chicago

Finley, M. I. (1959). 'Was Greek Civilization Based on Slave Labour?', *Historia* VIII 145–64; corrected reprint in Finley (1981)

Finley, M. I. (1960). 'The Servile Statuses of Ancient Greece', *Revue internationale des droits de l'antiquité*, 3rd ser., VII 165–89; corrected reprint in Finley (1981)

Finley, M. I. (1964). 'Between Slavery and Freedom', *Comparative Studies in Society and History* VI 233–49, also in French in Annequin (1975); corrected reprint in Finley (1981)

Finley, M. I. (1965a). 'La servitude pour dettes', *Revue historique de droit français et étranger*, 4th ser., XLIII 159–84; corrected reprint in English in Finley (1981), in German in Kippenberg (1977)

Finley, M. I. (1965b). 'Technical Innovation and Economic Progress in the Ancient World', *Economic History Review*, 2nd ser. XVIII 29–45; corrected reprint in Finley (1981)

Finley, M. I., ed. (1968). *Slavery in Classical Antiquity* (repr. with supp.). Cambridge and New York

Finley, M. I. (1973). *The Ancient Economy*. Berkeley and London

Finley, M. I., ed. (1974). *Studies in Ancient Society*. London and Boston

Finley, M. I. (1975). *The Use and Abuse of History*. London

Finley, M. I., ed. (1976). *Studies in Roman Property*. Cambridge

Finley, M. I. (1977a). 'The Ancient City: from Fustel de Coulanges to Max Weber and beyond', *Comparative Studies in Society and History* XIX 305–27; corrected reprint in Finley (1981)

Finley, M. I. (1977b). '"Progress" in Historiography', *Daedalus* CVI no. 3, 125–42

Finley, M. I. (1981). *Economy and Society of Ancient Greece*, ed. R. P. Saller and B. D. Shaw. London

Francotte, H. (1900–1). *L'industrie dans la Grèce antique*, 2 vols. (*Bibliothèque de la Fac. de Philosophie et Lettres, Univ. de Liège*, fasc. 7–8)

Francotte, H. (1916). 'Industrie und Handel', in *RE* IX 1381–1459.

Frank, T., ed. (1933–40). *An Economic Survey of Ancient Rome*, 6 vols. Baltimore

Frederikson, G. M., and Lasch, C. (1967). 'Resistance to Slavery', *Civil War History* XIII 315–29, reprinted in (and cited from) Weinstein/Gatell (1973) 118–33

Fustel de Coulanges, N. M. (1885). 'Le colonat romain', in his *Recherches sur quelques problèmes d'histoire*, pp. 1–186. Paris

Garlan, Y. (1972). 'Les esclaves grecs en temps de guerre', in *Actes du Colloque d'histoire social 1970*, 29–62. Paris

Garnsey, P. (1970). *Social Status and Legal Privilege in the Roman Empire*. Oxford

Garnsey, P., ed. (1980). *Non-slave Labour in Graeco-Roman Antiquity* (*Proceedings of the Cambridge Philological Society*, Supp. 6)

Genovese, E. D. (1974), *Roll, Jordan, Roll*. New York

Gernet, L. (1955). *Droit et société dans la Grèce ancienne* (reprint). Paris

Hahn, I. (1961). 'Freie Arbeit und Sklavenarbeit in der spätantiken Stadt', *Annales Univ. . . . Budapestiensis, Sectio historica* III 23–39

Hahn, I. (1971). 'Die Anfänge der antiken Gesellschaftsformation in Griechenland und das Problem der sogennanten asiatischen Produktionsweise', *Jahrbuch für Wirtschaftsgeschichte* II 29–47; reprinted in Kippenberg (1977) 68–99

Hahn, I. (1976). 'Sklaven und Sklavenfrage im politischen Denken der Spätantike', *Klio* LVIII 459–70

Heeren, A. H. L. (1826). *Ideen über die Politik, den Verkehr und den Handel der vornehmsten Volk der alten Welt* III 1, 4th ed., in his *Historische Werke* XV. Göttingen

Heitland, W. E. (1921). *Agricola*. Cambridge

Highet, G. (1973). '*Libertini Patre Natus*', *American Journal of Philology* XCIV 268–81

Himmelmann, N. (1971). *Archäologisches zum Problem der griechischen Sklaverei*, in *Akad. Mainz*, no. 13

Hobsbawm, E. (1964). Introduction to Marx (1964)

Hopkins, K. (1978). *Conquerors and Slaves*. Cambridge

Hume, D. (1752). 'Of the Populousness of Ancient Nations', cited from the World's Classics ed. of his *Essays* (London 1903), pp. 381–451

Ingram, J. K. (1895). *History of Slavery and Serfdom*. London

Jameson, M. H. (1977–8). 'Agriculture and Slavery in Classical Athens', *Classical Journal* LXXII 122–45

Jameson, R. P. (1911). *Montesquieu et l'esclavage*. Paris (reprinted New York, 1941)

Joly, R. (1969/70). 'Esclaves et médecins dans la Grèce antique', *Sudhoffs Archiv* LIII 1–14

Jones, A. H. M. (1964). *The Later Roman Empire 284–602*, 3 vols. Oxford

Kajanto, I. (1969). 'Tacitus on the Slaves. An Interpretation of the *Annales*. XIV, 42–45', *Arctos* n.s. VI 43–60

Kiechle, F. (1969). *Sklavenarbeit und technischer Fortschritt im römischen Reich*. Wiesbaden

Kippenberg, H. G., ed. (1977). *Seminar: Die Entstehung der antiken Klassengesellschaft*. Frankfurt

Klees, H. (1975). *Herren und Sklaven: Die Sklaverei im oikonomischen und politischen Schrifttum der Griechen in klassischer Zeit*. Wiesbaden

Kreissig, H. (1978). *Wirtschaft und Gesellschaft im Seleukidenreich*. Berlin

Kudlien, F. (1968). *Die Sklaven in der griechischen Medizin der klassischen und hellenistischen Zeit*. Wiesbaden

Kühne, H. (1962). 'Zur Teilnahme von Sklaven und Freigelassenen an der Bürgerkriegen der Freien im 1. Jahrhundert v.u.Z. in Rom', *Studii clasice* IV 189–209

Lange, R. (1899). Review of Ciccotti (1899), *Wochenschrift für klassische Philologie* XVI 761–70

Lauffer, S. (1960). 'Die Sklaverei in der griechisch-römischen Welt', *Rapports* (XIth Intl. Historical Congress) II 71–97. Uppsala

Lencman, Ja. A. (1966). *Die Sklaverei in mykenischen und homerischen Griechenland*, trans. M. Braüer-Pospelova. Wiesbaden

Lepore, E. (1970). 'Economia antica e storiografia moderna (Appunti per un bilancio di generazioni)', in *Ricerche . . . in memoria di Carrado Barbagallo* I 3–33. Naples

Letourneau, C. (1897). *L'évolution de l'esclavage dans les diverses races humaines*. Paris

Levy, E. (1948). 'Von römischen Precarium zur germanischen Landleihe', *ZRG* LXVI 1–30

McCulloch, J. R. (1845). *The Literature of Political Economy: a Classified Catalogue*. London

Marx, K. (1964). *Pre-capitalist Economic Formations*, trans. J. Cohen. London

Marx, K. (1973). *Grundrisse*, trans. M. Nicolaus. Harmondsworth

Mazza, M. (1977). Introduction to Ciccotti, E. (1977), reprinted in *Klio* LXI 57–83 (1979)

Mazzarino, S. (1966). *Il pensiero storico classico*, 2 vols. in 3. Bari

Meillassoux, C., ed. (1975). *L'esclavage en Afrique précoloniale*. Paris

Meyer, E. (1895). *Die wirtschaftliche Entwicklung des Altertums*, reprinted in (and cited from) Meyer (1924) 79–168

Meyer, E. (1898). *Die Sklaverei im Altertum*, reprinted in (and cited from) Meyer (1924) 169–212

Meyer, E. (1899). *Forschungen zur alten Geschichte*, vol. 2. Halle

Meyer, E. (1902). *Zur Theorie und Methodik der Geschichte*, reprinted in (and cited from) Meyer (1924) 1–78

Meyer, E. (1924). *Kleine Schriften*, 2nd ed., vol. I. Halle

Mickwitz, G. (1937). 'Economic Rationalism in Graeco-Roman Agriculture', *English Historical Review* LII 577–89

Mickwitz, G. (1939). 'Zum Problem der Betriebsführung in der antiken Wirtschaft', *Vierteljahrschrift f. Sozial- u. Wirtschaftsgesch.* XXXII 1–25

Milani, P. (1972). *La schiavitù nel pensiero politico: dai Greci al Basso Medio Evo*. Milan

Millar, J. (1771). *Observations concerning the Distinction of Ranks in Society*. Dublin

Mintz, S. A. (1977). 'The so-called World System: Local Initiative and Local Response', *Dialectical Anthropology* II 253–70

Momigliano, A. (1966). *Studies in Historiography*. London

Mommsen, T. (1961). *Römisches Strafrecht* (reprint of ed. of 1899). Darmstadt

Morrow, G. R. (1939). *Plato's Law of Slavery and Its Relation to Greek Law*. Urbana, Ill.

Nehlsen, H. (1972). *Sklavenrecht zwischen Antike und Mittelalter* (vol. I only so far). Göttingen

Nieboer, H. J. (1900). *Slavery as an Industrial System*. The Hague. 2nd ed. 1910

Oertel, F. (1925). Appendix to Pöhlmann (1925), reprinted in Oertel (1975) 40–98

Oertel, F. (1975). *Kleine Schriften zur Wirtschafts- und Sozialgeschichte*, ed. H. Braunert. Bonn

Patlagean, E. (1977). *Pauvreté économique et pauvreté sociale à Byzance, 4e – 7e siècles*. Paris and The Hague

Patterson, O. (1970). 'Slavery and Slave Revolts: A Sociohistorical Analysis of the First Maroon War, 1665–1740', *Social and Economic Studies* XIX 289–325; reprinted in (and cited from) Price (1973)

Patterson, O. (1977a). 'The Structural Origins of Slavery. A Critique of the Nieboer-Domar Hypothesis from a Comparative Perspective', *Annals of the N.Y. Acad. of Science* CCXCII 12–33

Patterson, O. (1977b). 'The Study of Slavery', *Annual Review of Sociology* III 407–49

Percival, J. (1969). 'Seigneurial Aspects of Late Roman Estate Management', *English Historical Review* LXXXIV 449–73

Pignoria, L. (1613). *De servis, et eorum apud veteres ministeriis commentarius*. Augsburg

Pippidi, D. M. (1973). 'Le problème de la main-d'oeuvre agricole dans les colonies grecques de la mer Noire', in *Problèmes de la terre en Grèce ancienne*, ed. M. I. Finley, pp. 63–82. Paris and The Hague

Pöhlmann, R. (1925). *Geschichte der sozialen Frage und des Sozialismus in der antiken Welt*, 3rd ed. by F. Oertel. Munich

Popma, T. (1608). *De operis servis liber*. Leiden

Price, R., ed. (1973). *Maroon Societies: Rebel Slave Communities in the Americas*. Garden City, N.Y.

Puglisi, A. (1977). 'Servi, coloni, veterani e la terra in alcuni testi di Constantino', *Labeo* XXIII 305–17

Raskolnikoff, M. (1975). *La recherche soviétique et l'histoire économique et sociale du monde hellénistique et romain*. Strasbourg

Reitemeier, J. F. (1789). *Geschichte und Zustand der Sklaverey und Leibeigenschaft in Griechenland*. Berlin

Richter, W. (1958). 'Seneca und die Sklaven', *Gymnasium* LXV 196–218

Rivet, A. L. F., ed. (1969). *The Roman Villa in Britain*. London

Roscher, W. (1871). *Ansichten der Volkswirtschaft aus dem geschichtlichen Standpunkte*. Leipzig and Heidelberg

Rostovtzeff, M. (1941). *The Social and Economic History of the Hellenistic World*, 3 vols. Oxford

Rostovtzeff, M. (1957). *The Social and Economic History of the Roman Empire*, 2nd ed. by P. M. Fraser, 2 vols. Oxford

Rostowzew, M. (1910). *Studien zur Geschichte des römischen Kolonates* (*Archiv f. Papyrusforschung*, Beiheft 1)

Salvioli, G. (1906). *Le capitalisme dans le monde antique*, trans. A. Bonnet. Paris

Sargent, R. L. (1924). *The Size of the Slave Population at Athens* (*Univ. of Illinois Studies in the Social Sciences* XII 3)

Sartori, F. (1973). 'Cinna e gli schiavi', in *Colloque* (*1971*) 151–69

Schiller, L. (1847). *Die Lehre des Aristoteles von der Sklaverei* (*Jahresbericht d. K. Studienanstalt zu Erlangen in Mittelfranken*). Erlangen

Schwartz, Ed. (1938). *Gesammelte Schriften* I. Berlin

Seyfarth, W. (1963). *Fragen der spätrömischen Kaiserzeit im Spiegel der Theodosianus*. Berlin

Shtaerman, E. (1964). *Die Krise der Sklavenhalterordnung im Western des römischen Reiches*, trans. from the Russian (1957) by W. Seyfarth. Berlin

Shtaerman, E. (1969). *Die Blütezeit der Sklavenwirtschaft in der römischen Republik*, trans. from the Russian (1964) by M. Bräuer-Pospelova. Wiesbaden

Shtaerman, E. M., and Trofimova, M. K. (1975). *La schiavitù nell' Italia imperiale, I–III secolo*, trans. from the Russian (1971). Rome

Spranger, P. P. (1960). *Historische Untersuchungen zu den Sklavenfiguren des Plautus und Terenz*, in *Akad. Mainz*, no. 8

Stier, H. E. (1945). *Grundlagen und Sinn der griechischen Geschichte*. Stuttgart

Stroud, G. M. (1856). *A Sketch of Laws relating to Slavery in the Several States of the United States of America*, 2nd ed. Philadelphia

Temperley, H. (1977). 'Capitalism, Slavery and Ideology', *Past & Present* LXXV 94–118

Thür, G. (1977). *Beweisführung vor den Schwurgerichtshöfen Athens: Die Proklesis zur Basanos*. Vienna

Tourmagne, A. (pseud. of A. Villard) (1880). *Histoire de l'esclavage ancien et moderne*. Paris

Verlinden, C. (1955). *L'esclavage dans l'Europe mediévale* (only vol. 1 published). Brugge

Vidal-Naquet, P. (1968). 'Les esclaves grecs étaient-ils une classe?', *Raison Présente*, no. 6, 103–12.

Vidal-Naquet, P. (1972). 'Réflexions sur l'historiographie grecque de l'esclavage', in *Colloque (1971)* 25–44

Villard, A. *see* A. Tourmagne (pseudonym)

Vittinghoff, F. (1960). 'Die Theorie des historischen Materialismus über dem antiken "Sklavenhalterstaat": Probleme der alten Geschichte bei den "Klassikern" des Marxismus und in den modernen sowjetischen Forschung', *Saeculum* XI 89–131

Vittinghoff, F. (1961). 'Die Bedeutung der Sklaven für den Übergang von der Antike ins abendländische Mittelalter', *Historische Zeitschrift* CXCII 265–72

Vlastos, G. (1941). 'Slavery in Plato's Thought', *Philosophical Review* L 289–304, reprinted in Finley (1968) 133–49

Vogt, J. (1974). *Ancient Slavery and the Ideal of Man*, trans. T. Wiedemann. Oxford

Vogt, J. (1978). 'Die Sklaverei in antiken Rom', *Antike Welt* IX, no. 3, 37–44

Volkmann, H. (1961). *Die Massenversklavungen der Einwohner eroberter Städte in der hellenistisch-römischen Zeit*, in *Akad. Mainz*, no. 3

Wallace, R. (1753). *A Dissertation on the Numbers of Mankind in Ancient and Modern Times*. Edinburgh

Wallon, H. (1847). *Histoire de l'esclavage dans l'antiquité*, 3 vols. Paris

Wallon, H. (1879). 2nd ed. of Wallon (1847)

Weber, M. (1891). *Die Römische Agrargeschichte*. Stuttgart

Weber, M. (1896). 'Die sozialen Gründe des Untergangs der antiken Kultur', reprinted in (and cited from) Weber (1924) 289–311

Weber, M. (1909). 'Die Agrarverhältnisse des Altertums', in *HWB der Staatswiss.*, 3rd ed., reprinted in (and cited from) Weber (1924) 1–288

Weber, M. (1924). *Gesammelte Aufsätze zur Sozial- und Wirtschaftsgeschichte*. Tübingen

Weinstein, A., and Gatell, F. O., ed. (1973). *American Negro Slavery: A Modern Reader*, 2nd ed. New York

Welskopf, E. C. (1957). *Die Produktionsverdältnisse im alten Orient und in der griechisch-römischen Antike*. Berlin

Welwei, K.-W. (1974–77). *Unfreie im antiken Kriegsdienst*, 2 vols. Wiesbaden

Westermann, W. L. (1935). 'Sklaverei', in *RE* Supp. VI 894–1068

Westermann, W. L. (1955). *The Slave Systems of Greek and Roman Antiquity*. Philadelphia

White, Lynn, Jr. (1964). *Medieval Technology and Social Change*, paperback ed. Oxford

Wilamowitz, U. von (1910). *Staat und Gesellschaft der Griechen und Römer* (with B. Niese). (2nd ed. 1923). Berlin and Leipzig

Will, Ed. (1954). 'Trois quarts de siècle de recherches sur l'économie grecque antique', *Annales, E.S.C.* IX 7–22

Yanoski, J. (1860). *De l'abolition de l'esclavage ancien au moyen âge et sa transformation en servitude de glèbe*. Paris

Yeo, C. A. (1952). 'The Economics of Roman and American Slavery', *Finanzarchiv*, n.F. XIII 445–85

INDEX
Compiled by Douglas Matthews

Abignente, G., 151*n*7
Académie des Inscriptions et Belles-Lettres, 24, 26, 155*n*51
Académie des Sciences Morales et Politiques, 15, 32–3, 42
Aegina, 90
Africa, 11, 29, 85, 130; *see also* North Africa
agriculture, techniques in, 137–9
Agrigento, 83
Alaric the Goth, 123
Alexander the Great, 47, 78
Alexandria, 169*n*3, 174*n*59
Allard, Paul, 15
Ambrose, St, 140
America (New World), 11, 19; Marx on slavery in, 41; and extraneous considerations, 66; as settlement area, 88; economic efficiency of slaves in, 91–2; attitude to slaves in, 100; fugitive and deserter slaves in, 113–14; abolition of slavery in, 127
Andocides, 108
Angola, 85
Antioch, 145
apotympanismos, 169*n*2
Appian, 98, 130, 177*n*96
Aquinas, St Thomas, 18
Aristophanes, 96, 119
Aristotle, on slavery, 18, 47, 73, 81, 117, 119–20; on torture, 94; cited, 87
Arles, 140
Athenaeus, 17, 30, 113, 171*n*118
Athens, French Revolutionary views of, 19; Müller denigrates, 21; slave population of, 34, 45, 48, 65, 80; origins of slavery in, 37, 86–9; types of slaves in, 78; Scythian slave police in, 85; coins in, 88; aid for poor in, 90; and slaves in military service, 99; and doctors, 106; slave informers in, 108; in Pelopennesian War, 112; torture in, 170*n*10
Attica, 86–9
Atticus, 130
Augustine, St, 121
Augustus, 110, 128, 139
Aulus Caecina, 133

Babington, Churchill, 16
Backhaus, Wilhelm, 62–4, 150*n*7, 157*nn*68, 72
bandits, 113
Bang, M., 180*n*66
Barbagallo, C., 50
Barrow, R. H., 107, 173*n*41
Barth, Karl, 15
Barthélemy, Abbé Jean-Jacques, 20
Bellen, H., 175*nn*72, 73
Beloch, J., 30, 88, 176*n*81
Berr, Henri, 51
Bible, 29; *see also* Christianity
Biot, E. C., 32–3, 151*n*12
Blair, William, 24–6, 36
Bledsoe, A. T., 152*n*17
Bloch, Marc, 70, 124, 131, 149
Boak, A. E. R., 183*n*58
Böckh, August, 25, 31, 39
Bodin, Jean, 20
Bömer, F., 56
Bradford, John, 141
Brazil, 11, 80, 114
brigands *see* bandits
Brosses, Charles de, 24

Bücher, Karl, 38, 42–4, 46, 48–9, 51–2, 57, 157n66, 158n76
Büchsenschütz, B., 25–6, 39, 51, 155n52
Buckland, W. W., 65
Burckhardt, J., 162n122

Caesar, Julius, 71, 109, 128, 143
Cairnes, J. E., 157n72
Calderini, A., 50
Caribbean, 11, 114
Carthage, 115, 144
Cassiodorus, 140
Cassirer, E., 19–20
Cassius Longinus, 118
Cato, 137
Charlemagne, 131, 138, 149
Chios, 17, 85, 113–14
Christianity, effect on slavery, 13–17, 27, 32–3, 42, 55, 64, 127–8; attitude to slaves, 121
Chrysippus, 120
Ciccotti, Ettore, 42–4, 48, 50, 58, 63
Cicero, Marcus Tullius, 81, 106, 112, 133; De republica, 27
Cincinnatus, 84
citizenship, 144
clientes, 70–71, 75, 133
Collinet, Paul, 126
coloni, 70, 123–4, 138, 140, 142, 145; development of word, 147
Columella, 92, 126, 130, 135, 138, 141, 143, 149, 166n33
Commodus, 144
Constantine, Emperor, 76, 122, 124, 127
contubernium, 75
Corcyra, 109–10
Corinth, 85, 90
corporal punishment, 93, 95; see also torture
Corpus Iuris, 19, 25
Crete, 71
Creuzer, Friedrich, 24–7
crop yields, 138–9
Cuba, 80
Cudjoe, Captain, 114

Cujas, Jacques, 19

Dante Alighieri, 18
Danubian provinces, 183n54
Darwin, Charles, 65
debt-bondsmen, 68, 70–72, 79, 87, 143
Demosthenes, 50, 52, 80, 93
Delphi, 129, 165n26
Dezobry, L. C., 153n25
Diakonoff, I. M., 70–72
Dictionnaire de Théologie catholique, 34
Diderot, Denis, 20
Diligenskii, G. G., 58
Dio Cassius, cited, 109
Dio Chrysostom, 121
Diocletian, 130, 140, 143
Diodorus, cited, 49
Diogenes the Cynic, 120
Dionysius (Cicero's slave), 112
Dionysius of Halicarnassus, 18
doctors, 105–7
Domesday Book, 138
dominium (word), 73
dominus (word), 73, 179n10
Domitian, 75
Dover, K. J., 170n15
Drimacus (slave fugitive), 113–14
Ducat, J., 164n15
Dureau de la Malle, A. J. C. A., 31
Dutilleul, J., 34

Edinburgh Philosophical Society 30
Egypt, 76, 106, 180n20
Encyclopédie, 20
Engels, Friedrich, 12, 40–42, 57, 62–4, 70
Enlightenment, 17, 19–21, 23, 28, 34
Epicrates, 171n18
Epictetus, 117, 121
Epidemics (Hippocratic books), 106–7
Erechtheum, Athens, 100

erus (word), 73
Erwig, King, 124
estates (land), 133–7, 140–41;
 see also latifundia
Eupatrids, 86–7
Euripides, 105, 120

Feith, Everhardt, 25
Ferrero, G., 50
foundlings, 180n17
Francotte, Henri, 44, 52
Frank, Tenney, 52
Franklin, Benjamin, 28–30, 100,
 138
freedmen, 83, 97–8; *see also*
 manumission
French Revolution, 19, 115
Frontinus, 134
fugitives, 111–13
Fustel de Coulanges, N. M., 67,
 142–3, 160n102

Gaius (jurist), 27, 99
Gaul, 79
Gelzer, M., 84
Germany, identification with
 Hellenism, 56–7, 59; post-
 war education, 58; ideological
 dispute in, 58–63; slaves from,
 129
Gibbon, Edward, 21–2
Gillies, John, 22–3
Glotz, Gustave, 51
Gortyn, 71
Goths, 123
governesses, 105, 107–8
Gracchus, Tiberius Sempronius
 (the tribune), 84
Greece, effects of slavery in, 12,
 14; spiritual excellence of, 17;
 authorities invoked, 20; and
 origins of slavery, 37, 67, 78–9,
 86; mode of production in,
 40, 43; manumission in, 50,
 97; slave occupations in, 81;
 and 'barbarian' slave supply,
 85; slave punishment in, 94;
 slave craftsmen in, 100–102;

medicine in, 106; absence of
 slave revolts in, 115
Grote, George, 22
Grotius, Hugo, 154n41
Grumentum, 104
Guiana, 114
Guiraud, Paul, 51
Gymnasium (journal), 59

Hadrian, 143, 173n41
Haiti, 115
Hannibalic Wars, 84
Harpocras, 106
Hartmann, L. M., 48
Heeren, Arnold, 12, 14, 162n127
Heitland, W. E., 52, 169n63
hektemoroi, 78, 81, 87
helots, helotage, 68, 70–72, 75,
 78, 86, 115
Hermann, K. F., 25
Hermippus (of Berytus), 177n96
Herodes Atticus, 133–4, 136
Herodotus, 99, 118–19
Heyne, Christian Gottlob, 35–6,
 154n42
Highet, G., 177n96
Hobsbawm, Eric, 41
Holbach, P. H. D. von, 20
homo (Latin word), 73
Horace, 96–7, 117, 134
Hugo, Gustav, 36
Hulsean Prize (Cambridge), 15
humanism, classical, 38–9, 56–7,
 59–60, 154n40
Humboldt, Wilhelm von, 56–7,
 59, 122
Hume, David, 25, 27–31, 36–7,
 40

Illyria, 123
informers (slave), 108–9
Ingram, J. K., 150n7
inquilini, 124
International Historical Congress (Stockholm, 1960), 56,
 60–62, 69
Isocrates, 165n32
Israel (ancient), 46

Italy, slave mode of production in, 40, 79; chain gangs in, 77; slave population, 80; slave occupations in, 81; land-holdings in, 89; slave revolts in, 115; land tax in, 145; *see also* Rome

Jaeger, Werner, 56–7
Jamaica, 113–14
Jaucourt, Louis, Chevalier de, 20
Jesus Christ, 16
Joly, R., 174*nn*53, 57
Jones, A. H. M., 129, 140
Julian (jurist), 107
Julian, Emperor, 145–6
Justinian, code, 107, 131, 142–3, 165*n*24, 173*n*41; and land tax, 145
Juvenal, 97

Kautsky, Karl, 158*n*74, 159*n*82
Kiechle, Franz, 62, 182*nn*42, 47
Kroll, Wilhelm, 52–3
Kronia, 96
Kudlien, F., 174*nn*53, 56
Kyllyrioi, 79

labour, nature of, 67–8; compulsory and hired, 68–70, 72, 77–9, 81; systems of, 69–70; and decline of slavery, 127; internal supply of, 141–2, 148
land-ownership and tenure, 89, 132–7, 143; *see also* estates; peasants
Lange, R., 44
laoi, 70, 133
Larcius Macedo, 103, 121
latifundia, 78, 92, 135, 147, 182*n*39
Lauffer, S., 56, 69, 71
Laureion, 56, 87
law codes, 124–6, 142–5; *see also* Justinian; *Theodosian Code*
Letourneau, C., 150*n*7
Letronne, J. A., 31
Leuctra, Battle of (371 B.C.), 72
Levesque de Burigny, Jean, 24

Lewis, G. C., 153*n*35
lex Poetelia Papiria, 84
Libanius of Antioch, 125–6
Licinian-Sextian laws (367 B.C.), 84
Livy, Titus, cited, 83–4
Locris, 168*n*63
Louis, Paul, 51
Lycurgus, 21–2
Lyons, 140
Lysias (orator), 80, 90

Macaulay, T. B., Lord, 34
McCulloch, J. R., 30–31, 153*nn* 32, 34, 155*n*46
Maecenas, 134
Maine, Sir Henry, 147
Mainz Academy, 55, 58–9, 62
Malthus, T. R., 31
mancipium (word), 172*n*31
Mandrou, Robert, 61, 63
Manso, J. C. F., 21–2
manumission, Augustan curbing of, 18; in America, 19; in Greece, 50, 97; qualifications to, 74–5; and *peculium*, 82; taxed (Rome), 83; effect of, 96–7; of church slaves, 128; cost of, 129; increase in, 131
Marathon, Battle of (490 B.C.), 99
markets (economic), 139–41
Marquardt, J., 24
maroons, *marronage*, 113–14
Marx, Karl, on evolution of society, 38, 40–41; on slavery and modes of production, 40–43, 45–6, 50, 62; attacked by West German historians, 62–4; relation to Bücher and Weber, 158*n*76; *18th Brumaire*, 19; *Grundrisse*, 40–41; *Kapital*, 41
Marxism, on slavery, 57–8, 67, 91; and Mainz project dispute, 60–64; on slave classification, 70–71; social theory, 164*n*17

Mazza, M., 151*n*7, 158*n*75
Mazzarino, S., 177*n*96
medicine, 105–7
Mehl, A., 163*n*140
Meillassoux, C., 69, 71
Meiners, Christoph, 156*n*62
Melania, 123, 128, 134
Menander, 119
Mesopotamia, 70
Messenia, 72
metics, 97, 108–9
Meyer, Eduard, theories, 44–9, 51–2, 57, 88, 90; influence on Westermann, 53–4; and German Hellenism, 56–7; and German ideological dispute, 60–61; on position of slaves, 74; and Rodbertus, 157*n*66
Michelet, Jules, 32–3, 151*n*12
Michell, H., 91
Micknat, Gisela, 56
Mickwitz, G., 137
Millar, John, 15, 19, 28, 36, 138, 154*n*42
Mitford, W., 22
Mnason, 168*n*63
Momigliano, A., 23, 56
Mommsen, T., 34–5, 44, 48, 94, 128
Montesquieu, C. de Secondat, Baron de, 19–20, 22
Montmaurin estate (Gaul), 134
Müller, Karl Otfried, 21

Naucratis, 169
Nenci, G., 169*n*63
Nepos, Cornelius, 130
Nero, 102
nexum, 84, 143, 166*n*33
Nieboer, H. J., 150*n*7
Niebuhr, B. G., 22
Nietzsche, Friedrich, 15
North Africa, 134, 149
noxal actions, 98–9
nursemaids, 105, 107–8

obaerati (*obaeraii*), 165*n*33
occupatio, 84

Oertel, Friedrich, 49–50
outlaws, 113
Overbeck, Franz, 15, 34

paedagogus, 105, 107
pais, 96
Palladius, Bishop, 123
Pareto, Vilfredo, 50
paroikoi, 133
patrocinium, 145–6
patronus (word), 179*n*10
Paul, St, 122
'Pauly-Wissowa' (encyclopaedia), 53, 55
Pausanias, 99
peasants, 143–6
peculium, 77, 82, 102, 131
Pedanius Secundus, Lucius, 80, 102, 117, 178*n*108
pelatai, 70, 78, 87
Pelopennesian War, 112
penestai, 70, 75
peregrini, 97, 106
Periander, Tyrant of Corinth, 54
Pericles, 89
Petit, Samuel, 25
Petronius, 96, 117, 129
Philip II, King of Macedon, 47, 165*n*32
Pignoria, Lorenzo, 23–4, 94
Pindar, 18
Pinianus, 123
Pisistratid tyranny, 85
Plato, 49, 106–8, 120–21
Plautus, 73–4, 120, 122
Pleket, H. W., 182*n*47
Pliny the elder, 92, 105, 109, 116, 141, 173*n*41
Pliny the younger, 103–4, 106, 121, 126, 133–6, 141, 143
Plutarch, 87, 107, 177*n*96
Pöhlmann, R., 44, 49–50
police, 168*n*62
Popma, Titus, 23–4, 158*n*78
population, slave, 30–31, 34, 45, 48, 53, 64–5, 79–80, 123; growth of, 167*n*55
Portugal, 85

Potgiesser, Joachim, 23
prostitution, 96
Ptolemais, in Egypt, 169n3
puer (word), 96
Punic War, 2nd, 83
Puteoli, 95

racism, 118
Reitemeier, J. F., 25, 35-9, 42
Rhodes, 54, 90
Richter, W., 121, 156n59
Riezler, Kurt, 50
Rodbertus, J. C., 38, 48
Rome, spiritual excellence of, 17; law invoked, 18-20; barbarian invasions of, 33, 123-4, 140, 146; labour and production in, 43, 67; colonate, 67; origins of slavery in, 67, 79, 83, 86; distribution of slavery in, 79; slave numbers in, 80; slave occupations in, 81, 102; manumissions in, 83, 97-8; punishment in, 93-4, 102; medicine in, 106; slave informers in, 109; law codes in, 124-6, 142-5; decline of slavery in, 127, 131-2; expansion and conquests by, 128-30; landownership in, 132-7, 143; slave system and structure in, 135-6; technology and invention in, 137-8; commodity production and markets in, 139-41; army supplies in, 139-40; taxation in, 145-6; bureacracy in, 146
Roscher, Wilhelm, 40
Rostovtzeff, M., 52-4, 135-6, 144
Rousseau, Jean-Jacques, 20
Russia, 57-8, 61-2, 151n8

Saeculum (journal), 61
Sainte Croix, Guilhem de, 31
Sallust, cited, 143
Salvioli, Giuseppi, 42-4, 50, 58
Samnite War, 3rd, 83

Sardinia, 76, 127
Saturnalia, 96
Savigny, F. C. von, 36
Schneider, A., 156n59
Schwartz, Eduard, 56-7, 65
Scirians, 123
Scythia, 85, 118
Seneca, 96, 104, 121-2
Serena, 'Empress', 123
serfdom, 46-7, 68, 70
servi, 124, 147
sex, slaves and, 95-6
Sextus Pompey, 110
Sextus Roscius, 133
Shtaerman, E., 91, 130-31, 135-6, 138, 174n64
Sicily, 79, 115, 134
slaves, slavery, and abolition question, 11, 13; numbers of, 29-30, 64-5, 79-80, 123; origins of, 36-7, 69, 82-90, 131-2; and nature of labour, 68; chattel, 68-9, 71-2; classification and terminology of, 69-72, 76, 99, 124-6, 146-8; rights of, 71-2; revolts, 71-2, 110-11, 114-15, 117; as property, 73-5, 77; kinlessness, 75; family dispersal of, 75-7; hierarchies among, 77; distribution of, 79-80, 89, 132; 'location' and occupations of, 81-2, 84, 101-2, 105, 148-9; and state of war, 82-6, 112; military service by, 84, 99, 109-10; profitability of, 91; relations with masters, 93, 103-5, 131; punishment of, 93-5, 98-9, 102, 117, 122, 148; sexual availability of, 95-6; treatment of, 96-7, 99-100; crimes by, 98, 111; ambiguities of, 99-100, 117; and medicine, 105-7; as nursemaids/governesses, 107-8; as informers, 108-9; fugitive, 111-14; acceptance of condition of, 116; ancient attitude to,

slaves—*contd*
117–22, 126; law codes on,
124–6; decline of, 126–7, 131–
2; branding and marking of,
127; sources of, 128–30; price
of, 129–30; breeding of, 130;
and land-holdings, 133–7; system and structure of, 135–6,
149; productivity of, 138–9,
141; definitions of, 165*nn*20,
23; *see also* manumission
Smith, Adam, 19–20, 28, 31, 91,
138
Social War (91–89 B.C.), 104
Society for the Defence of the
Christian Religion, 16
Solon, 22, 78, 87–8
Spain, 77, 79, 124
Sparta, helots in, 17–18, 37, 75;
French Revolutionary views
on, 19; Manso's history of, 21;
Müller on, 21; defeated at
Leuctra, 72; attacks on Ath-
ens, 89, 112; helot revolt in,
115
Spartacus, 24, 98, 104
Spengler, Oswald, 48
Stalin, J. V., 63
Statius, 75
Stier, H. E., 56
Stockholm Historical Congress
see International Historical
Congress
Stoicism, 42, 55, 121, 127
Suetonius, cited, 145
Symmachus, Quintus Aurelius,
52, 134, 136
Syracuse, 78–9

Tacitus, 97, 102–3, 107, 118,
145, 173*nn*41, 43
taxation, 88, 145–6
technology, 62, 138–9
tenants *see* land-ownership and
tenure
Terence, 73, 117
Thebes, 112
Theodosian Code, 125–7, 142, 146

Theopompus, 17
Thessaly, 70, 75, 179*n*15
Thirlwall, C., 22
Thompson, Edward, 62
threptoi, 147
Thucydides, 89, 108–9
Tiberius, 145
Timaeus, 168*n*63
Tocqueville, Alexis de, 100
Toledo, 16th Council of, 124
torture, 94–5
Tourmagne, A. (*pseud. of* A.
Villard), 150*n*7
Toutain, Jules, 51
Trajan, 109
Trier, 140
Troeltsch, Ernst, 15, 17
Turner, Nat, 114
Twelve Tables, 46

United States of America, 80,
114; *see also* America (New
World)

Valentinian I, Emperor, 124,
147
Vandals, 125
Van Effenterre, H. G. M., 61
Varro, Marcus Terentius, 143
Velleius Paterculus, 109
Verlinden, C., 129, 151*n*7
Vespasian, 145
Victor Vitensis, Bishop, 125–6
vilicus, 84, 92
Virgil, 18
Visigoths, 124–5
Vittinghoff, F., 61, 63
Vogt, Joseph, 16–17, 25, 45; and
Mainz project, 55–6, 58–60,
62, 64–5; and corporal pun-
ishment, 94; on slave nurse-
maids, 107; on slaves and
moral world, 122
Voltaire, François Marie Arouet,
called, 20

Wallace, Robert, 30–31, 36
Wallerstein, I., 79

Wallon, Henri, *Histoire de l'esclavage dans l'antiquité*, 12–17, 25, 32–5, 39; on slave numbers, 31, 64; on Reitemeier, 36; and corporal punishment, 94; and treatment of slaves, 116; translated into Russian, 151n8

war, state of, and slave supply, 82–6; slave actions in, 112

water-mills, 138

Weber, Max, and evolution of ancient society, 38; on slavery, 42–4; Meyer on, 48; on farm economy, 137; on Roman laws, 142; and Bücher, 158n-76; opposes Meyer, 159n94; Westermann praises, 161n109

Westermann, W. L., 13–14, 16, 45, 52–5, 65–6, 73, 94, 103

Wilamowitz, U. von, 56–7, 65

Wiskemann, Heinrich, 16

Xenophon, 81, 100

Yanoski, J., 32, 33, 151n12, 155n55